For Nicholas

RELIGIOUS EXPERIENCE

RELIGIOUS EXPERIENCE

Wayne Proudfoot

UNIVERSITY OF CALIFORNIA PRESS
Berkeley   Los Angeles   London

University of California Press
Berkeley and Los Angeles, California

University of California Press, Ltd.
London, England

Library of Congress Cataloging in Publication Data

Proudfoot, Wayne, 1939—
  Religious experience.

  Bibliography: p.
  Includes index.
  1. Experience (Religion) I. Title.
BL53.P819   1985   291.4'2   84-23928
ISBN 0-520-05143-2
ISBN 0-520-06128-4 (pbk)
Printed in the United States of America

1 2 3 4 5 6 7 8 9

CONTENTS

PREFACE

During the past two centuries, religious thinkers and scholars of religion have depended heavily on the concept of religious experience. That concept is a relatively recent one and was developed and shaped to meet the needs of those thinkers and scholars. I have tried to subject that concept to scrutiny, to show why it emerged when it did, and to reflect on the ambiguities in the concept that permit it to be used both for descriptive and apologetic purposes. Consequently, this investigation sheds light on important issues in the study of religion and religious thought that extend beyond the consideration of religious experience.

My research has taken me in directions that were unanticipated at the outset. As a result, I am indebted to friends and colleagues for introducing me to literature with which I was unfamiliar. Ruth Ellen Proudfoot first made me aware of current work in social psychology, and collaboration with Phillip Shaver on an article and a course in the psychology of religion helped me to discover what I could learn from that work about emotion, belief, and experience. Earlier versions of some parts of the manuscript were read to colloquia in various departments of philosophy and religion, and parts were read and commented upon by gracious colleagues and students. George Rupp and Jeffrey Stout must be singled out as close friends who read several drafts and who have been partners in extensive conversations during the time in which I have been working on this project. Joel Brereton, Arthur Danto, Arnold Eisen, Van Harvey, Gordon Kaufman, George Lindbeck, James A. Martin, Jr., Richard Niebuhr, Victor Preller, and James S. Preus were generous with their time and comments. Among students in the graduate program at Columbia, Ava Chamberlain, Robert Forman, Warren Funk, Jay Harris, John Newman, James Wetzel, and David Wisdo were particularly helpful. All comments were appreciated, though undoubtedly many were neither appropriated nor addressed with the thoroughness they deserved.

Earlier versions of some of the material that now appears in chapters two, three, and six were published as articles. Phillip Shaver and I collaborated on "Attribution Theory and the Psychology of Religion," which was published in the *Journal for the Scientific Study of Religion* 14 (1975) and some of which is incorporated into chapter three. "Religious Experience, Emotion, and Belief" appeared in the *Harvard Theological Review* 70 (1977) and is also used in chapter three. "Religion and Interpretation," which first appeared in *Soundings* 61 (1978), and "Religion and Reduction," published in the *Union Seminary Quarterly Review*, 37 (1981–1982), have been heavily revised and reworked as parts of chapters two and six. I am grateful to the editors of these journals for permission to use this material.

INTRODUCTION

For the past two centuries, the issue of religious experience has been central in the work of religious thinkers and of those who have contributed to the development of the study of religion as an academic discipline. Religion has always been an experiential matter. It is not just a set of credal statements or a collection of rites. A religious life is one in which beliefs and practices cohere in a pattern that expresses a character or way of life that seems more deeply entrenched in the life of that person or community than any of the beliefs or practices. When new evidence about pagan and primitive religious traditions became available through historical research and the translation of crucial texts, nineteenth-century students of religion read the myths and narratives about the gods not as cosmological beliefs or history but as expressions of particular forms of religious experience. In this respect they were more sophisticated in the study of this material than their Enlightenment predecessors had been. They did not treat pagan, primitive, and oriental myths and practices as erroneous doctrine or immoral conduct. Instead they viewed them as expressive of particular forms of the religious life, each of which highlighted some aspect of religious experience that was, in principle, available to all. This way of viewing ancient and religious texts has been particularly influential in shaping the course of biblical study during the course of the last two centuries.

Although religious experience seemed to be ubiquitous, the idea of religious experience was novel. Members of the cultures whose myths and practices were now being interpreted as expressions of the religious dimension of human experience did not understand what was happening to them or what they were doing in these terms. Both *religious* and *experience* are relatively recent concepts, whose provenance is in the modern West. Though that need not detract from their usefulness in describing or analyzing the religious life of other cultures, it does mean that members of those cultures did not employ these terms in their own attempts to understand their experience and behavior.

This book is about that idea of religious experience which has been so influential in religious thought and the study of religion in the past two centuries. It is an examination of some of the most important theories of religious experience, an elucidation of the idea or concept as it is presupposed by discussions of such topics as mysticism and reductionism in the study of religion, and a consideration of the implications of these theories and this idea for contemporary issues in the philosophy of religion. Particular attention will be given to the way people come to understand or interpret their behavior and what is happening to them, and under what conditions they label certain bodily or mental states religious. Recent work in psychology and in the philosophy of mind will be employed to understand what must be assumed in order to account for particular religious emotions or for a sense of finitude or of unity with the whole.

The emergence of the concept of religious experience in the late eighteenth century, and its centrality for the liberal tradition of religious thought which stems largely from the work of Friedrich Schleiermacher, can best be understood when set in historical context. Traditional appeals to metaphysical argument to justify religious belief were undercut by the criticisms set forth by a line of thinkers beginning with Descartes and culminating with Immanuel Kant. Hume's *Dialogues Concerning Natural Religion* dismantled the argument from design which some empiricists wanted to substitute for the scholastic theistic arguments. Kant's critiques effectively blocked both the appeal to metaphysics and the weighing of probabilities based on empirical evidence as methods for addressing the question of the existence of God. Appeals to ecclesiastical authority or to scripture to justify religious belief were rendered more difficult by the study of the historical development of scripture and the early church.

The turn to religious experience was motivated in large measure by an interest in freeing religious doctrine and practice from dependence on metaphysical beliefs and ecclesiastical institutions and grounding it in human experience. This was the explicit aim of Schleiermacher's *On Religion*, the most influential statement and defense of the autonomy of religious experience. In *The Christian Faith*, Schleiermacher provided a more careful statement of the relation between religious doctrine and experience and a systematic reconstruction of Christian doctrine on the basis of that statement. Religion could now be appreciated as an autonomous moment in human experience which ought not to be reduced to science, metaphysics, or morality. Religion had its own integrity, and religious belief and practice were properly viewed as expressions of the religious dimension or moment.

With this idea of religion as an experiential moment irreducible to either science or morality, belief or conduct, Schleiermacher sought to free religious belief and practice from the requirement that they be justified by reference to nonreligious thought or action and to preclude the possibility of conflict between religious doctrine and any new knowledge that might emerge in the course of secular inquiry. Religion is grounded in a moment of experience that is intrinsically religious, so it need not be justified by metaphysical argument, by the kind of evidence considered by the proponents of the design argument, or by appeals to its importance for the moral life. Moreover, because religion is autonomous, all possible conflict between religion and science or morality is precluded. Any attempt to assimilate religion to nonreligious phenomena is an attempt to reduce it to something other than it is. Reductionism is thus the chief error to be avoided in the study of religion.

Schleiermacher offered a careful description of the religious sense from the perspective of a member of the communities with which he was most familiar. He sought to convince his friends among the artists, poets, and critics of Berlin at the end of the eighteenth and the beginning of the nineteenth century that their sensibilities were more in tune with the genuine spirit of the religious life than much that went on in churches and synagogues. He set out to awaken this interest in his readers and to direct their attention to it. But the evocative language required for that task does not serve well as a theoretical account of religious experience. The sense of the infinite, or the feeling of absolute dependence, does not seem to those who experience it to be the result of inference or to presuppose concepts and beliefs. This moment seems unmediated by linguistic representation.

Accounts of religious experience in this tradition are constructed from the perspective of the subject. Any other perspective, or any attempt to explain the experience in terms other than those adopted by the subject, is regarded as reductive, and reductionism in any form is to be opposed. One result of this stance is that much contemporary philosophy of religion and theology takes the form of edifying discourses designed to elicit in the reader the experiences the author intends to communicate. Accounts of religious experience which are allegedly descriptive and theoretical actually serve to constitute or evoke the experience they purport to describe or analyze. This follows from the assumption that such moments of experience are immediate and thus can only be understood by direct acquaintance.

Schleiermacher's approach continues to inform much contemporary religious thought and philosophy of religion, even among those who think of themselves as having broken with that tradition. If they disagree with the claim for the autonomy of religious experience viewed as a sense of the infinite or the feeling of absolute dependence, they employ similar arguments to defend the irreducible character of religious experience construed as the experience of the sacred, or as limit experience, or of religious language, practice, or doctrine. In each of these cases, despite considerable differences, the autonomy of the religious life is defended in order to preclude inquiry and to stave off demands for justification from some perspective outside of that life. The result is a combination of genuine insights into the ways in which religion ought to be studied and protective strategies that serve apologetic purposes.

No topic is better suited for an examination of current issues in religious thought and the study of religion than religious experience. If we can understand how that experience has been variously described, and begin to distinguish between descriptive, analytical, explanatory, and evocative elements in the accounts of religious experience which have been most influential, we will be in a better position to assess the current state of the field.

Schleiermacher's program required that he show that religious experience is independent in the requisite sense. But concepts, beliefs, and practices are assumed by the descriptions he offers and the instructions he gives for identifying the religious moment in experience. Recent work in psychology and the philosophy of mind shows the extent to which our ascriptions of emotions to ourselves and to others and our identification of bodily and mental states depend on complex sets of beliefs and grammatical rules. These are not simple inner states identifiable by acquaintance, as Schleiermacher and others suggest. Such moments of experience are clearly dependent on the availability of particular concepts, beliefs, and practices. When that is recognized, Schleiermacher's program cannot be carried through as he envisioned it.

Most philosophers of religion would concur in their criticism of claims that religious experience is prior to or independent of beliefs and practices. But that concurrence is often misleading. Some who criticize Schleiermacher for naiveté on this point and who emphasize the degree to which all emotions, actions, and mental states are embedded in and presuppose concepts and linguistic practices, go on to argue for the autonomy of religious language, action, or doctrine and to denounce reductionism in ways that show a marked similarity to Schleiermacher's program. In both cases an ambiguity between descriptive analysis and explanatory commitments is built into an allegedly neutral account of religious experience or of religious language or practice. Strictures against reductionism are invoked to preclude critical inquiry from outside the religious life. The result is a powerful protective strategy.

It is possible to turn that protective strategy around and to use the warnings against reductionism as indicators of tacit criteria for what an author takes to be distinctive about the religious. For example, if someone claims that any attempt to offer a natural explanation of religious phenomena is reductive, one can infer that for this person the distinctively religious characteristic of those phenomena is that they elude natural explanation. In this way it is possible to tease out the distinguishing marks of the religious operating in these protective strategies.

The insistence on describing religious experience from the subject's point of view, the stress on the reality of the object of an experience for the person who has that experience, the avoidance of reductionism, and the distinction between descriptive and explanatory tasks are all important for the study of religion. Each, however, can and has been used to block inquiry for apologetic purposes. In the following chapters we shall examine the accounts that have been given and the claims that have been made for religious experience with a view toward distinguishing the genuine insights from erroneous theories and protective strategies.

The book proceeds by considering different topics in the analysis of religious experience, but special attention is given to two authors whose work has been particularly influential in shaping the development of the idea of religious experience during the past two centuries: Friedrich Schleiermacher and William James. Selected issues from Schleiermacher's *On Religion* and the introduction to *The Christian Faith* and from James's *The Varieties of Religious Experience* are considered. The *Varieties* has been widely read and commented upon, but its significance for contemporary issues in the philosophy of religion has often been overlooked.

The opening chapter is an examination and criticism of Schleiermacher's theory of religious experience, with particular attention to his claim that it is independent of concepts and beliefs and to his account of the way that experience is expressed in language. I argue that his program requires the experience to be both immediate and intentional, and that these requirements are incompatible. According to Schleiermacher, the experience must be both independent of language and thought and identified only by reference to concepts and beliefs.

Chapter two focuses on two traditions of thought about the concept of interpretation and the interpretation of experience. The concept is ambiguous with respect to its use in the statement that there is no uninterpreted experience and its use in the hermeneutic tradition that has focused on the interpretation of texts and cultural products. Some theorists have traded on this ambiguity in order to justify a neglect of issues concerned with explanation.

Chapter three is an analysis of the ascription of emotions to oneself and to others, drawing on recent work in cognitive psychology and the philosophy of mind. Emotions cannot be picked out without reference to rather sophisticated concepts, beliefs, and grammatical rules. These must be in place and certain conditions must be fulfilled in order for someone to identify what is happening to him or her as anger and thus to experience anger. The conditions under which people attribute certain emotional states to themselves and others are examined. These attributions typically include explanatory claims.

Chapter four is an analysis of mysticism. Mystical experience is often taken to be a paradigm of religious experience because it has seemed to many that evidence can be adduced for an experience that is invariant across cultures, even though the interpretation of that experience varies from one culture to another. I offer a new analysis of the two marks that James takes to be distinctive of mystical experience, its ineffability and its noetic quality. The latter mark again shows how deeply entrenched is the issue of the subject's explanation of his or her experience, despite attempts of theorists to disguise or deny it.

Chapter five is an explication of the concept of religious experience as it is employed in these accounts. By examining strictures against reductionism and the characterization of reductive accounts, one can tease out the implicit criteria of the religious which are at work. The most important ambiguity in the concept of religious experience emerges not from the term *religious* but from *experience*. An experience may be identified from the subject's point of view and regarded as neutral with respect to explanatory claims, or constraints on the proper explanation may be included in the criteria for identifying the experience. In this connection the parallels and dissimilarities between religious experience and sense perception are examined.

The final chapter is a consideration of different kinds of explanation of religious experience and the issue of reductionism. A distinction is proposed between descriptive and explanatory reduction, each of which has different implications for the study of religious phenomena. The former is to be avoided, but the latter is not. Some recent attempts to deny the appropriateness of explanation of religious phenomena are examined and shown to conceal protective strategies not unlike those of the tradition of Schleiermacher, even though these philosophers would reject Schleiermacher's claim that it is possible to identify an experience that is independent of concepts and beliefs.

I.
EXPRESSION

The early years of the nineteenth century figure prominently in the history of the idea of religious experience. Modern attention to religious experience, and the desire for an accurate description of that experience which would convey its distinctive character and avoid reductionism, stems from that period. Friedrich Schleiermacher's *On Religion: Speeches to the Cultured Among its Despisers*, published in 1799, is important for understanding both religious thought and the study of religion during the past two centuries. In his review of the origin and development of the concept of religion, Wilfred Cantwell Smith (1964: 45) wrote of *On Religion*: "It would seem to be the first book ever written on religion as such—not on a particular kind or instance and not incidentally, but explicitly on religion itself as a generic something."[1] In addition to its temporal priority, the influence of this book has been enormous. Schleiermacher has been described by supporters and critics alike as the seminal figure in nineteenth-century Protestant thought. The work of Ernst Troeltsch, Rudolf Otto, Joachim Wach, and other historians of religion is directly descended from this volume and from the work of his maturity, *The Christian Faith*.

Schleiermacher sets out to show the distinctive character of religion or piety. He proposes to attend to the religious sense or consciousness itself, apart from other thoughts or activities that may be associated with it, and to present it in its original, characteristic form. He is motivated in this project by two goals. The first is to present an accurate description of the religious consciousness. In his view, both orthodox Christians and Jews and Enlightenment critics of religion have erred in depicting religion as a system of beliefs or doctrines or as a moral code prescribing behavior. The religious component in experience has its own integrity and cannot be assimilated to the pursuit of knowledge or morality. Schleiermacher's early years spent among the Moravians and his participation in the original circle of young romantics in Berlin at the turn of the century prepared him to attend particularly to the aesthetic and affective character of the religious life. He wanted to show the artists and critics with whom he associated that what they despised was not religion but the dogmas and institutions that result from mistaking external forms for the inner life of the spirit, and that real piety is identical with the spiritual integrity and sense of harmony with the universe which they sought in the aesthetic and cultural life.

The second goal is more theoretical and apologetic. Schleiermacher hopes that by presenting religion in its original, characteristic form he will demonstrate the inapplicability of Enlightenment criticisms of religious belief, particularly of the Kantian critique of speculative metaphysics, to the actual phenomena of religion. Religion is a sense, a taste, a matter of feeling and intuition. Consequently, it remains unscathed by Kant's contention that our experience is structured by the categories and thoughts we bring to it and thus that we produce rather than reproduce the world we think we know. As a sense that precedes and is independent of all thought, and that ought not to be confused with doctrine or practice, religion can never come into conflict with the findings of modern science or with the advance of knowledge in any realm. It is an autonomous moment in human experience and is, in principle, invulnerable to rational and moral criticism.

Both the descriptive and theoretical goals of this program require that religion be shown to be original and autonomous, and that it not be reducible to something else. These interests and this requirement continue to shape much contemporary writing in the philosophy of religion, theology, and the history or science of religions.[2] For Schleiermacher and for the tradition that derived from him, descriptive accuracy is to be obtained and reductionism to be avoided by insisting on the immediacy of religious experience, and on its radical independence from beliefs and practices. It is a moment in human experience which remains unstructured by, though it is expressed in, thoughts and actions.

Schleiermacher's insistence on the immediacy of religious experience is descriptively accurate, but it is theoretically inadequate, as we shall see. The experience seems to the subject to be immediate and noninferential, but it is not independent of concepts, beliefs, and practices. This confusion between the phenomenological and theoretical senses of *immediate* is central to Schleiermacher's program and is important for understanding contemporary religious thought and the study of religion.

All knowledge, according to Kant, derives its authority from experience. But we have no direct grasp of the objects of our experience. These objects can be apprehended only through the forms of sense and the categories that structure the judgments we make. Kant addressed Hume's epistemological skepticism by drawing attention to the active role of the mind in experience, and to the ways in which it constitutes its perceptions. We have no access to any uninterpreted given. All the data to which we appeal are informed and categorized by antecedent judgments and interpretations. There are no data unshaped by the forms of sense and the categories of judgment, and those forms and categories cannot be legitimately employed to yield knowledge that transcends our experience.

Metaphysical speculation, and many of the claims of traditional religious doctrine, result from attempts to apply the forms of intuition and the categories of judgment beyond the limits of experience. The critical philosophy is an attempt to discriminate between the legitimate application of concepts and categories to the contents of experience and their illegitimate extension beyond the bounds of sense.

In each of the critiques that comprise his major work, Kant focuses on a different area of human experience: scientific, moral, and aesthetic. In each area he attempts to map carefully the limits of permissible judgments. When such limits have been articulated, he reasons, it will be possible to distinguish judgments that are securely rooted in experience from propositions that assume the form of experiential judgments but are actually attempts to extend concepts and categories to questions that exceed the limits of their proper application.

In the first critique Kant analyzes the concept of God as a transcendental ideal of pure reason and in the second as a postulate of pure practical reason. It is a concept of something about which we can have no knowledge, though it serves as a regulative idea that is required for the orientation and completion of our thinking both in science and in morals. Religious belief and practice is grounded in moral experience. It is a result of the dictates of practical reason and of our struggles with the moral law. When Kant turns to write a volume on religion that is structurally parallel to the three critiques, he does not set out to analyze our intuitions and judgments in the religious sphere, as he has earlier examined scientific, moral, and aesthetic experience. Rather he argues that religious doctrines and practices emerge from our experience of the moral law and our inability to adhere to it.[3] Religion, subjectively regarded, is the recognition of all duties as divine commands (Kant, 1960: 95). Jesus Christ is the exemplification of an archetypal ideal humanity, and the church approaches asymptotically the ideal of an ethical commonwealth, a concept developed with explicit reference to the contractual theories of political authority set forth by Hobbes and Rousseau. Religious language and images are interpreted in terms of universal moral ideals. The rational moral law provides the hermeneutic principle for the religious use of the Bible. Religious beliefs and practices are viewed as an outgrowth of the moral life.

Kant did not regard religious experience or religious judgments as autonomous but sought to account for them by an analysis of the moral life. This view of religion as grounded in the demands of the moral law may reflect his religious nurture in the biblical tradition as represented in German Protestantism. In the wake of Kant's account, religious thinkers found it necessary to reconsider the ways religious doctrine is related to experience. Is it possible to speak of distinctively religious intuitions and judgments? If so, is there a sector of experience analogous to the scientific, the moral, and the aesthetic, from which such judgments might arise?

Recently acquired knowledge of other religious traditions, especially those of the classical world, and a new appreciation of pietism prepared Schleiermacher to reject Kant's identification of the religious and the moral. He sought to provide a description and an analysis of religious doctrine and practice which would parallel Kant's analysis of moral judgments but would do greater justice to the autonomy of religion and the distinctive character of religious experience.

Persuaded by Kant's analysis of the activity of the mind in constructing its world, some philosophers of religion sought a domain of experience in which that formative activity is circumvented, and in which there is some direct contact with a reality that transcends the mind and its categories. If a moment of experience not shaped by language could be identified, it might plausibly be claimed that this moment is untouched by the active forming and categorizing that Kant demonstrated, and thus that it is not subject to his critique. Kant himself provided a model for this search in his claim that reason in its practical function assumes an immediate relation to noumenal reality in the apprehension of human freedom, though he was careful to add that this is not an epistemological relation, and thus it yields no knowledge. Each individual experiences, in a practical rather than a theoretical intuition, himself or herself as free. A person's sense of obligation or duty to the moral law is inexpungable, and it assumes a will that is free (Kant, 1956: 28–30).

Within the Kantian context, the search for a moment of religious experience unstructured by the forms and categories of the mind presents a dilemma. Should such a moment be identified, it would not be knowledge and would have no epistemological significance. To the extent that it did have such significance, it would be shaped by the forms and categories. In his early work Schleiermacher held that such piety was a sense or moment of consciousness that did have cognitive import. Later he denied that the religious affections provide knowledge of any kind, but he continued to describe them as a sense or consciousness of something and to attribute to them a content that can only be described in propositional terms.

Even if one holds to the Kantian position that knowledge is limited to the theoretical realm, however, the question arises as to whether there can be distinctively religious judgments and religious experience, as there are moral and aesthetic judgments and experience. Schleiermacher was the earliest and most systematic proponent of the autonomy of religious experience and of religious judgments and doctrine. The religious is governed by its own rules and ought not to be assimilated to scientific or moral paradigms. This claim for the autonomy of religious experience, religious language, and religious judgments has become prominent in the work of contemporary religious thinkers and philosophers of religion. It has become the chief strategy for protecting religious beliefs and practices from the possibility of conflict with the conclusions of science or with the assumptions that inform our perceptual and moral experience.

In resisting Kant's identification of religion with morality, Schleiermacher gave priority to the religious affections. In doing so, he contributed to a tradition in which religious experience, conceived chiefly as affective experience and differentiated from both intellect and will, has been regarded as the original and characteristic form of religion. Among the representatives of this tradition are figures as diverse as Jonathan Edwards, William James, and Rudolf Otto, each of whom has offered a description and a taxonomy of the varieties of religious experience. They differ chiefly over whether or not there is a single and distinctively religious moment of consciousness, but they agree that the original and characteristic form of religion is a sense or feeling that is not to be identified with either belief or practice.

James is typical of this tradition in his contention that "feeling is the deeper source of religion" and that philosophical and theological formulations are secondary. Intellectual operations in the philosophy of religion "presuppose immediate experience as their subject matter. They are interpretative and inductive operations, operations after the fact, consequent upon religious feeling, not coordinate with it, not independent of what it ascertains" (James, 1902: 433). Because it is direct and unmediated by concepts and judgments, religious experience is akin to sensations and can only be known by acquaintance. James argues that mystical states defy expression and must be directly experienced. Unlike scientific laws or moral rules, they cannot be communicated linguistically. Words can be used only to indicate the direction toward which the reader must look in his own experience. Schleiermacher attempts to awaken his readers to the moments of piety in their own consciousness.

The claim that religious experience can only be understood by acquaintance, and the contention that it is a distinctive kind of experience, are most clearly represented in Otto's description of the sense of the numinous. He regards this sense not as a feeling but as a distinctive mental state, and he holds that it can be understood only by awakening the experience in the reader.

> This mental state is perfectly *sui generis* and irreducible to any other; and therefore, like every absolutely primary and elementary datum, while it admits of being discussed, it cannot be strictly defined. There is only one way to help another to an understanding of it. He must be guided and led on by consideration and discussion of the matter through the ways of his own mind, until he reaches the point at which "the numinous" in him perforce begins to stir, to start into life and into consciousness. We can cooperate in this process by bringing before his notice all that can be found in other regions of the mind, already known and familiar, to resemble, or again to afford some special contrast to, the particular experience we wish to elucidate. Then we must add: "This X of ours is not precisely *this* experience, but akin to this one and the opposite of that other. Cannot you now realize for yourself what it is?" In other words our X cannot, strictly speaking, be taught, it can only be evoked, awakened in the mind; as everything that comes "of the spirit" must be awakened. (Otto, 1958: 7)

According to this view, in order to elucidate the experience one must elicit it in the reader. Anyone attempting to describe religious experience must employ evocative rather than analytical language. Otto, following Schleiermacher, does exactly that. Confusion arises, however, when language that is meant to function evocatively is also presented as analysis or as a theoretical account of religious experience.

Consider the relation between descriptive and theoretical accounts of religious experience. Is direct acquaintance required in order to understand religious experience, and what role does the understanding that comes from such acquaintance play in a theoretical account of the experience? The place to begin an inquiry into these issues is with Schleiermacher.

The Priority of the Affective Mode: Schleiermacher's *On Religion*

Schleiermacher's speeches on religion were addressed to his friends and fellow members of a circle of romantic poets and critics in Berlin. These young intellectuals were devoted to the cultivation of sensibilities, tastes, and personal relationships, and to the achievement of the finest artistic expressions, but they could see no value in religion as conventionally understood and practiced. Schleiermacher wrote the book in response to their request.[4] He sought to show in it that true religion is not to be identified with the doctrines and practices that they held in contempt but is a "sense and taste for the infinite" presupposed by the cultivation and art to which they were devoted. In the second speech, in which his view of the nature of religion is set forth, Schleiermacher is particularly concerned to distinguish it from both science and morality and to demonstrate that it is a third and autonomous region of human experience. The book, and especially the second speech, is a treatise on the nature of religion which has as its chief aim the combatting of reduction. Religion must be apprehended in its integrity, not reduced to something else.

Religion, or piety, argues Schleiermacher, is distinct from both the theoretical and practical functions of reason, if the latter is viewed as exclusively concerned with the making of moral judgments. Religion is neither a way of thinking nor a way of acting, neither a set of beliefs nor a collection of practices. By a series of Socratic questions, Schleiermacher elicits the recognition that one may be learned yet lack piety, and one may be pious yet ignorant of theoretical matters. Likewise, one may be morally admirable yet not especially religious, and a religious person may not have engaged in sophisticated reflection upon ethical issues, yet his piety provides a ground for both his knowing and his actions. One cannot be pious and immoral, and the cultivation of science or morals itself constitutes

a kind of piety. Religion is not unrelated to thought and
practice, but it cannot be identified with either.

> Only when piety takes its place alongside of science and prac-
> tice, as a necessary, an indispensable third, as their natural
> counterpart, not less in worth and in splendour than either,
> will the common field be altogether occupied and human
> nature on this side complete. (Schleiermacher, 1958: 37–38)[5]

A sustained argument against reductionism, the treatise is
paradigmatic for many recent exhortations to respect the
autonomy of religion.

It is not enough to contend only that religion is original and
distinct. If it is not a matter of belief or practice, then how is it
to be characterized? For Schleiermacher, religion is a sense, a
taste, an affection.

> True science is complete vision; true practice is culture and
> art self-produced; true religion is sense and taste for the
> Infinite. (39)

> In itself [religion] is an affection, a revelation of the Infinite
> in the finite, God being seen in it and it in God. (36)

Piety is a matter neither of the intellect nor of the will, but of
feeling, where feeling is assimilated to sense or taste. It is
directly experienced and is not shaped by thought. The religious consciousness is original, immediate, and "has not yet
passed through the stage of idea, but has grown up purely in
the feeling" (54). It provides, however, the requisite affective
ground and orientation for right knowing and acting. "To wish
to have true science or true practice without religion, or to
imagine it is possessed, is obstinate, arrogant delusion, and
culpable error" (39).

Schleiermacher sometimes speaks of the unity of intuition
and feeling (40). In the first edition of *On Religion*, after which
substantial revisions were made, he speaks boldly of an intuition of the whole.[6] But even in the later editions, religious feeling is said to be "immediate, raised above all error and

misunderstanding" (43). The sense of the infinite is portrayed as feeling, in order to differentiate it from thought and knowledge, but it is also characterized as an intuition and said to transcend error and misunderstanding. Schleiermacher is trying to have it both ways. The religious consciousness is said to have the immediacy and independence from thought which are characteristic of sensations, and yet to include an intuitive component whose object is the infinite. It is both intentional, in that it is directed toward the infinite as its object, and immediate.[7] It is not dependent on concepts or beliefs, yet it can be specified only by reference to the concept of the whole or the infinite. This combination, required for Schleiermacher's program, is an impossible one. If the feeling is intentional, it cannot be specified apart from reference to its object and thus it cannot be independent of thought. But Schleiermacher claims that it is immediate and has not passed through the stage of idea or concept. He thinks that he has identified a moment of consciousness independent of thought and yet still having cognitive significance.

Since piety is neither doctrine nor precept but an immediate sense or taste, it cannot be understood by description but only by acquaintance (9). Schleiermacher asks his readers to turn their attention away from any preconceived notions of religion and to regard only inward emotions and dispositions. Like Otto, he says that piety can only be known by discovering it in oneself. To this end, he provides instructions to aid his readers in locating and identifying that "original relation of intuition and feeling" that is the religious consciousness. His instructions are worth quoting at some length in order to see what is presupposed by that identification.

> But I must direct you to your own selves. You must apprehend a living moment. You must know how to listen to yourselves before your own consciousness. At least you must be able to reconstruct from your consciousness your own state. What you are to notice is the rise of your consciousness and not to reflect upon something already there.

Your thought can only embrace what is sundered. Wherefore as soon as you have made any given definite activity of your soul an object of communication or of contemplation, you have already begun to separate. It is impossible, therefore, to adduce any definite example, for, as soon as anything is an example, what I wish to indicate is already past. Only the faintest trace of the original unity could then be shown. (41–42)

In knowing an object, one actively directs one's attention toward the object, and the object gradually impresses itself on the mind. In acting, one impresses one's own intention on the object or material on which one acts, but that intention and the resulting action are also shaped by the object. This growing preponderance of receptivity over activity, or of activity over receptivity, points toward a unity underlying that polarity. This unity is the moment from which the religious consciousness arises.

Sense and object mingle and unite, then each returns to its place, and the object rent from sense is a perception, and you rent from the object for yourselves, a feeling. It is this earlier moment I mean, which you always experience yet never experience. . . . It is the holy wedlock of the Universe with the incarnated Reason for a creative, productive embrace. It is immediate, raised above all error and misunderstanding. (43)

These are difficult passages. They are offered to direct the listener or reader to a particular moment in his or her own experience. For this reason, the language ought to be viewed as evocative rather than descriptive. Schleiermacher has formulated rules governing the identification of a moment of experience as religious. In order to count as such a moment it must be prior to and thus unstructured by the distinction between subject and object. It is a unity that precedes the differentiation that is present in perception, thought, or feeling. As soon as one focuses on a particular thought or attends to a particular object, the moment is lost. These conditions are presented as attempts to describe an experience that eludes words and thought and therefore must be evoked by indirect ostension and necessarily vague expression. In fact, however, the "description" consists of a rather precise stipulation to the effect that whatever can be captured in language or thought is not the religious consciousness. That moment precedes and underlies all differentiation. The belief that a particular moment of consciousness is immediate and prior to all concepts and beliefs may well be constitutive of the experience. In that case, Schleiermacher's account would be theoretically inaccurate because the experience would be dependent on a rather sophisticated set of concepts and beliefs (e.g., infinite, whole, the belief that the experience is prior to all concepts), but it would be effective as rhetoric that serves to evoke such an experience.

Schleiermacher is convinced that piety is an original and underived moment of consciousness, and that the study of religion and of religious thought ought to be approached as the attempt to describe that experience through an examination of its expressions. He thinks that mysticism and mythology have infected much religious thought and theology because descriptions of feelings have been taken for a science of the religious object (49). Ideas and principles, however, are foreign to religion (46). They belong to the intellect and not to feeling. Religious ideas can and ought to be nothing more or less than descriptions of religious affections with which their authors are acquainted at first hand (48).

In order to direct his reader toward the religious moment in consciousness, Schleiermacher offers distinguishing marks to enable one to identify the appropriate feeling. Though he argues that the experience is prior to concepts and beliefs, piety is identified as a sense and taste "for the Infinite." The religious moment cannot be specified without reference to God, the infinite, or the whole.[8] Reference to such concepts is required for the description or identification of the experience. Beyond that, Schleiermacher even says that a criterion of the religious experience is that one believes it to be produced by

God or the universe. Reference to a belief about the cause of the experience is built into the rules for identifying the experience.

> Your feeling is piety, in so far as it expresses, in the manner described, the being and life common to you and to the All. Your feeling is piety in so far as it is the result of the operation of God in you by means of the operation of the world on you. (45)

> The sum total of religion is to feel that, in its highest unity, all that moves us in feeling is one; to feel that aught single and particular is only possible by means of this unity; to feel, that is to say, that our being and living is a being and living in and through God. (49–50)

> The religious man must, at least, be conscious of his feeling as the immediate product of the Universe; for less would mean nothing. (90)

The first of the above quotations suggests that one of the criteria for identifying an experience as religious is that it be caused by God. Were some affection not the result of the operation of God, it would not be religious. The second and third suggest that the relevant criterion is not that the experience be the result of divine operation but that it be regarded as such by the one who has the experience. The religious person must be conscious of his feelings as the immediate product of the universe, or must believe them to be such a product. Thus the criteria for identifying the religious consciousness include reference not only to concepts but also to a specific belief about how the experience is to be explained. This despite Schleiermacher's insistence that religious ideas be restricted to descriptions of religious affections, and his claim that explanation has nothing to do with the childlike intuition that informs those affections (127).

To summarize, the account of piety as an affective state which Schleiermacher offers in *On Religion* contains two components. First, he contends that ideas and principles are foreign to religion and that piety is a matter of feeling, sense, or taste distinct from and prior to concepts and beliefs. Second, he identifies piety as a sense and taste for the infinite, an identification that requires reference to God, to all, or the universe. The identification of a moment of feeling as religious assumes not only reference to God or the infinite as the object of the feeling but also a judgment that this feeling is the result of divine operation. Both of these components are required by Schleiermacher's program, and they are incompatible. Piety cannot be independent of concepts and beliefs and at the same time an intentional state that can only be specified by reference to objects of thought and explanatory claims. In his later work Schleiermacher renders each of these components more precise, but the incompatibility remains.

The Feeling of Absolute Dependence: *The Christian Faith*

On Religion constitutes a programmatic statement of a romantic account of religion. Schleiermacher set forth a conception of religion which had roots in eighteenth-century pietism but had not been given a clear intellectual formulation in that context and had been ignored by representatives of the Enlightenment, who were preoccupied with the assessment of the evidence for and against religious beliefs. He incorporated the insight of the pietists that religion is chiefly a matter of the heart within an anthropology that was informed by his studies of Spinoza and Kant. The language of *On Religion* is rhetorical and is well suited to its content. But the thesis that religion is chiefly a matter of the affections provides no criteria for discriminating between more or less adequate theological formulations. If the essence of piety consists in the immediate relation of the self to the infinite, a relation that precedes reflection and action, how can one critically assess religious doctrine? Is theology, or its parallels in nontheistic traditions, possible? Twenty-two years later, as an established professor at the University of Berlin, Schleiermacher addressed these questions. In *The Christian Faith,* Schleiermacher develops a new method for theology which grows out of his earlier view about religion. His conception of the task of systematic or dogmatic theology is novel, and it remains his most important contribution. Systematic theology is not the product of metaphysical speculation or a set of beliefs about the world. It is the science that systematizes the doctrine prevalent in a particular community at a specific time. What is that doctrine if it is not a collection of beliefs? It is the expression of the religious affections in that community. "Christian doctrines are accounts of the religious affections set forth in speech" (CF 15).[9] The subject matter of theology is neither God nor evidence of divine creation and governance in the world but the self-consciousness of the religious believer in the context of his or her community. Metaphysical speculation of the kind that Kant had shown to be illegitimate is precluded.[10] The theologian is an empiricist, and his aim is to provide an accurate account of the religious affections within a particular communion.[11]

Religious communities, like individuals, are characterized by their own peculiar states of affection. These states are expressed in primary religious language, which is the relatively un-self-conscious language of hymns, prayer, personal journals, and preaching. The theologian examines this primary language for its coherence and its clarity in expressing the religious affections of that community. He then systematizes it in the secondary language of his discipline. Schleiermacher's remark, in the preface to the second edition, that he has invented nothing "except my order of topics and here and there a descriptive phrase" may be somewhat disingenuous, but it is consistent with his conception of the task of the theologian (CF xxix). That task is not to invent or to construct but to describe, arrange, and systematize. The authority for any theo-logical claim must be sought in the state of affections of a par-ticular religious community. "God created the world" is not a metaphysical claim or a belief about how the world came to be; it is the expression of the feeling of absolute dependence, or the religious self-consciousness insofar as it expresses the rela-tion between God and the world.

In the body of *The Christian Faith*, Schleiermacher writes as a theologian. The propositions that comprise the introduction, however, do not belong to theology but are propaedeutic to it. They are borrowed from ethics, by which is meant the histori-cal and moral, in contrast to the natural, sciences.[12] Philosophy of religion is a branch of historical science whose task is to exhibit "in a completely exhaustive way, according to their affinities and gradations," the totality of religious communities and their distinctions from one another (CF 4). Before under-taking to describe and systematize the affections of a particular religious community, the author must clarify what he means by the religious affections and how those affections are set forth in speech.

The conception of piety proposed in the introduction to *The Christian Faith* is developed from that in *On Religion*, but it is more carefully formulated. The care can be seen in the manner in which Schleiermacher's dual thesis, that piety is independ-ent of thought and practice and that it has an intentional object, is made more precise. The common element in the reli-gious consciousness is now specified not as a sense and taste for the infinite, nor as an intuition of the unity of self and universe, but as a feeling of absolute or total dependence upon a source or power that is distinct from the world. The edifying language of *On Religion* has been supplanted by a careful analy-sis of the religious self-consciousness. In the earlier work, the religious sense was defined chiefly in terms of its object (i.e., sense of the infinite or of the whole), but at several points Schleiermacher said that affections are religious insofar as they result from the immediate operation of God or the universe on the self. Now this causal criterion has come more directly to the fore. Piety is identified not chiefly by reference to its indeterminate object but as a feeling of absolute dependence. It is a sense of finitude, or of oneself and one's world being causally dependent on a source or power.

The conception of piety is set forth in propositions 3 and 4. The first states that piety is "neither a knowing nor a doing, but a modification of feeling, or of immediate self-consciousness" (CF 3). It is immediate in the sense that it is independent of thought or representation of any kind. The second proposes the marks by which piety can be identified and distinguished from all other feelings. Those assume the concept of dependence and of an indeterminate object toward which the feeling is directed. As in *On Religion*, Schleiermacher defends the incoherent thesis that the religious consciousness is both independent of thought and can only be identified by reference to concepts and beliefs.

Piety is distinct from knowing and doing. It is a feeling that is not reflexive and thus does not assume concepts or beliefs. When a feeling is mediated by representation or self-contemplation, it is no longer a genuine state of feeling.

> Thus joy and sorrow—those mental phases which are always so important in the realm of religion—are genuine states of feeling, in the proper sense explained above; whereas self-approval and self-reproach, apart from their subsequently passing into joy and sorrow, belong in themselves rather to the objective consciousness of self, as results of analytic contemplation. (CF 3.2)

Schleiermacher erroneously assumes that thought enters into emotions only in such explicitly reflexive moments. As we shall see in chapter three, joy and sorrow are not independent of concepts and beliefs but are in part constituted by them. Schleiermacher explicitly denies this, as he must in order to argue that the religious self-consciousness is immediate in his sense.[13]

Schleiermacher exploits an ambiguity in his conception of immediacy. Joy and sorrow may be phenomenologically immediate in the sense that when those moods are dominant one is not aware of thoughts or inferences on which they are dependent. An analysis of these emotions, however, shows that they assume rather complex concepts and beliefs, including reflexive ones. Confusion is caused by the employment of an account of how an emotion or experience seems to the subject as an account of what must be assumed in order to have such an experience.

Religion is a modification of feeling, but what is it that distinguishes religious affections from other states of immediate self-consciousness? How are they to be identified?

> The common element in all howsoever diverse expressions of piety, by which these are conjointly distinguished from all other feelings, or, in other words, the self-identical essence of piety, is this: the consciousness of being absolutely dependent, or, which is the same thing, of being in relation with God. (CF 4)

The religious consciousness is specified as a feeling of total dependence.

The feeling of absolute dependence is a plausible candidate for a core that underlies the various manifestations of religious affections in diverse traditions, though it is biased toward theism and the conception of a creator. Schleiermacher is pointing to what others have called a sense of finitude. Piety so defined, however, is certainly not independent of concepts and beliefs. To say that the religious person is conscious of being absolutely dependent is to attribute to him or her the concept of dependence and that of complete dependence. The concept of dependence is not only a sophisticated one but one that is concerned with causal explanation. In fact, Schleiermacher's characterization of the feeling more nearly resembles a transcendental version of the cosmological argument than an attempt to direct the reader to a particular aspect of experience.

Our self-consciousness in relation to objects, Schleiermacher contends, is always polar. It includes a moment of activity and one of receptivity, a moment in which we shape objects and one in which objects shape us. Though both are present in all consciousness, the former predominates in action and the latter in knowing and feeling. No person ever exists apart from an other, so one's total self-consciousness in relation to the world remains within the limits of this polarity. But accompanying all activity is a feeling of absolute dependence or "the consciousness that the whole of our spontaneous activity comes from a source outside of us in just the same sense in which anything towards which we should have a feeling of absolute freedom must have proceeded entirely from ourselves" (CF 4.4). This sense of finitude or dependence accompanies every moment of consciousness.

The feeling that Schleiermacher specifies assumes the concept of absolute dependence and appears also to assume the concept of God. The sense of finitude is equated with the consciousness of being in relation to God. But Schleiermacher realizes that his project requires that the feeling of absolute dependence be prior to and specifiable apart from any reference to God.

> As regards the identification of absolute dependence with "relation to God" in our proposition: this is to be understood in the sense that the *Whence* [*Woher*] of our receptive and active existence, as implied in this self-consciousness, is to be designated by the word "God," and that this is for us the really original signification of the word. (CF 4.4)

Schleiermacher argues that the feeling of absolute dependence is not mediated by any representation. He explicitly states that it is not conditioned by some previous knowledge about God (CF 4.3). It is radically independent of concepts and beliefs. The word *God*, he argues, derives its meaning solely from the feeling of absolute dependence and is quite innocent of any use or connotations that it might have in speculative contexts.

So that in the first instance God signifies for us simply that which is the co-determinant in this feeling and to which we trace our being in such a state; and any further content of the idea must be evolved out of this fundamental import assigned to it. (CF 4.4)

The content of the concept of God is derived from the immediate moment of consciousness, rather than the religious consciousness being derived from or shaped by the concept of God.

The concept of God is given in an immediate self-consciousness. The word *God* presupposes an idea that is "nothing more than the expression of the feeling of absolute dependence" (CF 4.4). The concept of expression will be used by Schleiermacher to argue that religious beliefs and practices are the products of religious experience and not vice-versa. The concept of God is conditioned only by the feeling of absolute dependence and not by any independent knowledge or speculation. It is untouched by the activity of the mind in its construction of representations and is thus invulnerable to the Kantian critique that all thought is shaped by the forms and categories of the mind.

Despite Schleiermacher's claims to the contrary, to attribute to a person the consciousness of absolute dependence is to ascribe to him or her the concept of dependence as well as that of some source on which one is totally dependent. In chapter three we shall examine how even apparently simple feelings of joy and sorrow assume particular concepts and beliefs. As regards Schleiermacher's claim for the cognitive value of the feeling of absolute dependence, there can be two positions, depending on which part of his dual thesis is emphasized. If one stresses the point that this moment of self-consciousness is independent of thought and of theoretical knowledge, and draws a close analogy to the Kantian critiques, then this feeling yields no knowledge whatsoever. Schleiermacher does disclaim any attempt to do natural theology or to show that the principles of the Christian faith are consonant with reason

(CF 2.1). The feeling of absolute dependence is not a source of theoretical knowledge. Emphasizing this pole, many have criticized Schleiermacher for equating religious experience with a subjective feeling that has no cognitive component and may be an artifact of personal or cultural factors. Even if the feeling is original and not culturally derivative, how can it tell us anything about God? The "object" of the feeling might be only a grammatical object and have no independent existence.

If one chooses to emphasize Schleiermacher's characterization of piety as one in which "God is given to us in feeling in an original way," one can argue that he is claiming that the religious self-consciousness has a cognitive component, but the way in which God is given in that consciousness is to be distinguished from any theoretical or speculative knowledge (CF 4.4). Williams (1978: 23–56) argues that Schleiermacher anticipates Husserl, and that the feeling he is describing is "a direct, prereflective apprehension of reality." Williams even claims that Schleiermacher's account of the religious consciousness provides a pretheoretical version of the ontological argument. He points to Schleiermacher's distinction between faith as "the certainty which accompanies a state of the higher self-consciousness" and the certainty which accompanies the objective consciousness (CF 14.1). The former is not theoretical, but it is no less certain. Though Williams anachronistically reads Husserl back into Schleiermacher, he may be correct in attributing to him a cognitive claim for the pretheoretical religious self-consciousness, but he is wrong to suggest that such a claim can be cogently defended.

In *On Religion*, the specification of piety always includes reference to its object, and Schleiermacher suggests that the identification of an experience as religious assumes that it is produced by God. In *The Christian Faith*, this second criterion comes to the fore. To ascribe the religious consciousness to a person is to attribute to that person a sense or feeling that he and the world of which he is a part are dependent on a power that is distinct from that world. It is to attribute to the person some rather sophisticated concepts and beliefs, including a belief about the cause of his or her existence and that of the world. Schleiermacher, of course, claims that the religious consciousness is prior to and independent of such concepts and beliefs, but he cannot specify that consciousness without reference to those concepts and beliefs.

Religious Language as Expression

Schleiermacher's opposition to reductionism enters in his claim that the religious moment in consciousness is original. By holding that it is original, he means to emphasize two points: (1) it can be accurately described only as a feeling of absolute dependence and is distinct from other moments of immediate self-consciousness; and (2) it is not an artifact and is not dependent on concepts, thoughts, or cultural representations of any kind. Religious language derives from the distinctive moment of immediate self-consciousness which is piety, and that moment is not conditioned by any antecedent concepts or representations. Religious language is to be explained by reference to the religious affections, and not vice-versa.

In support of his claim that religious affections are prior to and independent of their linguistic expression, Schleiermacher adumbrates a theory of religious language and its relation to experience which informs several recent approaches to the history and philosophy of religion, even when the practitioners of these approaches are not familiar with his work. Religious language is not used to make judgments or to advance claims. The expressive function is dominant. Religious language expresses the peculiar piety that is distinctive of a particular religious community, and the common element expressed in religious language is that which is common to all piety.

In *On Religion* Schleiermacher said that the religious consciousness is awakened in another by the natural expression of that consciousness in the life of the religious person (Schleiermacher, 1958: 119). What is "natural expression"? What does it mean to say that "Christian doctrines are accounts [*Auffassungen*] of the Christian religious affections set forth in speech" (CF 15)? How is an affection set forth in speech, and how does language express the self-consciousness of an individual or community? Schleiermacher addresses these questions directly in the introduction to *The Christian Faith*. The result is a sketch of a theory by which religious language is to be interpreted and explained by reference to the religious affections of which it is the expression.

Primary or original religious language, according to Schleiermacher, is an extension of natural expression. Feelings can determine speech in either of two ways. They can naturally and spontaneously manifest themselves in language, or language can be employed in reflection upon one's mental states. The first is a natural expression of piety in speech; the second is figurative expression, indicating its object by comparison and delimitation rather than directly. Natural expressions function as do involuntary cries, ejaculations, or gestures. They are not attempts to describe affective states but are direct manifestations of them. The more reflective figurative expressions gain their authority from the fact that they are extensions of natural expressions. This is the central thesis of Schleiermacher's doctrine that religious language is determined by the religious affections and not by antecedent thought. The emotions spontaneously manifest themselves in language. They are immediately identified by our acquaintance with them in our own experience and require no knowledge of language or convention. Our knowledge of our own affective states enables us to understand the linguistic expressions of the emotions of others.

> All religious emotions, to whatever type and level of religion they belong, have this in common with all other modifications of the affective self-consciousness, that as soon as they have reached a certain stage and a certain definiteness they

manifest themselves outwardly by mimicry in the most immediate [*unmittelbarsten*] and spontaneous way, by means of facial features and movements of voice and gesture, which we regard as their expression. Thus we definitely distinguish the expression of devoutness from that of a sensuous gladness or sadness, by the analogy of each man's knowledge of himself. (CF 15.1)

In fact, religious affections may be expressed in sacred signs and symbolic acts for repetition and propagation within a tradition without words or thoughts having been associated with them at all. They are independent of concepts and thoughts, though they naturally express themselves in language.

As persons and cultures develop, people increasingly reflect on their mental states. Gradually this reflection is cultivated until these states can be represented outwardly in speech and real doctrine is produced. Christianity has always emphasized preaching; it could not have emerged before the culture had reached this stage of reflective expression. Two forms of primary and original doctrine can be identified in every religious community that has reached such a stage: the poetic and the rhetorical. Poetic language results from the natural expression of a mental state, in which the impetus for expression comes strictly from within; rhetorical language is elicited by a stimulus from without. Primary religious language includes both. A third type, didactic language, is derivative and secondary. It results from the attempt to comprehend what is given in a direct way in the poetic and rhetorical forms. The primary forms may give rise to apparent contradictions, and didactic propositions are formulated in order to achieve definiteness and coherence. Didactic language is independent of the momentary stimuli, internal and external, that give rise to the primary forms. As doctrinal conflicts arise, the need is felt for language that is clear, definite, and free of contradiction. Didactic propositions are furthest removed from the immediate utterances of the religious self-consciousness. They do not arise from intellectual speculation, however, but solely from logically ordered reflection on those utterances. Dogmatic and speculative propositions are entirely different, even when they look similar and may actually be couched in the same words. Doctrinal propositions have always emerged from religious moods, and their real function is the expression of these moods. Their authority stems from the religious consciousness that they express and represent.

Schleiermacher has here offered a theory of religion in which religious language and practice are derived from religious experience conceived as feeling, and not the other way around. The emphasis is on religious language because, as Schleiermacher recognizes, one might ask whether what he takes to be the common element in all piety is an artifact of a culture in which certain concepts and beliefs are widespread. Perhaps the monotheism of the culture deriving from the religion of Israel has given rise to the feeling of absolute dependence. Though originally shaped by beliefs about God as creator and governor of the world, that sense of finitude and dependence appears to remain when the beliefs are bracketed, set aside, or even after they have waned. Were that the case, then the feeling of absolute dependence would not be original and immediate in the sense that Schleiermacher claims for it. The claim that the feeling of absolute dependence is original and not the product of antecedent beliefs or cultural legacies does not guarantee the validity of the belief that the self and its world are dependent on some power beyond the world, a belief Schleiermacher takes to be an expression of the religious consciousness but we have seen to be assumed in the identification of that feeling. It does, however, preclude an explanation of that feeling in nonreligious terms.

Others have followed Schleiermacher in viewing religious language as expressive and consequently not subject to the critical questions and requests for justification which are appropriately applied to language that is employed to make assertions. Ernst Cassirer's (1946, 1953–1957) differentiation of mythological language and thought from the discursive language of science stands in this tradition. Cassirer (1946: 7) refers to the "curse of mediacy" harbored by all symbolism. He wants to escape this curse by discovering the roots of language in our primitive and spontaneous responses to immediate experience. He attempts to map a spectrum from natural spontaneous expressions to more reflective and derivative ones. The intuitive and creative form of myth provides the key by which we may gain access to the original forms of language. The ultimate basis of myth is the primitive power of feeling. Mythical thought does not relate and compare but is captivated by the intuitions of immediate experience (Cassirer, 1946: 32). From these moments of immediacy, a process of increasing objectification takes place. Religious symbols and myths preserve the immediacy and power that have been lost in discursive and scientific language. This power varies inversely with the distance of a linguistic form from immediate experience.

The claim that religious statements neither represent nor assert but are used to express a dimension of experience which is immediate and primitive has been influential in the comparative study of religion, in part through the work of two Schleiermacher scholars, Rudolf Otto and Joachim Wach.[14] Both emphasize the irreducible character of religious experience and the need for an autonomous approach to the study of religion. Despite the attraction of such an approach for those who wish to preclude reductionism in the study of religion, scholars who follow in this tradition often find that the phenomena they are studying belie their methodological commitments.

A recent study demonstrates clearly the inappropriateness of the attempt to assimilate logically articulated linguistic forms to expressions of prelinguistic states. Streng (1967) set out to study the meaning of the term *śūnyatā* (emptiness) in the thought of Nagarjuna, a second-century Buddhist philosopher in India. In his opening and concluding chapters, Streng says

that religious statements are expressions of what is variously
described as religious awareness, a living experience, or an
existential situation. A religious statement is expressive rather
than descriptive or analytical, and religious language is only
one of several different forms of religious expression (Streng,
1967: 171, 175). His portrayal of the intellectual context of
second-century India is organized around a typology of different structures of religious consciousness and their linguistic
and nonlinguistic expressions.

Streng's analysis of Nagarjuna's dialectic in the central chapters of his book requires that he pay careful attention to the
highly articulated and grammatical structure of the argument.
A striking discrepancy emerges between Streng's announced
theory of religious experience and its expression in religious
language on the one hand, and his analysis of Nagarjuna's text
on the other. Nagarjuna's language is analytical language, and
his arguments turn on a tetralemma that is part of a subtle
and sophisticated grammatical analysis. This language cannot
plausibly be assimilated to natural nonlinguistic expressions.
Streng's commentary appropriately emphasizes grammar, syntax, and logic.[15] Consequently, his actual practice is inconsistent
with the theory of religious expression which he has taken
from Cassirer and Wach, and within which he has embedded
his commentary. The details of Nagarjuna's logical and grammatical arguments are much more important for understanding the experience he is describing than that theory would lead
one to suppose. In the commentary Streng exhibits an awareness of the power of Nagarjuna's dialectic to shape religious
experience, but his theoretical reflections imply that it can only
express that experience.

Wittgenstein offers a very different suggestion. In his discussion of the noncognitive status of avowals, he considers the
possibility that some linguistic forms might function as natural
expressions and be located on a spectrum with moans, cries,
and other involuntary behavior. Wittgenstein suggests that

certain psychological verbs in the first person present are not really statements at all; they cannot be true or false. They therefore ought to be assimilated to behavioral manifestations of psychological states. He was struck by the observation that a person who utters the sentence "I am in pain" cannot possibly doubt it or be mistaken, and that consequently it makes no sense to say that he knows that it is true (Wittgenstein, 1953: 256).[16] Such sentences are not statements and therefore cannot be judged true or false. They replace the natural non-linguistic expression of pain. "I am in pain" differs from "He is in pain" roughly as moaning differs from saying that someone is moaning (Wittgenstein, 1958: 68). How does a person learn the meaning of sensation words?

> Here is one possibility: words are connected with the primitive, the natural, expressions of the sensation and used in their place. A child has hurt himself and he cries; and then adults talk to him and teach him exclamations and, later, sentences. They teach their child new pain-behavior.
>   "So you are saying that the word 'pain' really means crying?"—On the contrary: the verbal expression of pain replaces crying and does not describe it. (Wittgenstein, 1953: 244)

Psychological verbs, as Wittgenstein characterizes them, are those in which a statement in the third person present is verified by observation but the first person present is not. I infer from observation that you feel anger or he feels anger, but neither observation nor inference is required for me to say that I feel angry. Such avowals as "I think," "I believe," "I feel," and "I want" function to express and not to describe. The suggestion that avowals may be manifestations of behavior rather than statements about it appears throughout the *Philosophical Investigations* and is closely connected with Wittgenstein's argument against the possibility of a private language.[17]

Although Wittgenstein suggests only that avowals, certain psychological verbs in the first person present, might best be construed as extensions of natural expressions, and Schleier-macher claims that all primary religious language develops out of natural and spontaneous expressive behavior, both posit a continuity between certain linguistic forms on the one hand, and moans, cries, and other primitive behavior on the other. But this position runs into considerable difficulty. Unlike physiognomic patterns, gestures, cries, and other primitive behavior, "I am in pain" and "I feel angry" are linguistically articulated, as is "God created the world." Their expressive function is not natural but conventional. These sentences have a grammatical structure. They can and do enter into logical relations (e.g., contradiction or entailment) with other sen-tences, they can be combined to form complex sentences, and they can be transformed into other tenses. Their logical status is quite different even from facial features and gestures, which are more likely to be governed by conventions than involun-tary cries. Any attempt to assimilate such obviously linguistic forms to nonlinguistic ones is implausible.[18]

The assimilation of religious language to natural and spon-taneous expression is an integral part of Schleiermacher's program. He claims that the common element in religious experience is intentional in that it must be described as the feeling of absolute dependence, and that it includes reference to a codeterminant of that feeling, a "whence" that cannot be specified and is not given in consciousness but which is the source of the religious use of the term *God*. He also argues that this experience is immediate, original, and underived. It is independent of any concepts and beliefs. For this independence to be maintained, the distinctive character of doctrine must be produced by the religious consciousness. Schleiermacher can-not allow the possibility that the common element in religious experience itself derives from or is essentially dependent on the language employed to express it. Were that to be the case, the descriptive and explanatory priority he attributes to the religious consciousness would be compromised. He wants to avoid reduction of the feeling of absolute dependence either by descriptions of that feeling which omit reference to the "whence," or codeterminant, of the feeling, or by purported explanations of piety which portray it as consequent upon antecedent concepts or beliefs. For Schleiermacher, piety is original and underivative, and it includes reference to a codeterminant other than the self and its world.

Expression and Thought

Schleiermacher's conception of religion was inspired by the pietistic tradition in which he was nurtured, and it was intended as a response to Kant's critiques. Piety is chiefly a matter of feeling, and feeling, as distinct from knowing and doing, is a receptive mode of consciousness which is unstructured by the forms and categories of the mind. Religious experience may be expressed in thought, but thought is not constitutive of the experience. The success of this program rests on three theses: (1) the distinctive moment in the religious consciousness is radically independent of concepts and beliefs; (2) that moment is best described as a sense of the infinite or a consciousness of absolute dependence; and (3) religious language and doctrines are properly viewed, not as assertions or judgments, but as extensions of the natural and spontaneous expressions of this sense or consciousness.

The first thesis is intended to show that the common element in piety is not an artifact of the constructive activity of the mind or of the historical development of conceptions of creation and governance in a particular cultural tradition. It is a moment of consciousness that is prelinguistic, prereflective, and therefore irreducible. The second thesis characterizes that moment by reference to its object, or to the codeterminant of the feeling. The relation of the self to that codeterminant is one of total dependence, of being sustained by some power. The third thesis is intended to show that the connection between the religious consciousness and the language of a religious community is an unproblematic one. Primary religious language is an extension of the natural, spontaneous, and involuntary expressions of inner states in direct and immediate physiognomic and vocal manifestations. As in the case of a cry or a wince, no thought need come between the inner state and its expression. To characterize this expression as natural is to deny that it is governed by convention, and thus to assert that the connection between the religious consciousness and its linguistic expression is independent of cultural influences and constructive thought. Secondary religious language develops out of an attempt to understand or interpret the religious consciousness expressed in primary language. Though concepts are employed that have not been given directly in the religious consciousness or its primary expressions, it is in principle unaffected by speculative thought and judgments about the world.

The first two theses are incompatible. If reference to the concept of dependence and to an intentional object or codeterminant is required in order to identify the distinctive moment of religious experience, then it cannot be independent of language or thought. In the absence of the concepts of cause and dependence, or of the thought that the entire causal nexus we call the world might depend on some more comprehensive power distinct from it, the consciousness of absolute dependence Schleiermacher describes would not be available. As we shall see in chapter three, the attribution of emotions to a person presupposes the ascription to that person of certain concepts, beliefs, and attitudes. Fear of flying assumes the belief that airplanes, or other vehicles for air travel, are dangerous. The feeling of absolute dependence assumes the belief that my activity and the world in which I am situated and with which I interact owe their origin and sustenance to some other power.

The religious consciousness as described by Schleiermacher is an intentional state, which is to say that it can be identified only by reference to an object, and that object is given by the prepositional object used to specify the state.[19] Schleiermacher recognizes this when he says that the common element in piety cannot be described without mention of the codeterminant of the feeling. Attitudes, emotions, and beliefs are intentional. The intentional character of these states is sometimes represented by saying that they are always directed toward objects. A thought is always a thought of something. I must be angry at someone, cool toward some particular proposal, or believe that some state of affairs obtains. Intentional objects need not exist.[20] I might be afraid of a ghost or bear that is only a figment of my imagination, or of a plane crash that I worry about; or I might believe falsely that it is raining in Chicago. But the ghost, the bear, the accident, and the rain at this time and in that place must be mentioned in order to specify accurately my fear or my belief. An intentional object must always be specified under a certain description, and that description must be one that is available to the person to whom the emotion, attitude, or belief is ascribed. If Jones is afraid of what he takes to be a bear but which I know to be a clump of bushes moving slowly in the wind, then the object of his fear is the bear and not the bushes. There is no bear, but his thought of the bear must be cited in order to describe his fear. The object of the religious consciousness as described by Schleiermacher is a peculiar one that cannot be specified in a determinate way. This is true of the "infinite" or the "universe" of *On Religion* as well as of the "whence" of *The Christian Faith*. But neither the "sense and taste" of the early work nor the "immediate self-consciousness" of the latter can be characterized without reference to its object. Therefore Schleiermacher's claim that piety is prior to and unaffected by any concepts or thoughts is incompatible with his characterization of it.

The third thesis, that religious language is grounded in and continuous with the natural expression of inner states, and that therefore the connection between those states and that language is unproblematic, is a more complicated one. It is an attempt to assimilate religious language to nonlinguistic phenomena and yet to claim that it can develop naturally to such a point that it is an account or an interpretation of the religious consciousness. The assimilation of this language to natural expressions assumes that the religious consciousness is akin to sensations in that it is independent of concepts and beliefs. The portrayal of religious doctrines as interpretations of that consciousness assumes that it is intentional, characterized by a certain grammatical and logical structure, and is thus a fit object of interpretation. Schleiermacher's thesis that religious language is expressive of the religious affections, then, is intended to hold together the claim that those affections are independent of all thought and the claim that they are intentional and have a certain cognitive structure. He wants to show that the language of religious belief and doctrine emerges from those affections without being contaminated by thoughts and claims about the world which might make it vulnerable to philosophical criticism or to contradiction by advances in knowledge. To that end, he represents the link between the religious consciousness and its expressions as a natural one. Religious doctrine must be viewed as originating in direct utterances [*Äusserungen*] of the religious moment in self-consciousness, and not as dependent on thought or convention. The link between the two is not a logical or grammatical one but a causal one. Schleiermacher's theory of the expressive character of religious language is offered as an explanation of the emergence of that language. It is set over against alternative explanations, in particular the hypothesis that the religious consciousness is a product of antecedent concepts and beliefs.

The argument that religious language is exclusively expressive, that it is not used to make judgments about the world and thus cannot conflict with the assertions of science or philosophy, and that it is related to feeling in a way analogous to a cry or grimace, has been defended recently by the logical positivists. Ayer's characterization of religious language and his view of its origins might have been acceptable to Schleiermacher, but the two thinkers differ radically in their conclusions because they differ in their descriptions of the religious consciousness and their judgments about its source. Schleiermacher thinks that piety has a cognitive component, whereas Ayer does not. Ayer writes about moral and religious statements:

> They are pure expressions of feeling and as such do not come under the category of truth or falsehood. They are unverifiable for the same reason as a cry of pain or a word of command is unverifiable—because they do not express genuine propositions. (Ayer, 1970: 108–109)

Ayer concludes that religious statements have no cognitive significance.[21]

> Thus we offer the theist the same comfort as we gave to the moralist. His sentences cannot possibly be valid, but they cannot be invalid either. As he says nothing at all about the world, he cannot justly be accused of saying anything false, or anything for which he has insufficient grounds. (Ayer, 1970: 116)

Schleiermacher would agree that religious statements are not true or false in the same sense that either scientific or philosophical statements are, and that they do not make claims about the world. He thinks, however, that they can be assessed for their coherence and their adequacy in expressing the religious consciousness.[22] Such assessments assume that they have a logical structure and that the religious consciousness has a conceptual component.

We have seen that Schleiermacher's account requires that the religious consciousness be intentional and that it be independent of all concepts and beliefs, and we have seen that these two claims are contradictory. He is correct to view primary religious language as the expression of a deeply entrenched moment of consciousness but incorrect to portray that moment as independent of thought and belief. Schleiermacher has mistaken a felt sense of immediacy for a guarantee that piety is not formed or shaped by thought or inference.

To identify some linguistic or other behavior as an expression of religious experience is to judge that it provides evidence for an attribution of that experience to the person. To describe a certain kind of behavior as an expression of fear is to say that an inference is warranted from that behavior to an ascription of fear (Tormey, 1971: 39–60). Certain kinds of actions when performed before embarking on an airplane warrant an ascription of fear or anxiety about air travel, and we say that such behavior expresses a fear of flying. We cannot, however, identify the behavior as expressive in the absence of such an inference. No distinguishing mark enables us to identify some language or behavior as expressive. We take it to be expressive if we think that it provides evidence for the ascription of the state that we take it to express. To label something an expression is to make and to license such an inference. We speak of expressing emotions, attitudes, and beliefs, but not pangs, twitches, or even a sensation of warmth. For something to be expressed, it must have a conceptual component. When we describe certain behavior as the expression of pain, we understand pain to be not a simple sensation but a condition that includes concepts and beliefs about that sensation (cf. Tormey, 1971).

Schleiermacher says we can identify an expression of devoutness and distinguish it from an expression of gladness because we have direct acquaintance with each of these emotions in our own experience. We know something to be an expression of a certain feeling because we are acquainted with that feeling and its natural expressions. But we cannot directly distinguish between expressive and nonexpressive behavior or language and between the expressions of different inner states by inspection alone. I may describe something as a sad expression, and yet have no reason to take it as an expression of sadness (Tormey, 1971: 39–51). A clown's mask or the face of a beagle may be described as having a sad expression without anything at all being expressed. To say that something has a sad expression is to characterize certain observable features of a situation. To say of some behavior that it is an expression of sadness, however, is to say that it provides evidence for an attribution of sadness to the agent. A sad expression can occur without sadness, but an expression of sadness cannot. There is a logical connection between an identification of something as an expression of sadness and the attribution of sadness to a person. The context must be taken into account in identifying some behavior as an expression.

The identification of linguistic or other behavior as expressive assumes an explanation of that behavior. Were I to overhear someone engaging in invective and angry expressions, I would initially take that as evidence of his anger. If I then noticed that I had wandered onto a stage and had overheard an actor rehearsing his lines, I would discount his words and gestures as evidence of what he was feeling. He might indeed be angry, but those words in that setting are not sufficient to warrant that inference. If the setting were a ceremonial one in which a pastor were leading his congregation in the recitation of the Apostles' Creed, one would be less likely to accept those words as a direct expression of the beliefs of the pastor or of his parishioners than one would in another context. That is because an alternative explanation is available. The conventions governing the service dictate that those words are to be said at that time and in that place. The Creed may be an accurate expression of the beliefs of those reciting it, but the evidence is insufficient to warrant that conclusion.

No class of behavior, including linguistic behavior, can be designated as expressive without qualification. A tic or a facial feature may or may not be expressive, depending on the circumstances in which it appears. It is expressive only when it provides evidence that warrants an inference to some belief, desire, emotion, or attitude. There are no natural expressions of inner states in the sense of the direct manifestations that Schleiermacher's theory requires. To identify something as an expression is to offer an explanation of that phenomenon and to regard it as evidence for the ascription of an intentional state.

Whereas Schleiermacher claims that any speculative or theoretical interests are irrelevant to the task of the theologian or philosopher of religion, his description of the religious consciousness is formulated in order to preclude the reduction of that consciousness and thus to rule out as illegitimate several kinds of criticism of religious doctrine and belief. He dismisses explanations of the feeling of absolute dependence as an artifact of antecedent concepts or cultural influences. It is an original moment within the mind which must be taken as a given and cannot be explained away. This is not, of course, an argument for the validity of the feeling. It might be original and yet the self and cosmos might not be dependent on some power that is distinct from both. But the exclusion of alternative explanations is itself a kind of explanation, and Schleiermacher's theory of the expressive character of religious language is also offered as an explanation that precludes reduction of the religious experience.

The religious consciousness is given, is original, and includes a sense of a codeterminant distinct from the self and the world. The notion of a codeterminant is ambiguous with regard to whether it should be understood as an intentional object without any assumption regarding its existence outside the consciousness, or as something that determines the consciousness. Schleiermacher's denial of speculative and theoretical interests and his restriction of his task to an elucidation of the religious consciousness requires the first interpretation, but his rejection of alternative explanations for the feeling appears to assume the second. In fact, Schleiermacher makes no distinction between what we will later differentiate as descriptive and explanatory reduction, and thus is able to appeal to an elucidation of the religious consciousness to rule out nonreligious explanations.[23] Suppose that the actual source on which the self and world are dependent is the cosmos itself. Schleiermacher considers this possibility and proposes to exclude it by appeal to the intentional object of the religious consciousness.

> It is possible to give a non-religious explanation of the sense of absolute dependence; it might be said that it only means the dependence of finite particulars on the whole and on the system of all finite things, and what is implied and made the center of reference is not God but the world. But we can only regard this explanation as a misunderstanding. For we recognize in our self-consciousness an awareness of the world, but it is different from the awareness of God in the same self-consciousness. (CF 32.2)

The nonreligious explanation is rejected on the grounds that it is not a proper elucidation of the religious consciousness.[24] This argument, and the claim that the feeling of absolute dependence is original, both appear to be designed to stave off criticisms of the belief that is assumed by the religious consciousness. The confusion between the proper description or elucidation of religious experience and its proper explanation is not unique to Schleiermacher, and we shall see that it plays a crucial role in the protective strategies that have been employed by some recent philosophers of religion.

The recognition that religious language is often expressive remains one of Schleiermacher's contributions to the study of religion, though the affections that are expressed are not independent of concepts and beliefs. Although religious language is expressive and thus shaped by certain affections, it is also formative and shapes emotions and experiences. It can be highly evocative and can prepare the conditions under which a person will attend to a particular moment and identify that moment as an experience of a certain kind.

While claiming to give a description of an experience that is independent of thought, Schleiermacher attempts to create the conditions necessary to evoke it by establishing the appropriate thoughts.

> What you are to notice is the rise of your consciousness and not to reflect on something already there. Your thought can only embrace what is sundered. Wherefore as soon as you have made any given definite activity of your soul an object of communication or of contemplation, you have already begun to separate. It is impossible, therefore, to adduce any definite example, for, as soon as anything· is an example, what I wish to indicate is already past. (Schleiermacher, 1958: 41–42)

Whatever the reader focuses on is, according to Schleiermacher, not the moment under discussion. That moment is, by definition, one that underlies and precedes our reflective consciousness. The passage appears to be pure description, but it actually serves to direct one's attention and to form one's judgments in such a way as to support the inference that there is an undifferentiated moment that cannot be given a determinate characterization. The use of the empty term *whence* as a placeholder for that indeterminate source or power that is the object of the feeling of absolute dependence plays an important role in this process. Religious language is not only the expressive, receptive medium Schleiermacher takes it to be. It also plays a very active and formative role in religious experience.

II.
INTERPRETATION

Religious beliefs and practices are interpretations of experience, and they are themselves fit objects of interpretation. Numerous scholars have recently argued for the primacy of the method of interpretation in the study of religion and culture. Clifford Geertz (1973) has called for a semiotics, and Ricoeur (1970, 1976) for a hermeneutics, of culture. Both view religion as central to any culture, and both argue that cultures are properly studied through some kind of interpretative approach. A myth serves as an interpretation of the experience of a community, and it is itself a text that calls for interpretation. The study of religion, like a page of medieval exegesis of the Bible or the Talmud, is a succession of commentaries on texts that are themselves interpretations of texts. The two ends of the series are arbitrarily fixed by canonical decision and the most recent commentator, but the possibilities for expansion are endless.

Students of religion, both classical and contemporary, would agree that a major function of religious language and practice is to enable persons and communities to make sense of, or to interpret, their experience. Much of the literature that comprises the Hebrew Bible can be read as the record of attempts to interpret the actions of a particular people and the events that befell them and to discern the purposes behind those actions and events. Early Christian literature consists largely of attempts to interpret the events surrounding the life and death of Jesus in the light of the Jewish tradition and the contemporary Hellenistic context and to understand the experiences of individuals in the light of those events. Augustine's *Confessions* stands as a paradigmatic instance of the interpretation of the course of a life in religious terms, and *The City of God* has served as a model for subsequent interpretations of social and political processes. All religious communities are preoccupied, in good measure, with the interpretation of sacred scripture, myths, stories, or legal documents that have been bequeathed to them by previous generations. Myths are interpretations addressed to questions of origin, of moral ambiguity, of the meaning of suffering and death, and of anomalous phenomena that cannot be assimilated to existing conceptual systems. Rituals serve to dramatize and to permit the acting out of such interpretations, thereby increasing their power to convince. Crises of interpretability create demands for innovation in interpretation and for solutions to the problems that have led to the crises.

Any term or concept that can serve, even with some stretching, as an umbrella under which to group so many diverse approaches to the study of religion and culture must be difficult to make precise. What is an interpretation? Does it include description, evaluation, explanation, and application? Is it possible to speak of a valid or true interpretation, or ought they to be assessed in some other way? Can a person interpret his or her own behavior? The recent literature, dominated as it is by the hermeneutic tradition stemming from Schleiermacher, exhibits agreement only on the point that the interpretative method differs from methods of explanation employed in the sciences of nature. It is designed to achieve understanding of systems of meaning and of cultural symbols and artifacts. For this purpose, it is argued, the paradigmatic inference of the natural scientist from observation to a causal hypothesis that can be experimentally tested is inappropriate. The scientist's search for explanations that can be couched in terms of general laws and initial conditions must be replaced by special guidelines for the interpretation of texts, actions, and other embodiments of meaning.

There is an ambiguity that runs through discussions of interpretation in religion, and it can be seen in the dual statement that religious beliefs and practices are interpretations of experience and are themselves fit objects for interpretation. Both parts of this statement are true, but the relevant concept of interpretation differs from one part to the other. Religious beliefs and practices are interpretations of experience in that they are attempts to make sense of and to account for the phenomena and events with which one is confronted, including one's own behavior. They are attempts to understand, where understanding can be construed as seeking the best explanation. It is in this sense that there is no uninterpreted experience. Our experience is already informed and constituted by our conceptions and tacit theories about ourselves and our world. All observation is theory-laden. We can design procedures in which certain hypotheses can be tested, but any perception or experience is already shaped by the concepts and implicit judgments we bring to it. In this sense, we are constantly engaged in interpretation and reinterpretation. As problems arise, inquiry is initiated and we search for solutions. Thought has been characterized as the search for increasingly adequate explanations.[1]

When we say, however, that interpretation is the proper method for understanding texts, myths, actions, and other cultural products, the meaning of *interpretation* is more specific. Here interpretation is conceived as the method required for grasping the rules that govern a certain system of symbols or conventional practices. I cannot understand a text unless I know the grammar of the language in which the text is written, and I cannot interpret an action unless I understand the institutional context in which the action was performed and the language and concepts available to the actor. I cannot understand what he was doing, or identify the action under a description that he might accept, unless I know what grammatical rules and conventions governed the situation as the actor perceived it. This kind of interpretation does not preclude explanation but must precede it. It is necessary in order to properly identify the belief, the text, the action, or the emotion that is the object of inquiry. Here interpretation refers specifically to the elucidation of a text or practice by reference to the rules and conventions that govern a particular symbolic system.

The difference between these two uses of the concept of interpretation has not always been kept in mind, and its neglect has fostered confusion in discussions of interpretation in religion. In this chapter, two traditions of thought about interpretation will be examined. The two ways of construing the term will be compared and contrasted with particular attention to their implications for the study of religion and religious experience.

The issue of how one comes to understand the various expressions of human consciousness has been addressed in a tradition of reflection on the methods employed in the interpretation of texts. Does the interpretation of literature, works of art, actions, and other expressions of the intentions, emotions, and beliefs of persons and communities require an approach that differs from the methods for the study of the phenomena that are the objects of the natural sciences? Schleiermacher is a major figure in the development of philosophical reflection on hermeneutics, or the theory of interpretation. Recent interest in his work from outside the disciplines of philosophy of religion and theology has centered on his contributions to this tradition.

Schleiermacher's hermeneutical theory is not unrelated to his analysis of religious experience. If the religious consciousness is expressed in gestures, primary language, and in certain practices, then those expressions require interpretation in order to understand that consciousness. His conception of the nature of religion has definite implications for how it ought to be studied. Religious language should not be regarded either as an instance of ordinary language or as a vehicle for scientific or philosophical assertions. It functions in a special way as an expression of the various forms of the religious consciousness. In order, then, to study that language as religious language, one must adopt a distinctive approach. One might, of course, investigate the same language and practices for other purposes. A social scientist might study anchorites or monastic communities in order to see what light they shed on the dominant social order and why individuals sometimes leave family and other institutions for the desert or the cloister. A literary or art historian might study Christianity in order to trace the influence of religious motifs and biblical allusions in the art of medieval Europe. An economist might attempt to correlate certain kinds of religious attitudes with particular economic data. The language of worship in a Reformed parish in Berlin might be studied as an example of early nineteenth-century German, or as the language of a particular social class. But each of these requires an understanding of the particular form of the religious consciousness that has shaped the relevant intentions, symbols, attitudes, and language. To study religion is to seek to grasp these varied data as expressions of diverse modifications of the religious consciousness. To view them in some other way is to engage in a reductive approach and to lose the distinctive character of the religious.

In its broadest sense, the term *interpretation* is employed to refer to the active moment in perception, or to the mind's construction of reality. It is in this sense that one can say there is no uninterpreted experience, but that fact alone provides no warrant for contrasting interpretation with the explanatory methods of the natural scientist. Interpretation, in this Kantian sense, refers to the role of the imagination and to the activity of the mind in knowing. The mind, to a greater or lesser extent, depending on the specific formulation of this view, constitutes the reality it perceives. Everything is an object of interpretation, and all of the contents of consciousness are the result of interpretation. This poses one of the quandaries of post-Kantian thought: if everything is the result of interpretation, then what is the object of interpretation? Is there such a thing as a primitive or uninterpreted datum? This question has inspired searches for things-in-themselves, absolute ideas, sense data, and other candidates for the role of the given.

As a step toward the elucidation of the concept, and to bring out the two meanings at work in the contemporary discussion, let us consider two traditions of thought about interpretation: the hermeneutic and the pragmatic. Both are indebted to Kant, and proponents of both would subscribe to the broad sense of interpretation mentioned above. Each assumes a particular paradigm that is originally derived from a limited sphere but is eventually extended and extrapolated to provide a general theory of interpretation. Representatives of the hermeneutic tradition have typically argued that the study of human history and culture requires an approach that differs from that employed in the study of natural phenomena, whereas pragmatists have stressed that the processes of inquiry and inference are invariant with respect to the object of study.

In his *Tractatus Theologico-Politicus*, Spinoza argues that Scripture ought to be interpreted by employing the same method that we use to interpret nature.

> I may sum up the matter by saying that the method of interpreting Scripture does not widely differ from the method of interpreting nature—in fact, it is almost the same. For as the interpretation of nature consists in the examination of the history of nature, and therefrom deducing definitions of natural phenomena on certain fixed axioms, so Scriptural interpretation proceeds by the examination of Scripture, and inferring the intention of its authors as a legitimate conclusion from its fundamental principles. (Spinoza, 1951: 99)

Spinoza recommends that the same method of inquiry be applied to Scripture that is applied to any secular text or natural phenomenon and says that the aim of the inquiry is to infer the intention of the authors of the text.

The two traditions to be considered here are distinguished from one another with respect to this issue of whether or not the interpretation of scripture, or of any other text, differs widely from the interpretation of nature. Can texts and natural phenomena be assimilated to one another? In the hermeneutic tradition, the concept of interpretation is employed chiefly to distinguish the study of persons and their cultural expressions from that of nature, and thus to establish a dualism with respect to the methods and objects of knowledge. In the pragmatic tradition, the same concept is used to emphasize the unity of thought and the seamless character of the web of belief. The hermeneutic tradition stems from and continues to have affinities with literary interpretation and the humanities, whereas the pragmatic tradition emerges from reflection on the interpretation of empirical data. For the first tradition, the interpretation of texts is paradigmatic; for the second, the study of perception and the interpretation of laboratory data provide the model.

These two traditions will be briefly compared and contrasted, with particular reference to the early formulations of each in the work of Schleiermacher and Peirce. We shall see that the hermeneutic tradition derives from an important insight, but that an erroneous conclusion is drawn from that insight. The insight is that an experience, emotion, intention, action, or belief must be identified under a description that accords with the rules governing the subject's language and behavior, and therefore that the subject's point of view has a certain priority for one who wants to understand that experience or that action. The erroneous conclusion is that we can only know the experience, emotion, or intention of another by sharing it, by evoking it in ourselves, by applying it, or by participating in it in some way. By contrast, the pragmatic tradition does not sufficiently take account of the distinctive problems posed by the interpretation of texts and practices. Each has a contribution to make to our understanding of the proper method for the study of religious experience.

The Hermeneutic Tradition

This tradition originates with the recognition that the interpretation of texts differs from the formulation and assessment of scientific hypotheses. Early attempts to account for that difference were built upon the assumption that the understanding of a text or of any form of human expression requires empathy with the author, or something approaching a direct experience of what the author has expressed. The history of the hermeneutic tradition can be traced from the assumption that some such direct acquaintance with what is expressed in the text is required, to the recognition that it is often neither necessary nor possible, and finally to an attempt to account in some other way for the difference between the interpretation of texts and the interpretation of data. According to this account, the difference lies in the fact that one must master the grammatical rules and conventions that govern a text or other cultural product in order to understand it. A message or an action must be identified by reference to those rules and conventions.

Though one can cite precursors, Schleiermacher's lectures on hermeneutics may be regarded as the first general theory of interpretation. Drawing on the legacy of special traditions for the exegesis and application of biblical and legal texts, on the work of classical philologists, and on his own philosophical psychology, he proposed a theory that was intended to account for the understanding of any linguistic expression, whether spoken or written. Schleiermacher spent years engaged in editing and translating Plato's dialogues. On the basis of his study of their literary form, he worked to establish an accurate chronological order and criteria for determining the authenticity of the dialogues. He also lectured on the New Testament, and he preached nearly every Sunday of his adult life. Consequently, his hermeneutic theory grew out of actual practice and constant reflection on the problems posed by the interpretation of texts whose languages and cultures are foreign to those of their interpreters. He understood the task of interpretation to be that of grasping the original intention of the author and the relation of that intention to the language in which it is expressed.

Schleiermacher (1959) distinguishes two moments in the interpretative process, both of which are necessary and each of which complements the other. The first is the grammatical interpretation, which refers to the study of the history of a language, of the relation of the language to its culture, and of the general historical and social context of the discourse to be interpreted. The second is the psychological or technical interpretation.[2] The psychological moment is intended to enable the interpreter to grasp or to reconstruct the individuality of the author. This method requires an analysis of the author's style, or the particular way he has chosen to present his thoughts, and of what he has excluded. Beyond this stylistic analysis, which need be no less rigorous than the grammatical, the interpreter must draw on his or her own sensitivity to reconstruct the unity of the author's intention as it is expressed in the discourse. This reconstruction calls for what Schleiermacher terms the divinatory procedure, in which the interpreter attempts imaginatively to share in the author's meaning. To use the word *empathy* here might be to place too much emphasis on the pathic, or on the element of feeling. But in the broadest sense the aim is surely empathic. The divinatory moment is balanced by a comparative procedure in which the individuality of the author is set alongside that of others in order to heighten his peculiar characteristics. It is facilitated by comparison with one's own individuality as well as with that of others.

Much discussion has focused on the divinatory procedure in Schleiermacher's hermeneutics. It must be remembered that the psychological moment is always to be correlated with and complemented by the historical and linguistic competence demanded by the grammatical interpretation, and that the comparative and divinatory procedures assume one another. They must be held in continual tension, and consequently the process of interpretation is never completed. But Schleiermacher knew that even after substantial linguistic and historical competence has been acquired, interpretation demands something more. It requires an ability to perceive the situation as the author of the text perceived it, to grasp his intention, and even, if possible, to appropriate the experience expressed in the text. The history of Platonic and biblical scholarship provided Schleiermacher with ample evidence of scholars who had acquired the requisite technical competence but who were unable to grasp the spirit of the texts. A pianist whose technical skills are unassailable might still be unable to bring to life the music of Chopin or Mozart. The interpreter must grasp the tone of the whole.

The divinatory and comparative methods are distinguished and characterized as follows:

> The divinatory [method] is that by which one, by turning himself, as it were, into the other, seeks to grasp immediately the individual in him. The comparative [method] first places him under a universal type in order to understand him, and then attempts to find his distinctive traits by comparing him with others of the same general type. (Schleiermacher, 1959: 109)

Each method refers back to the other. Comparison assists in the process of divination, but without the latter component there would be nothing to compare. Despite its being correlated with and balanced by the other methods, however, the divinatory moment is at the heart of Schleiermacher's hermeneutics. The interpreter aims to grasp the original intention of the author as it is expressed in the text, and this grasp is immediate and intuitive.

To say that the author's individuality is to be intuitively apprehended is not to say that this apprehension requires no activity on the part of the interpreter. The intuitive moment is not a passive one. The author's intention must be actively reconstructed, but that reconstruction leads to an apprehension that is finally immediate. It is not inferred or hypothesized from the external data.

Why does Schleiermacher characterize this moment in the interpretative process as immediate and intuitive? In *On Religion* he argues that in order to understand the nature of piety the reader must reproduce the religious moment in himself or herself. It cannot be understood by representation but only by participation. In the lectures on hermeneutics he says that the individuality of an author cannot be grasped conceptually but only intuitively, and that both immediate intuition and comparison must be combined in a continual dialectic.

> Immediate intuition cannot be communicated; comparison never quite reaches the true individuality. The two ways must be combined by relating them to the totality of possibilities. (Schleiermacher, 1959: 119)

Immediate intuition is required because the author's originality eludes concepts and can be known only by direct acquaintance. The divinatory procedure is based on the assumption that each individual is responsive to the uniqueness of every other and can also share in the other's experience (Schleiermacher, 1959: 109). The assumption of a common humanity guarantees that it will always be possible for the interpreter to cultivate himself in such a way as to be able to elicit in his own mind the experience expressed by the author of the text on which he is working. When that happens, interpreter and author meet, the interpreter "turns himself into the author," and the individuality expressed in the text is immediately grasped.

> For him [Schleiermacher], the walls of time and of the historical transmission or mediation process disappear, and the two—the original and the interpreter—are directly and, therefore, in unaltered shape present to each other in a heterogeneity which is at the same time a mutual fitness, affinity, or even homogeneity. (Frei, 1974: 290)

Some recent representatives of the hermeneutic tradition have criticized Schleiermacher for requiring that the interpreter empathize with the author, or grasp some prelinguistic feeling (Kimmerle, 1959: 9–24; Gadamer, 1975: 162–173). They deplore what they take to be the psychologism that emerges in the later notes and addresses and applaud the focus on language as opposed to authorial intent which they find in the early notes.[3] This contrast has been overdrawn, but in any case it does not affect Schleiermacher's claim that there is an immediate and intuitive moment in the experience. Hans Frei (1974: 295–300) draws attention to the fact that, in contrast to his work on religion, and despite their contemporaneity, Schleiermacher mentions feeling only rarely in the notes on hermeneutics, and then with none of the freight that it carries in either *On Religion* or *The Christian Faith*. Frei argues that the divinatory method yields an intellectual intuition that is a cognitive matter and not an affective one. He suggests that Schleiermacher may have been influenced in this regard by Schelling's concept of an intellectual intuition or an immediate cognitive act, which had replaced what he had earlier claimed was an aesthetic intuition that rested on immediacy of feeling. But the characterization of divination as affective or intellectual intuition is not the crucial issue, nor is it a matter of psychologism versus attention to language. Were Frei's suggestion correct, Schleiermacher would be cleared of the charge of relying upon a prelinguistic empathy as the capstone of the act of interpretation, but his insistence on the immediate and intuitive character of that act would remain intact.

The influence of Schleiermacher's hermeneutical theory was greatly extended by Wilhelm Dilthey, who carried the theory beyond its application to written texts and employed it for the interpretation of all cultural expressions. While still a student, Dilthey wrote a prize essay on Schleiermacher's hermeneutics. Later he edited Schleiermacher's letters, and at his death he was at work on a biographical study that, though unfinished, remains the best written about the theologian. In 1900, Dilthey published an essay entitled "The Development of Hermeneutics," in which he portrayed Schleiermacher as the critical systematizer of the subject and as the founder of scientific hermeneutics (Dilthey, 1976: 247–260).

Once hermeneutics had been defined as the art of understanding and Schleiermacher had argued that the aim of the interpreter is to grasp the original intention of the author and its relation to the particular form in which that intention is expressed, there was no reason to restrict the act of understanding to linguistic expressions. The painter's canvas or sketchbook, the composer's score, or the craftsman's artifact is as much a vehicle for the expression of the intention and individuality of an author as is a written or spoken text. Gestures, actions, and cultural products of all kinds are expressions of lived experience (*Erlebnis*) and thus, for Dilthey, appropriate objects of interpretation. The hermeneutic method was to provide the basis for all study of human history and culture.

Schleiermacher employed the traditional distinction between physics (the study of nature) and ethics (the study of man), a distinction that received support from Kant's differentiation between the theoretical and practical employments of reason. Dilthey sharpened this distinction into a separation and argued that cultural expressions could and should be treated as texts, embodiments of meaning which can be studied in order to understand the experiences of authors and actors, just as Schleiermacher had suggested that we could share the meaning and experience of the author of a text. He argued that the method of interpretation is required for all human studies (*Geisteswissenschaften*), in contrast to the sciences of nature (*Naturwissenschaften*), and that the study of human history and culture must not be reduced or assimilated to the natural sciences. Human studies could be as rigorous and as successful as the sciences of nature, but they must be autonomous.

It was Dilthey who gave currency to the term *verstehen*, employing it to refer to the process of reconstructing the subjective understanding of another and of coming to view the world as others view it. This concept is often traced, perhaps anachronistically, back to Vico and his claim that we can understand the motives of historical actors because we are also actors and the products of human culture because we produce similar expressions ourselves.[4] We are uniquely equipped to understand the feelings, intentions, and actions of other persons because we share similar experiences and have acted similarly. Consequently, we are better able to understand the world of mind than the world of nature.

The method of *verstehen* has figured prominently in the work of many social scientists concerned with the study of religion, beginning with Max Weber's (1968) description of his approach as *verstehende Sociologie*. It is difficult, however, to determine exactly what the method is, and it has been the subject of much controversy in the social sciences and philosophy.[5] Defense of the method, or of some variation of it, has proceeded hand in hand with defense of the sharp distinction between the *Geisteswissenschaften* and the *Naturwissenschaften* which was drawn in Dilthey's work. Appeals to *verstehen*, and to the contrast between interpretation or understanding on the one hand and explanation on the other, have come to serve as reliable indicators of those who argue that the methods of the social and natural sciences are qualitatively distinct and that the former cannot be reduced to the latter.[6] The distinction has developed into a commitment that is characteristic of the hermeneutic tradition.

Schleiermacher held that the aim of the interpreter is to grasp the intention of the author, but that aim can only be approached through a careful balancing of the grammatical and psychological interpretations and of the comparative and divinatory procedures. Dilthey claims somewhat more boldly that the aim of interpretation is to relive the experience of the author. He introduces the term *Nacherlebnis* to designate this process of reexperiencing what is expressed in the text or cultural artifact under scrutiny (Dilthey, 1927: 213–216). The author, whether a person or a cultural movement, is a historical individual whose uniqueness and creativity can be grasped only by the hermeneutic method. Following Schleiermacher, Dilthey thought this could be effected by the interpreter's reproduction of the experience in himself.

> By transposing his own being experimentally, as it were, into a historical setting the interpreter can momentarily emphasize and strengthen some mental processes and allow others to fade into the background and thus reproduce an alien life in himself. (Dilthey, 1976: 258)

This does not mean that the interpreter can or should shed his skin or his culture. When he describes the reliving of the experience of another as immediate and intuitive, Dilthey does not imply that it can be accomplished without careful study and imaginative construction. Finally, however, like Schleiermacher, he holds that interpretation must be built on some form of direct acquaintance.

Dilthey's chief illustration of *Nacherlebnis* is the historian's understanding of the past. He proposed, but never completed, a critique of historical reason which would stand as a complement to the Kantian critiques of theoretical, practical, and aesthetic reason. His concepts of *nacherleben* and *verstehen* were part of an attempt to formulate the special conditions that make historical knowledge possible. Dilthey agreed with the romantics in their claim, against Kant, that an intellectual intuition is possible, but he criticized the attempt to locate this intuition in man's relation to nature. He tried to defend a mode of intuitive understanding in the knowledge of history rather than in the knowledge of nature. History is the product of the thoughts and actions of persons, and therefore it is possible for an interpreter to gain access to the inner processes that move history.

The most influential contemporary representative of the Continental hermeneutic tradition, Hans-Georg Gadamer, has criticized Dilthey for what he calls his psychologism (Gadamer, 1975: 192–214). Gadamer argues that it is an error to represent the interpreter as empathically entering into the mind and grasping the intentions of the author of a text. No one can step outside of his own mind and culture to enter into that of another, and the meaning of a text is not limited to that which its author intended it to have. Gadamer stresses the ubiquity of prejudice (*Vorurteil*) and the necessity for the interpreter to acknowledge the tradition in which he stands. The historian is always immersed in his own culture, shaped by the beliefs and interests of his time, and cannot escape that context to enter fully into that of another time and place. A nineteenth-century history of Rome is not difficult to identify. It reflects the beliefs and interests of the author and of his culture rather than those of Rome.[7] This holds for the natural scientist as well as for the cultural historian, though the effect of diverse interests in shaping the interpretation of data may be more dramatic in the latter instance.

Dilthey's defenders have argued that the emphasis on the subjective experience of the author is characteristic only of his earlier writings. He later came to emphasize the logical rather than the historical character of interpretation and to see that the aim of the interpreter is to grasp the meaning of the text and not the experience of the author.[8] Close study of the writings of Hegel, and especially of Husserl's *Logische Untersuchungen*, led him to focus on the intentional object of a linguistic expression rather than on authorial intent. The object of a text is a logical one and is not meant to be apprehended by attending to the subjective state of its author. Meaning is a logical matter, and not a psychological one.

The shift of focus from the subjective state of the author to the intentional object that is discovered by grammatical analysis of the text is a step in the right direction, and it provides a satisfactory answer to Gadamer's critique of the attempt to grasp a prelinguistic intuition. But it need not affect Dilthey's characterization of the task of interpretation as one of reproducing the experience of the author or the interpreter. After reading Husserl, Dilthey could see that the experience could not be reproduced by focusing on the consciousness of the author; rather, the interpreter must direct his attention to the object of the author's consciousness. For example, if a text expresses a thought about elephants or a fear of snakes, the interpreter can share in the experience only by imaginatively attending to elephants or snakes, and not by attending to the author. In this way the interpreter can draw on his own experience to reproduce the author's thought or emotion in himself. The change in Dilthey's formulations may render them more adequate, but it does not alter his conviction that the meaning of linguistic and cultural expressions can be understood only by drawing on our common humanity and seeking to share the mind of their authors.[9]

For the hermeneutic tradition, the interpretation of texts is paradigmatic. We come to understand the natural world by seeking lawlike connections and explanations for phenomena that may initially appear mysterious, but we come to understand a speaker or author by interpreting a text or discourse in order to recover the meaning he intended to convey. Just as Dilthey extended the method of interpretation to the study of individual and cultural expressions, contemporary hermeneutic theorists begin by considering the interpretation of written texts but quickly resort to metaphorical extensions of text. Ricoeur moves first to dreams and then to actions, and Geertz to such events as a Balinese cockfight or a royal cremation ceremony. What are the limits within which something can validly be considered a text? Though it is often tacit, a judgment is required to determine whether or not something is a proper object of interpretation.

Something is interpretable if it is a message, whether its form be a written text, the spoken word, an obscure code, or the conventions of a composer or painter. In order for something to be a text in this broad but still restricted sense, it must have been written or encoded by someone who intended the signs to communicate. Where no such intention can be presumed, interpretation is inappropriate. For instance, radio astronomers, upon intercepting nonrandom blips from the far reaches of space, might think the blips could constitute a message from a distant world.[10] People might set to work trying to decode the message. Later an explanation might be proposed to account for this particular pattern of blips on the basis of natural cosmic phenomena such as quasars. Were this explanation to be generally accepted, people would stop trying to decode the blips. Where an explanation can be given in physical terms, and the phenomenon is not governed by grammatical rules or conventions, we have no text and therefore nothing to interpret. Such considerations have led to the contrast between interpretation and explanation.

Ricoeur (1970), commenting on Freud, views dreams and myths as perhaps the most fruitful objects of interpretation. They differ from the stricter notion of text only in not having been formulated with the intention to communicate, unless one is prepared to admit unconscious intentions. Yawns, facial expressions, and involuntary gestures may also be objects of interpretation. While yawns do not normally admit of interpretation in terms of intentions and purposes, actions do. Several theorists have recently proposed a hermeneutics of action.[11] We observe a person behaving unusually and ask ourselves what he or she means by that. Interpretations of actions are generally couched in terms of intentions, desires, and beliefs that we attribute to the actors and in the light of which the actions have meaning.

The phrase "the interpretation of history" is a familiar one; it has engendered much discussion in writings on the philosophy of history. Is the interpretation of historical events merely a case of interpreting actions in the aggregate? Do we interpret a historical event in terms of the purposes of individuals, or do we assume a larger context, a *Geist*, or locus of purpose beyond the sum of individual intentions? What do theologians mean when they speak of interpreting biblical history? Are they interpreting the Bible or the history?

Interpretation of texts, actions, and cultural expressions is contrasted by the hermeneutic theorist with the explanation of natural phenomena. Bayle and Voltaire ridiculed attempts to interpret Halley's comet and the Lisbon quake because that meant taking them as signs or messages rather than as natural events. As natural explanations of the comet and the quake came to be widely accepted, people ceased to interpret them, as in the case of the cosmic blips. Is this because they are deemed already to have a sufficient interpretation, or because they are now viewed as phenomena that don't admit of interpretation? A physicist interprets meter readings or spots on photographic plates. These could be construed as texts, even in the extended sense mentioned above, only by the most avid Parisian semioticist. They surely are natural phenomena, yet it seems more appropriate to talk of interpreting meter readings than of interpreting an earthquake. Perhaps this is because the readings are given in terms governed by conventions and require to be read according to certain rules. The readings and the spots on the plate are viewed as signs, though they differ in the mode of signifying, but they are not presumed to embody the intention to communicate. The physicist interprets data in the light of certain experimental manipulations he has performed. They are to be interpreted within the context of the experiment and of his antecedent beliefs and purposes.

Recent proposals for an interpretative method for the study of culture are not directly derived from the Continental tradition and thus do not display the romantic and idealist assumption that understanding aims at participation in or appropriation of that which is to be understood, an assumption that sometimes seems to persist even in the work of Gadamer.[12] Geertz (1973: 3–30) has argued for what he calls an interpretive theory of culture. Interpretation is required to identify, or to arrive at a "thick description" of, a practice or other cultural expression. The interpreter must master the grammatical rules or cultural conventions that govern this particular practice and the concepts assumed by it. The interpreter of a text must master the grammar of the language in which the text is written in order to understand what has been said. A similar competence is required of the ethnographer. To distinguish a ritual practice from instrumental behavior and to specify the kind of ritual it is, or to differentiate a relatively spontaneous expression of emotion from a conventional phrase or gesture, the interpreter must understand the rules that govern those concepts, practices, and expressions in that culture. Texts, actions, and other cultural symbols are all governed by grammatical rules and conventions. They assume a system of representations which must be understood before one can identify a practice, emotion, belief, or action. The peculiar interpretative task that differentiates the social from the natural sciences is a consequence of the need to understand these systems of representation. To identify a belief or practice by reference to the cultural rules by which it is governed can itself serve as a kind of explanation, and some have thought this to be the characteristic mode of explanation in the social sciences. Such identification does not, however, preclude causal explanation.

The Pragmatic Tradition

When it is said that there is no uninterpreted experience, the concept of interpretation which is assumed is not that of the hermeneutic tradition. To say that there is no uninterpreted experience is to say that all observation is theory-laden. We are unable to isolate and describe brute data against which to test our theories, because the data we gather is already shaped by the assumptions and questions that have informed our inquiry. Our tacit theories and hypotheses have already played a constitutive role in the perceptual judgments that make up our experience. To say that experience is always interpreted is to say that any experience assumes particular concepts, beliefs, hypotheses, and theories about ourselves and the world. In this context, interpretation means not the decoding of texts or cultural symbols, but the construction and assessment of hypotheses. Reflection on the conduct of inquiry and the interpretation of experience has been central to the pragmatic tradition.

This tradition originates in the work of Charles Sanders Peirce.[13] Though Peirce developed a theory of signs which has captured the interest of those working in the hermeneutic tradition, his analysis of inquiry emerges from reflection upon the interpretation of empirical data rather than of written texts. Schleiermacher translated Plato and interpreted the Bible to his congregation, but Peirce spent most of his life in and around scientific laboratories. His father was an eminent mathematician, and he himself was a working scientist. His work is informed by the questions of the experimental scientist. How do we solve problems, make correct inferences, formulate hypotheses, and fix belief? How is a theory to be justified? How does one distinguish and adjudicate between two hypotheses advanced to explain the same phenomenon? Peirce was sensitive to the social character of scientific practice, well versed in the history of science, and appreciative of its moral and aesthetic dimensions, but his attack on foundationalism and his pragmatic theory of meaning and inquiry were inspired by the procedures of the experimentalist.

In a series of essays on scientific and philosophical method, Peirce attacks all forms of "the myth of the given."[14] These essays constitute an explicit and persuasive criticism of foundationalism in epistemology. Introspection, radical doubt, the certainty of the *cogito*, and the assessment of ideas according to their clarity and distinctness are all considered and found wanting. In their place, Peirce offers his description of the method of fixing belief which he thinks has been perfected by science but is also characteristic of our more informal habits of inquiry. Three themes in these papers are relevant for our consideration: (1) the denial of the possibility of intuitive cognition; (2) the denial of any immediate self-consciousness; and (3) the theory of doubt and inquiry.

Schleiermacher described piety as a sense of the infinite or a feeling of absolute dependence. The former he characterized as intuition and the latter as a modification of immediate self-consciousness. In these cases, as well as in the divinatory moment in interpretation, Schleiermacher thought it possible to achieve an immediate and intuitive consciousness of something that cannot be known as the result of inference. Peirce argues that no such intuition is possible. He shows the necessity of distinguishing between a feeling of immediacy and an immediate feeling. A moment of consciousness may seem to be immediate and noninferential, but that in itself provides no assurance that it is not the result of inference or that it does not assume antecedent concepts. The claim that an experience is unmediated by concepts and beliefs is itself a hypothesis that must be assessed. Peirce sets out to do just that.

Peirce defines an intuition as "a cognition not determined by a previous cognition of the same object, and therefore so determined by something out of consciousness" (CP 5.213). This is exactly what Schleiermacher claims for the feeling of absolute dependence. How could we ever know whether a cognition has been shaped by antecedent thoughts? How do we know that the sense of the infinite is not an artifact of romantic theories of the infinite, or that the feeling of absolute dependence has not been determined by religious speculation about a divine creator and governor? An intuition would have to be self-authenticating. We would need to have an intuitive power of distinguishing an intuition from some other cognition. But this begs the question. Peirce points out that the only evidence in favor of the faculty of intuition is that we seem to feel we have such a faculty. But the relevance of that evidence depends on our ability to determine whether that feeling is itself the product of habits of thought and former associations. The weight of the evidence depends on the assumption we set out to examine. Our only evidence for the claim that some moment of consciousness is immediate and intuitive is our feeling that it is (CP 5.214). This is clearly insufficient, however.

The historical record provides ample evidence of cases in which something was thought to be intuitively known but was later discovered to be the product of inference. Peirce cites several examples. Before Berkeley's treatise on vision, it was thought that the third dimension of space was immediately intuited, but we now know it to be constructed by inference from subtle cues in the visual field. Witnesses in a courtroom often testify sincerely regarding what they have seen, only to have evidence introduced that shows them to be wrong. We constantly discover that something previously thought to have been directly experienced is actually a product of beliefs that are subject to revision in the light of new knowledge. Any cognition for which intuitive status is claimed may well suffer the same fate. A confusion between the sense that a thought or feeling is immediate and the claim that it is in fact not dependent on other cognitions is widespread, and it lies at the heart of Schleiermacher's program. The cognitive value of a particular experience can be shown only by constructing the best theory to explain that experience, and not by appeal to its felt quality.

Any simple concept or theory that seems to unify the facts soon becomes appropriated and internalized. We don't see bent sticks in the water but straight ones. If a person believes that the world is dependent on divine causality, he is likely to feel that he experiences this dependence directly. A sense, feeling, or experience apprehended as immediate and intuitive may in fact be the legacy of previous education and speculation. Intuitions are hypotheses for which we have no viable alternatives. The subject does not perceive them as such, but they are corrigible beliefs.[15] At present they may be indubitable in the sense that no real doubt has been elicited with respect to them, but they are not incorrigible. New information or further reflection may lead one to question and revise them. Even sensations result from perceptual judgments, and emotions follow from the application of particular predicates to our representations of some object. To regard these cognitions as intuitive is to endow them with an authority that is unjustified.

These arguments and examples may serve to demonstrate that we have no intuitive consciousness of external objects. But what about self-consciousness? Is a sharp distinction to be drawn between our knowledge of ourselves and our knowledge of others? Peirce argues that self-consciousness is not immediately given but is the product of inference. Young children come to use the word *I* only rather late, long after they have mastered such complicated inferential procedures as are involved in the trigonometry of vision, for instance. Once again a distinction must be drawn between the felt quality of a cognition and the best explanation of that cognition. Peirce says that the only argument worth noticing for the existence of an intuitive self-consciousness is that we are more certain of our existence than of any other fact, that a conclusion cannot be more certain than the premises from which it follows, and that therefore we cannot have inferred to our own existence from any other fact. But, he argues, this is faulty reasoning. A conclusion can be more certain than any of the facts that support it. A dozen witnesses may testify to the occurrence of an event. If they concur, we are more certain that the event took place than we would have been on the basis of any one of the testimonies. Such reasoning has the strength of a cable made up of many interwoven strands rather than of a chain that is only as strong as its weakest link. "In the same way, to the developed mind of man, his own existence is supported by every other fact, and is, therefore, incomparably more certain than any of these facts" (CP 5.237). The question of whether we have an intuitive self-consciousness cannot be answered by introspection.

Do we have an intuitive power of distinguishing between the subjective elements of different cognitions? Can I tell by introspection whether something is the result of a dream, or distinguish between what I believe and what I merely entertain? Hume thought that one could distinguish between a proposition that was entertained and one that was believed by the feeling of greater vivacity that accompanies the latter. But conviction is a matter of judgment rather than feeling. The difference that I feel between the experience of climbing Mount Rainier and imagining that I am climbing Mount Rainier is accounted for, not by the content of the image or its vivacity, but by my judgment about the connection of that image to the rest of my experience.

Our knowledge of ourselves is not privileged. We have access to data and to knowledge of the context in which to interpret that data which may not be readily accessible to others, but the manner of reasoning by which we learn about ourselves is in principle no different from that which others can and do employ when they attribute to us certain emotions, intentions, and beliefs. Emotions might seem to be the most likely candidates for mental states that can be known by introspection alone, but emotions are also the result of judgments. We come to ascribe emotions to ourselves in much the way we ascribe them to others. Peirce concludes that the only way to investigate a psychological question is by inference from external facts, and that all ascriptions to ourselves of internal states must be construed as hypotheses to explain those facts (CP 5.249, 5.266). The denial of intuitive cognition and of immediate self-consciousness together constitute the claim that there is no uninterpreted experience.

How does one clarify and assess the concepts and beliefs that we constantly assume and that inform our experience? Much of Peirce's work is devoted to a theory of inquiry. Our concepts cannot be clarified by introspective examination of the sort that Descartes counseled. An idea may appear to be clear and distinct even when it is not. The pragmatic maxim was formed as a rule for clarifying the meaning of a concept by specifying its consequences. Appeals to intuition are rejected in favor of a procedure that is public and corrigible. Inquiry is elicited by real doubt, and its purpose is to settle opinion and fix belief.

Descartes recommended that the philosopher begin by doubting everything. But this is as impossible as it is undesirable. When he professed to doubt that he had a body or that the external world exists, Descartes was feigning doubt. Nothing was at stake. We can begin inquiry only *in medias res*, with the problems that actually confront us and the beliefs we currently accept. Descartes' method of feigned doubt does not generate real inquiry, so it is not surprising that he concluded by restoring all he had allegedly doubted. Peirce sums up pragmatism with the maxim "Dismiss make-believes" (CP 5.416). Serious inquiry and real solutions are occasioned only by real problems.

Beliefs are identified by specifying the consequences that would follow from acting on them. If two beliefs lead to the same expectations and actions, then they do not really differ though they may be expressed in different words.

> The essence of a belief is the establishment of a habit; and different beliefs are distinguished by the different modes of action to which they give rise. If beliefs do not differ in this respect, if they appease the same doubt by producing the same rule of action, then no mere differences in the manner of consciousness of them can make them different beliefs, any more than playing a tune in different keys is playing different tunes. (CP 5.398)

At this point the difference between Peirce's concern with interpretation of experience in the context of scientific inquiry and the hermeneutic theorist's interest in the interpretation of texts and symbolic action becomes clear. Peirce wants to distinguish between hypotheses that make a real difference in inquiry and those that don't. Two hypotheses that are couched in different terms but that lead to the same predictions do not differ in a way that is relevant to scientific inquiry. But the fact that they are couched in different terms, assume different concepts, and employ different metaphors may make a real difference to the persons who hold them, and may affect their thoughts and behavior. The interpreter of a text or a cultural product wants to understand the grammar of that text and the rules for thought and action in that culture. He tries to identify a belief or action in terms of those rules.

The hermeneutic theorist and the pragmatist have different interests, and consequently their judgments as to what constitutes a relevant difference between interpretations vary. Peirce's concern with sifting and testing hypotheses is not always appropriate for the task of understanding the thoughts or practices of another. This becomes clear with regard to an example he employs. In order to illustrate his claim that "there is no distinction of meaning so fine as to consist in anything but a possible difference of practice," Peirce refers to the Roman Catholic doctrine of transubstantiation (CP 5.400–401). He observes that, although Catholics claim that the elements of the sacrament are literally meat and blood and Protestants hold that they are bread and wine, they do not disagree on the sensible properties they expect of these elements. Catholics admit that the elements possess the perceptible qualities of bread and wine. Consequently, Peirce concludes, Catholics and Protestants do not really disagree on the matter.

This may show that the disagreement is not one that can be resolved by empirical inquiry, but to conclude that the Catholic and Protestant views of the sacrament are identical is to miss important theological differences that deeply affect belief and action. If my aim is to understand the beliefs and practices of another person or another culture, or to interpret an unfamiliar text or action, I must try to identify concepts and practices under descriptions that accord with those of the text or culture that is the object of my study. In fact, diverse views on transubstantiation might be expected to produce relevant differences in expectation and behavior. A Roman priest and a Methodist minister will be likely to dispose of leftover elements from the celebration of the sacrament of the eucharist in different ways. The place of the eucharist in one's religious life, and the implications of being deprived of it for several months, differ according to a person's theological views and the form of his piety.

Peirce is correct in his observation that this dispute does not display the characteristics that would make it appropriate for scientific inquiry, but his dismissal of any difference should be seen as a consequence of his particular interests. The chief insight of the hermeneutic tradition is that beliefs, practices, emotions, and intentions must be identified under descriptions that can properly be attributed to those to whom the beliefs and practices are ascribed. Each of these assumes certain representations of the world, and a proper identification must take account of those representations. The hermeneutic method is an attempt to enable an interpreter to arrive at an understanding of those representations.

Peirce's rejection of foundationalism, his denial of the possibility of intuitive cognition and of immediate self-consciousness, and his attempt to formulate public criteria for explicating meaning and assessing beliefs anticipated and influenced much in contemporary philosophy. Many of the contributions of the pragmatists have become an integral part of current work in the empiricist tradition. Willard Quine, Nelson Goodman, and Wilfrid Sellars are all deeply and explicitly indebted to the pragmatists.[16] For our purposes it is important to remember that the recognition that there is no uninterpreted experience is based on a construal of interpretation that differs from that of the hermeneutic tradition.

Understanding and Explanation

We have seen that two different conceptions of interpretation inform the hermeneutic and pragmatic traditions. The hermeneutic theorist is occupied with the problem of interpreting texts, practices, and other cultural expressions. Interpretation, for him, consists in understanding the representations assumed in those texts and practices by mastering the rules that govern them. The pragmatist is chiefly interested in the construction and assessment of hypotheses in order to arrive at the best explanation of the evidence. Both generalize the theories of interpretation and inquiry that are developed in order to account for the interpretation of texts and of scientific evidence.

Care must be taken not to confuse the two conceptions. When that happens, it is assumed that an attack on the myth of the given, and the recognition that there is no uninterpreted experience, leads to the conclusion that the hermeneutic method is appropriate for all inquiry and that it precludes explanation. This lends support to the idealism that is always a risk in the Continental hermeneutic tradition. This problem can be seen most clearly in the work of Josiah Royce.

Royce was an avowed idealist, but he was very much influenced by pragmatism, particularly by the essays by Peirce which we have considered. He is an important link in the transmission of the pragmatic approach to interpretation and inquiry through C. I. Lewis to Quine and Goodman. In his last major work, *The Problem of Christianity*, which many take to be his masterpiece, he develops a theory of interpretation and a metaphysics based on it. The move from the claim that all experience is interpreted to a metaphysical idealism is made by an equivocation on the word *interpretation*.

Royce begins by noting that we have no experience without interpretation. He cites Kant and Peirce to the effect that the mind is active in constructing its experience and that we have no intuitive cognitions. Then he asks what is the proper object of interpretation and concludes that it "is either something of the nature of a mind, or else is a process which goes on in a mind, or, finally, it is a sign or expression whereby some mind manifests its existence and its processes" (Royce, 1913: II, 129). As we might now say, the object of interpretation is a representation or a set of representations. Here Royce is using *interpretation* in the hermeneutic sense, in which the paradigm is the interpretation of texts and other expressions of the human mind or spirit. Now the idealism follows directly. Reality, he says, consists of signs and their interpretations, both of which are expressions of mind (Royce, 1913: II, 282–283). His argument is as follows: (1) there is no uninterpreted experience; (2) the only object of interpretation is a mind or an expression of mind; (3) therefore, reality consists of mind. The recognition that we have no uninterpreted experience does not necessarily lead to idealism, however. The slip in the argument is easy to detect. The meaning of *interpretation* changes from premise (1) to premise (2). In (1) it means any theory or account, and in (2) it means the technique of understanding language or signs.

The equivocation in Royce's argument is clear, but some contemporary instances of this equivocation are more difficult to discern. Gadamer's emphasis, following Heidegger, on what he calls the linguistic character of being, exhibits a similar assumption. Richard Rorty (1980, 1982) assimilates the hermeneutic and pragmatic traditions. He claims that there is little important difference between them. But in Rorty's reconstruction the hermeneutic tradition is dominant. The pragmatist's concept of inquiry is rendered as conversation, and literature is viewed as the center of culture, with science and philosophy regarded as "at best, literary genres" (Rorty, 1982: 141). The interest of Peirce, James, Dewey, and Quine in scientific inquiry is regarded as accidental, and their common attack on foundationalism is taken as sufficient grounds for assimilating the pragmatic tradition to the hermeneutic.

Now that we have distinguished these two kinds of interpretation, what is meant by the interpretation of religious experience? It could be either one. Understanding the experience of another requires mastery of the concepts and rules assumed by that experience. An experience is already interpreted and thus is constituted in part by the description under which the subject identifies it. To understand the experience of another or even my own experience requires that I identify it under the appropriate description. When it is said that there is no uninterpreted experience, or one attends to the interpretative component in religious experience, the reference is to the concepts within which the subject has tried to make sense of his experience, and to the tacit theoretical framework he has employed. Interpreting religious experience may include both an understanding of the description under which the experience is identified by the subject or in the culture in which it is embedded, and an attempt to arrive at the best explanation of the experience.

The hermeneutic tradition originated in the recognition that the interpretation of texts differs from the method employed in the natural sciences. We have seen that this difference does not assume that some kind of direct acquaintance is required. It has been suggested that *verstehen* can be understood as the imaginative construction of fruitful hypotheses.[17] The dawning of an idea or the recognition of a pattern is often experienced as immediate and intuitive; it may approximate what Schleiermacher refers to as the divinatory moment and what he takes to be an insight that is not the result of inference.

Gestalt recognition is sometimes offered as an example of noninferential learning. The experience of insight on completing a gestalt is a striking one; however, it is the experience of discovering a hypothesis that works. The insight is especially dramatic when the successful hypothesis is illumined against a background of frustrated attempts. A professor of psychology at Columbia is reported to have illustrated insight learning by asking his students to specify the operation that would generate the following series: 14, 18, 23, 28, 34, 42, 50, 59, 66, 72, 79, 86, 96, 103, 110, 116, and so on. Gradually it dawned on the students that these were the local stops on the Broadway line of the New York City subway system. The insight is sudden, but the experience is one of entertaining, after some frustration, a hypothesis that works. In this case the students were required to consider a sequence based on contingent facts of the environment rather than one derived from the formal properties of arithmetic. When asked to discover two figures in the Jastrow duck-rabbit drawing, one tries to look at it in different ways until the images appear. The experience is again a striking one, but the perception of the figure as a duck or rabbit is dependent on having tested certain hypotheses and on an ability to recognize conventional caricatures of ducks and rabbits which are accepted in this culture. It is not independent of thought and inference.

The sudden dawning of an insight is as common in the natural sciences as it is in the study of texts and symbolic action. This cannot sufficiently account for the method of *verstehen*. That method ought rather to be regarded as the understanding of the grammatical rules that govern a particular text or practice.[18] The insight of the hermeneutic theorist is that an experience, emotion, intention, or action must be identified under a description and with reference to the rules that can plausibly be ascribed to the subject. Before trying to arrive at an explanation of Napoleon's deeds, I must describe those deeds and ascribe to him intentions, desires, and motives in terms that would have been available to him. In order to do that, I must understand the concepts and the grammar that were constitutive of his views of himself and his world. To understand a ritual practice I must grasp the concepts that are presupposed and the set of cultural conventions in which it is embedded. Anger can be specified only by reference to the subject's beliefs about the object of his anger, and fear only by citing the relevant beliefs about the present danger. This requirement that an emotion, action, or experience be identified under a description that can be ascribed to the subject does not obtain in the natural sciences.

The identification of a practice in terms of the concepts and rules that govern a particular culture can itself be a kind of explanation, and some have held that this is the characteristic form of explanation in the social sciences. To identify the notching of sticks in a particular setting as voting behavior, or a peculiar posture and chant as prayer, is to extend greatly one's understanding of what is taking place. But this requirement that the practice be identified in terms available to the actors does not preclude the possibility of further explanation.

Were a person to report that he had an experience of Krishna in which Krishna revealed himself and spoke to him, the scholar who sought to study that experience could not describe it as an experience of God or of internalized social norms. The experience must be identified under the description employed by the subject and with reference to his concepts and beliefs. He had an experience which he took to be of Krishna, in which Krishna instructed him in a particular way. It is that experience that must be explained. To identify it as something other is to attend to something different from the experience of the subject.

No such constraints are placed on possible explanations of the experience. One may conclude that it is best explained as an hallucination or by reference to early socialization. A theist may be convinced that what was taken to be Krishna was actually the one God in another guise. The subject's concepts and beliefs must be cited for the identification of the experience because it is his experience that is to be explained. Any proposed explanation must account for why it was Krishna that was experienced and not some other deity, why he spoke that particular language, and why he said what he did. The explanation must account for the details of the experience as given in the subject's report.

The identification of a belief or a practice under the appropriate description is the distinctive task of the social sciences and humanities; it accounts for the difference between the method of interpreting a text and that employed in the natural sciences. But that task does not preclude the further step of seeking the best explanation for the practice or the belief. Representatives of the hermeneutic tradition often imply that the interpretative method and the inferential procedures used in the natural sciences are mutually exclusive. Geertz is explicit about the fact that hermeneutics is a matter of mastering a grammar and decoding meanings, and not one of empathy or participation. He does not directly oppose the tasks of interpretation and explanation, but his attitude toward the latter is one of extreme reserve. While he says that the anthropologist of religion should analyze systems of symbolic meaning and relate them to social-cultural and psychological processes, he shows little interest in detailing these relations (Geertz, 1973: 125). His use of the term *relate* in this connection, his portrayal of the appropriate level of theorizing in anthropology as clinical inference that is confined to generalizing within cases, and his description of anthropology as an interpretative science, all place the emphasis on interpretation at the expense of explanation (Geertz, 1973: 24–30). But these tasks need not be regarded as reciprocally related. They are different tasks. Both are required for a full account of phenomena that are in part constituted by concepts, beliefs, or other representations.

III.
EMOTION

The phrase *religious experience* has in some quarters come to be reserved almost exclusively for aspects of experience which are allegedly prereflective, transcend the verbal, or are in some way free of the structures of thought and judgment which language represents. Reports of religious experience appear to testify to the intensity, the privacy, the ineffability, and the engagement that characterize our emotional lives in contrast to the formulation of doctrines and the making of inferences. Some have adopted the traditional tripartite division of the mind into intellectual, volitional, and affective components and have tried to assimilate religious experience to the affections or emotions.

In addition to the shared qualities mentioned above, two reasons can be given for the assimilation of religious experience to the affections or emotions. The first arises from the search for what is common among different experiences we call religious; the second emerges from attempts to differentiate the religious from other dimensions of experience. The first is roughly descriptive and the second apologetic, though they cannot be easily separated. Both are given their first and most explicit expression in Schleiermacher's addresses on religion.

The first reason is based on the judgment that religion, with its experiential roots, is more deeply entrenched in the lives of persons and communities than are particular doctrines or explicit beliefs. Emotions or feelings and their expressions in language and behavior prove to be more reliable indicators of character or long-term behavioral dispositions than do either explicit statements of belief or individual actions. Deliberate acts and statements are subject to voluntary control to an extent to which emotions and their expressions are not. Feelings cannot be manipulated as easily as statements and actions can be. If piety is deeply rooted in the character of a person or community and shapes the thoughts and actions that constitute the form of life we would attribute to that person or community, then it appears to be more fundamental than the beliefs or behavior.

Emotions appear to be invariant across cultures that vary greatly in thought and action. Beliefs and acts are thought to be dependent on language and concepts in a way that emotions are not. Those who regard religious experience as a universal dimension of human experience which underlies differences in doctrine and ritual behavior often assume that this invariance is a consequence of feeling being more fundamental than thought or action and thus less susceptible to variation according to the content of particular cultural traditions. William James (1902: 504) thought that if one surveyed the field of religion he would discover a great variety of thoughts but a similarity of feeling and conduct. He took this to show that religious theories are secondary and that feelings and conduct are the constant and therefore essential elements in religion. Jonathan Edwards (1959: 95) said that true religion consists in holy affections. Schleiermacher describes religion first as a sense and taste and then as a peculiar modification of feeling. Rudolf Otto (1958: xxi) describes his phenomenological analysis of the holy as "a serious attempt to analyze all the more exactly the *feeling* which remains where the concept fails" (original emphasis). Each of these authors assumes that emotions, affections, or feelings are more deeply entrenched and more characteristic of religion than the doctrines or actions by which they are expressed.

The consideration raised by James is an important one. Religious emotions such as fear, awe, hope, and even the bliss attested to by some mystics appear to be widespread across different cultures and across traditions whose languages and doctrines vary enormously. The conclusion that James draws, however, may be an artifact of the level of generality at which the feelings, conduct, and thoughts are described. Fear may be universal though theistic belief is not, but belief in the inadequacy of natural explanations to account for our experience may be more invariant across cultures than the fear of God or even the feeling of absolute dependence. The description under which a particular feeling, belief, or action is identified proves crucial for the comparison. One can identify a feeling under a description that is sufficiently general to guarantee that it can be attributed to all persons and identify a belief with reference to particular concepts characteristic of a single tradition, or one can identify the belief in general terms and the feeling by reference to a specific object. Similar considerations hold for the identification of an action. The outcome of the comparison depends crucially on the way the actions, thoughts, and feelings are described.[1]

Schleiermacher's characterization of religion as feeling and his attempt to distinguish it from thought and action have been extremely influential for subsequent definitions of religion and debate about the proper study of religious experience. But sophisticated reflection on the religious affections antedates the nineteenth century. Augustine, Thomas Aquinas, Luther, Calvin, and Edwards, to mention only the most obvious figures in the Christian tradition, were astute analysts of the subtle distinctions between different religious emotions. They tried to articulate the marks that distinguish religious fear, hope, joy, and anxiety from the nonreligious instances of those emotions.

Why does the identification of religion with emotion become so much more pronounced and programmatic in Schleiermacher's *On Religion*? This question leads us to the second reason for characterizing religious experience as affective, a reason that derives from apologetic concerns. Enlightenment arguments against traditional religious authority, against rational arguments for the existence of God, and criticism of the parochial character of religious loyalties, followed by Kant's critique of theoretical reason and discrediting of speculative metaphysics, led defenders of religion to try to characterize it in such a way as to free it from any theoretical doctrine, including even belief in the existence of God. In the wake of Kant's critiques, many students of religion and theology sought immediate access to the real and a foundation for doctrine and belief in religious experience. Some thought that a mode of experience might be identified which was unscathed by the activity of the imagination in the construction of the forms and categories but would provide an alternative to Kant's exclusively moral account of religion. They searched for some channel of cognitive immediacy, and the most likely candidate was the affections. Religion must be identified with feeling or emotion in order to remove it from the arena in which it is dependent on particular beliefs or claims about the world, vulnerable to conflict with scientific beliefs, and open to the criticisms that Kant leveled against metaphysical speculation.

Both of these reasons for characterizing religious experience as emotion assume that emotions and feelings are independent of concepts and thoughts. Unlike a thought, a feeling cannot accurately be conveyed to another in words but can be known only by acquaintance. Evocative language must be employed to point another person to a particular aspect of experience in order to direct his attention to the relevant sector of his own mind. Because the experience is held to transcend conceptual forms and categories, language is in principle inadequate to it. Words can serve only as reminders of an experience that has already been enjoyed, or as catalysts or signposts that enable an individual to discover an aspect of his experience he has hitherto overlooked.

The relationship between the language used to describe or point and the experience itself is a contingent one, to say the very most. Unless the experience can be located in one's own consciousness, no words will suffice to convey it. Otto's instruction to his readers, in a passage that invariably causes students to smile, is typical:

> The reader is invited to direct his mind to a moment of deeply-felt religious experience, as little as possible qualified by other forms of consciousness. Whoever cannot do this, whoever knows no such moments in his experience, is requested to read no farther; for it is not easy to discuss questions of religious psychology with one who can recollect the emotions of his adolescence, the discomforts of indigestion, or, say, social feelings, but cannot recall any intrinsically religious feelings. (Otto, 1958: 8)

Otto's statement is presented as a straightforward invitation to attend to an experience that is simple, irreducible, and can be picked out by acquaintance. We shall have to examine carefully, however, exactly how such instructions operate. What does Otto mean by the "intrinsically religious"? In fact, he lays down very strict conceptual constraints that govern the reader's identification of particular experiences as religious. The rules that are incorporated into Otto's description allow him to develop an apologetic strategy while avoiding direct examination of the criteria for identification of a religious experience.

A brief review of traditional and contemporary theories of the emotions will enable us to assess the claim that affective experience is independent of concepts and beliefs and to examine the criteria for specifying emotions. Then we will be in a position to consider the similarities and differences between the rules for identifying emotions and those for identifying religious experience.

Hume and the Traditional Theory

In the modern period, beginning with Descartes' treatise on the passions of the soul but clearly articulated in Hume's discussion of the passions in his *Treatise of Human Nature*, the view of an emotion as an impression, a feeling, or a unique sort of internal experience came to dominate the analysis of emotions. Emotions were assimilated to sensations. The term *passion* is appropriate because it suggests something suffered by or impressed upon the soul, and not shaped by any cognitive activity on the part of the person who suffers it. The experience is a private one, and it can be named by attaching a word to it like a tag to a particular sense impression. People understand the words we employ to identify emotions because they are familiar with the same impressions in their own mental lives. These emotions cannot be analyzed or described, however, because they are simple and lacking in cognitive content.

> The passions of PRIDE and HUMILITY being simple and uniform impressions, 'tis impossible we can ever, by a multitude of words, give a just definition of them, or indeed of any of the passions. The utmost we can pretend to is a description of them, by an enumeration of such circumstances as attend them: But as these words, *pride* and *humility*, are of general use, and the impressions they represent the most common of any, every one, of himself, will be able to form a just idea of them, without any danger of mistake. (Hume, 1965: 217)

According to Hume, the passions are simple and therefore assume no conceptual or interpretative framework. Words can be employed to express and to indicate them. They cannot be fully captured in words any more than one can exhaustively describe the taste of honey, the smell of camphor, or Hume's missing shade of blue. But words can be used to suggest comparisons, to set a context, and to enable others to discern similar impressions in their own experience. In this view there is no way to insure that the passions indicated or expressed by two people using the same word are the same passions. The feeling that I identify by the word *pride* might be the feeling that you indicate by the word *anger*. As long as the words were consistently employed, such a discrepancy would never come to light. The problem is the same as that often discussed with respect to perception as the problem of the inverted spectrum.

In this view, thoughts are extrinsic to emotions. The word *pride* represents an emotion, but the emotion itself does not depend on any thought or concept. Passions are independent of cognitive representations of any kind. They are prior to thoughts and are unstructured by them. Hume is explicit about this.

> A passion is an original existence, or, if you will, modification of existence, and contains not any representative quality, which renders it a copy of any other existence or modification. When I am angry, I am actually possessed with the passion, and in that emotion have no more a reference to any other object than when I am thirsty, or sick, or more than five feet high. 'Tis impossible, therefore, that this passion can be oppos'd by, or be contradictory to truth and reason; since this contradiction consists in the disagreement of ideas, consider'd as copies, with their objects, which they represent. (Hume, 1965: 415)

Passions cannot enter into grammatical or logical relations because they are simple impressions and possess no conceptual structure. A sensation cannot agree with or contradict a thought; such relations require a logical or grammatical structure.

According to Hume, the connection between an emotion and its object is a causal one. My discovery that Tom has cheated me causes anger in me, but the feeling of anger can be specified without reference to how it was produced and thus without mentioning either Tom or cheating. The concept of a particular emotion gives us no information about the object of that emotion, because it might be related to any object at all. It is only by experience that we know that certain emotions are associated with certain objects and thoughts. Hume (1965: 368) says there is no reason why love and hatred need be connected with any desires at all, or why they could not be reversed. Hatred could be correlated with the desire to make the object of one's hatred happy, and love with the desire to make the loved one miserable. That we discover the opposite correlation is a contingent fact of experience. Because passions are independent of thoughts and desires, they are compatible with any combination thereof.

Hume's account of the passions has recently been subjected to considerable criticism. There are problems with the account even on its own terms. Hume says that passions are associated in memory according to their similarities and differences. But something that is absolutely simple cannot be similar to or different from anything else. Resemblance is always resemblance in some respect, and the specification of that respect requires reference to particular characteristics. But the greatest difficulty with Hume's theory is that he is unable to account for the fact that emotions can be justified and unjustified, can conflict with one another, and can enter into conceptual relations with one another.[2]

A conception of emotion which differs from that of Hume but shares with it the assumption that emotions are directly perceived or intuited and are thus unscathed by conceptual presuppositions and interpretations, is the view that was first proposed by William James and has become known as the James-Lange theory. James held that emotions are identical with perceptions of bodily changes. Like Hume, he conceived of an emotion as an internal event that is directly perceived and that is then expressed, described, or indicated through the use of language. The emotions are independent of representation and judgment.

> Our natural way of thinking about these coarser emotions is that the mental perception of some fact excites the mental affection of the emotion, and that this latter state of mind gives rise to the bodily expression. My theory, on the contrary, is that *the bodily changes follow directly the perception of the exciting fact, and that our feeling of the same changes as they occur IS the emotion.* Common sense says, we lose our fortune, and are

sorry and weep; we meet a bear, are frightened and run; we are insulted by a rival, are angry and strike. The hypothesis here to be defended says that this order of sequence is incorrect, that the one mental state is not immediately induced by the other, that the bodily manifestations must first be interposed between, and that the more rational statement is that we feel sorry because we cry, angry because we strike, afraid because we tremble, and not that we cry, strike, or tremble, because we are sorry, angry, or fearful, as the case may be. (James, 1890: 2.449–50; original emphasis)

The James-Lange theory has served as the foil against which several contemporary theories of the emotions have been formulated. It can be understood as a translation into physiological or physicalist terms of the traditional empiricist view. Emotions are directly perceived, as are other impressions. In James's theory, however, they are passions of the body rather than passions of the soul. The location has changed, but the mode of perception remains direct, immediate, and intuitive.

It is ironic that Schleiermacher and the romantics, who regarded themselves as radically opposed to the conception of human nature proposed by Hume and other representatives of the Enlightenment, share with that tradition a conception of the emotions as immediate, distinct from and unstructured by thought or representation of any kind, and knowable only by direct acquaintance. The irony is compounded by the fact that affections or feelings are regarded by Schleiermacher as the mode of mental life which is most expressive of individual character. The traditional view of emotions as internal events that are directly known was, in fact, a relatively recent one. Classical and medieval thinkers held a very different theory of the emotions.

Aristotle on Emotion

Though modern philosophers have until recently contrasted the emotions with thought and action, and though this kind of faculty psychology can claim roots in Plato's *Republic*, it has not always been dominant. In his analysis of the emotions in the second book of the *Rhetoric*, Aristotle is explicit about their conceptual structure. In order to specify an emotion one must specify the thought that is constitutive of that emotion. The thought allows one to identify both the object of the emotion and the grounds on which it is based. Without reference to both object and grounds, an emotion cannot be identified.

It is significant that Aristotle's chief discussion of the emotions is in the *Rhetoric*. He is addressing the practical question of how specific emotions can be aroused. In this respect his approach resembles Wittgenstein's attention to how one would teach another the proper use of certain words that apparently name private experiences. A proper analysis of such words would require a stipulation of the conditions under which they might appropriately be used and might show that they do not function as names at all.

All emotions are accompanied by feelings of pain and pleasure. Pain and pleasure are treated as sensations, and Aristotle regards them as free of conceptual content or assumptions. But the emotions are modifications or interpretations of pain and pleasure in accord with particular concepts and judgments about the world.

> The emotions are all those feelings that so change men as to affect their judgments, and that are also attended by pain and pleasure. Such are anger, pity, fear, and the like, with their opposites. We must arrange what we have to say about each of them under three heads. Take, for instance, the emotion of anger: here we must discover (1) what the state of mind of angry people is, (2) who the people are with whom they usually get angry, and (3) on what grounds they get angry with them. It is not enough to know one or even two of these points; unless we know all three, we shall be unable to arouse anger in any one. The same is true of the other emotions. (Aristotle, 1924: 1378a)

Specific cognitive structures and capacities for judgment must be presumed for certain kinds of emotion to be possible. An emotion is not a simple impression that is prior to or unstructured by concepts. It is a complex composed of both feelings and thoughts. It includes a feeling, an intentional object, and a set of beliefs which provides the reason or grounds for the emotion.

In contrast to Hume, Aristotle holds that an emotion cannot be discriminated from other mental states without attention to the appropriate object and the beliefs that provide relevant grounds for the emotion. Reference to concepts and thoughts is required for the specification of an emotional state. Aristotle details rather sophisticated concepts that must be assumed for specific emotions. He describes anger, for instance, as pain accompanying an apparent slight that is unjustified.

> Anger may be defined as an impulse, accompanied by pain, to an apparent revenge for an apparent slight directed without justification towards what concerns oneself or towards what concerns one's friends. If this is a proper definition of anger, it must always be felt towards some particular individual, e.g. Cleon, and not 'man' in general. It must be felt because the other has done or intended to do something to him or to one of his friends. It must always be attended by a certain pleasure—that which arises from the expectation of revenge. For since nobody aims at what he thinks he cannot obtain, the angry man is aiming at what he can attain, and the belief that you will attain your aim is pleasant. (Aristotle, 1924: 1378ab)[3]

The concept of a slight is a subtle one. It assumes self-respect and thus a reflexive concept of self. A person devoid of self-respect and of the elaborate cognitive structure it presupposes could not feel anger. In addition, the requirement that the slight be perceived as unjustified assumes a set of rules, customs, and moral institutions such that one has criteria for distinguishing between justified and unjustified slights. According to Aristotle, a person cannot be angry if he thinks he has been treated justly. This is a conceptual or logical requirement; it follows from the rules that govern the proper application of the concept of anger. Moral assessments enter into almost all the emotions Aristotle describes. His analysis demonstrates that rather sophisticated concepts and rules are implicit in the use of everyday language about fear, anger, and other emotions.

Consider how Aristotle's definition of shame differs from Hume's description of pride and humility.

> Shame may be defined as pain or disturbance in regard to bad things, whether present, past, or future, which seem likely to involve us in discredit; and shamelessness as contempt or indifference in regard to these same bad things. If the distinction be granted, it follows that we feel shame at such bad things as we think are disgraceful to ourselves or to those we care for. . . . And, generally, we feel no shame before those upon whose opinion we quite look down as untrustworthy (no one feels shame before small children or animals); nor are we ashamed of the same things before intimates as before strangers, but before the former of what seem genuine faults, before the latter of what seem conventional ones. (Aristotle, 1924: 1383b, 1384b)

Judgments about the status of the person before whom one is standing and the relative ignominy of one's actions are required conditions for the feeling of shame. Shame is not prereflective, nor does it transcend conceptual structures. It depends on an interpretative framework, and it assumes particular judgments about oneself and the world. Shame presupposes considerable cognitive achievement, in particular the ability to take the role of another and to see oneself through his eyes.

The distinction popular among some anthropologists and historians between shame cultures and guilt cultures is founded on the recognition that guilt requires even more cognitive development and conceptual differentiation than does shame.[4] Kierkegaard's (1954: 146–207) elaborate analysis of different forms of despair reveals the layers of self-consciousness, or conceptual distinction and moral assessment, which characterize the several forms. It is implausible to suppose that the richness of our language for distinguishing emotions could be accounted for by the differences between simple impressions that impinge upon the mind. The diversity of our emotional experience must rather be a function of the complexity of the concepts and thoughts that can enter into that experience.

Each of Aristotle's examples suggests that emotions assume and are in part constituted by concepts and judgments. To say that a concept is constitutive of an emotion is to say that the emotion cannot be specified without reference to that concept. The same point has been made by moral philosophers about the role of moral intuitions and key ethical concepts in defining certain actions. Murder, theft, and the making of promises are not simple descriptions of human acts. They presuppose complex institutional structures and values. Murder refers to unjustified homicide; thus it would be unintelligible in the absence of concepts for distinguishing between persons and nonpersons and of rules for distinguishing between justified and unjustified actions. Theft can be differentiated from other forms of acquisition only in the context of a well-defined concept of property and of rules for the transfer of property rights. The making of a promise assumes the existence of the institution of promising and the expectation that one's word is to be honored. None of these actions would be intelligible in a state of nature.

An emotion, like an action, must be identified under a description. The emotions described by Aristotle would also be unavailable in a state of nature. They presuppose concepts, rules, and institutions. Consequently, it seems likely that there are whole classes of emotions that are accessible only within particular cultures.[5] Because of these conceptual presuppositions, it is reasonable to ask whether some emotions are excluded by the presence of others. If emotions assume particular judgments about the context in which they occur, the requisite conditions for two different emotions may conflict. This suggests that there is a kind of logic to the emotions.

The relation between an emotion and its object is a conceptual or logical one. It is not a contingent or causal relation, as Hume supposed it was. It would make no sense to speak of certain emotions in the absence of appropriate objects. We would think it odd for someone to declare that he was proud of the sky or the sea (Foot, 1978: 113). Were a person to profess to be ashamed of the rain, we would conclude either that he was unaware of or unfaithful to the logic of the word *ashamed*, or that he possessed strange beliefs about his relation to the rain. We can sometimes recognize an emotion without knowing what its object is, but we must know what type of object it takes. The relation between an emotion and its object is not simply one of causal conjunction. Emotions are identified by the specification of their objects (Kenny, 1963: 52–75).

We speak of justified and unjustified emotions. Were emotions simply physiological events or some primitive mode of experience that contrasted with and was independent of thought and action, there would be no way to account for the cognitive presuppositions or logical relations among the emotions. It makes no sense at all to speak of a pang or a twitch as justified or unjustified. When Otto (1958: 7) coins the term *numinous* "to stand for 'the holy' *minus* its moral factor or 'moment,' and . . . minus its 'rational' aspect altogether," he seems to be saying that, like a pang, the sense of the numinous is uninformed by conceptual presuppositions and moral assessments. According to him, concepts and judgments are employed to schematize or interpret an affective experience that is independent of thought. But emotions require reference to concepts and beliefs for their identification. Otto's definition employs sophisticated concepts to incorporate into the rules for the identification of an experience of the numinous the claim that the experience transcends all concepts and judgments.

Many theorists have been convinced that emotions have a cognitive component and have tried to frame proper descriptions of it. If, however, one begins by defining emotions in contrast to thought or conceptual relations, it is impossible to describe the noetic or cognitive elements in emotional experience. Aristotle's approach accounts for these elements by showing that concepts and judgments are constitutive of and internal to the emotions themselves. According to him, emotions are not to be defined in contrast to intellect and will. In order to describe anger it is necessary to specify (1) the state of mind of an angry person, (2) the appropriate objects of anger, and (3) relevant grounds for anger. The first component refers to the quality of feeling, or the unpleasant sensation that accompanies anger. To specify that alone is insufficient. Aristotle (1931: 403a) says that to characterize anger as a boiling of the blood around the heart is to attend only to the matter and not to the form of the emotion. The second and third components are cognitive. The object of one's anger must be specified under the description by which it is identified by the person who is angry. Anger must be felt toward some particular individual. And there must be grounds for anger. My anger at Cleon may be grounded in my belief that he insulted me. The truth of my belief is unimportant for the description of the emotion. That is what Aristotle means by "an apparent slight." It is my belief that must be cited in order to specify both the object and the grounds for my anger, even though I might have mistaken someone else for Cleon and an affectionate remark for an insult.

Recent theorists have followed Aristotle and have elaborated on his analysis of the relevant concepts that must be specified in order to identify an emotional state. We shall see that similar conclusions have been reached by philosophers and social psychologists studying emotion.

A Philosophical Critique of the Traditional View

Theories in which emotions are thought to be directly or intuitively known and independent of cognitive assumptions have been challenged by recent work in philosophy and psychology. Each of these challenges takes its departure from difficulties in the traditional theory as represented by Hume and James, and each continues the kind of analysis begun by Aristotle and attempts to elucidate the interpretative component in the emotions.

Some philosophers who have been influenced by the later work of Wittgenstein have drawn on that work to criticize conceptions of emotions as private internal events that are intuitively known. Errol Bedford (1957) argues that emotion words are not names for feelings, for private experiences, or for anything else. They are not names at all. Bedford describes what he calls the traditional theory as one in which emotions are viewed as feelings and emotion words are regarded as names of feelings.

> It is assumed that to each word there corresponds a qualitatively distinct experience which may, although it need not, find "expression" in outward behavior. If it does, this behavior entitles us to infer the existence of the inner feeling, and therefore to assert, with some degree of probability, statements of the form "He is angry." (Bedford, 1957: 218–282)

Anger is regarded as a specific feeling that moves a person to a certain behavior that is characteristic of the emotion. If an emotion is a feeling of bodily changes, an impression, or an intuited inner state, then emotion words function as names. But emotions are not inner states or events, nor are they somatic sensations or even experiences of any kind. The confusion arises, according to Bedford, with the assumption that emotion words are names. This leads to a misconception of their function and to a search for the states, events, or processes that are being named.

Two considerations render implausible the classification of emotion words as nominative. First, we have no evidence to suggest the existence of a multitude of different internal states corresponding to the varied and subtle linguistic differentiation that is available for discussing emotion. The postulation of such subtle differences in inner states becomes even less plausible if one accepts James's identification of emotions with the perception of bodily changes. Are we ready to posit physiological differences, or even different states or events, to correspond to the subtle differentiation between the various forms of despair described by Kierkegaard in *The Sickness Unto Death*, or even to correspond to the difference between pride and joy, or annoyance and indignation, and between various modifications of each? Is it plausible, as Hume suggests, to think we identify these emotions by direct inspection of the qualitative difference in feeling which marks one off from the other? Psychologists have not been able to discover peculiar physiological or mental states that are correlated with each of the emotions. An emotion cannot be identified at that level.

Second, if emotion terms were names for private experiences, we could never explain the expression "feels angry" to someone. We might attempt to provoke that person to anger and then tell him that feeling angry refers to what he is now feeling. But how would we know whether or not we had succeeded in evoking the correct feeling in him? We would be faced with the problem of the inverted spectrum. There would be no way to insure that his conception of the meaning of the expression was the same as ours. Our provocations may have caused him to experience what we identify as a feeling of embarrassment. The point is even clearer if we take as our example, not the feeling of anger, but the sense of the numinous or the feeling of absolute dependence. When Otto asks his readers to attend to the numinous in their own experience, what guarantee does he have that they will attach the label to the same kind of experience with which it is associated in his mind?

On the basis of such considerations, Bedford argues that the ascription of anger is logically prior to the identification of an angry feeling. I don't need information about someone's feelings in order to conclude that he is angry. On the strength of my assessment of his behavior and of the context within which it occurs, I may describe him as angry. Anger is predicated of a person in a particular situation on the basis of cues drawn from observing his behavior and its relation to the surrounding context. This predication justifies the use of the phrase "feels angry," but it does not rely on my observation of his feelings or inner states. The ascription of anger is logically prior to the ascription of feelings of anger, and therefore being angry does not strictly entail having any feeling at all (Bedford, 1957: 284). We judge a person to be angry on the basis of the public evidence. We use this evidence not to infer inner states or feelings but to infer that the person is angry. If we have good grounds for believing that someone is angry or jealous, we don't discard that belief upon learning that he does not feel angry or jealous. People are often mistaken about their own emotions. The person who is angry, jealous, envious, or in love may be the last one to realize it. An emotion is not identified by the special quality of the feelings of the person to whom it is ascribed. Nor is he the final authority on the emotion terms that are properly to be attributed to him.

If this analysis is correct, we don't identify our own emotions by introspection, nor have we any privileged access to special inner states which would enable us to claim final authority on the emotions that ought properly to be ascribed to us. There is no essential distinction between first and third person attribution of emotions.

> It seems to me that there is every reason to believe that we learn about our emotions essentially in the same way that other people learn about them. Admittedly, it is sometimes the case that we know our own emotions better than anyone else does, but there is no need to explain this as being due to the introspection of feelings. One reason for this is that it is hardly possible for a man to be completely ignorant, as others may be, of the context of his own behavior. (Bedford, 1957: 285)

I don't appeal to private inner states in ascribing emotions to myself any more than I do in ascribing them to others. I often come to know what I am feeling by interpreting physiological changes or my behavior in exactly the same way in which another might interpret them if the data were available to him. Suppose I am involved in a heated discussion. Someone tells me I am angry. I deny it, but then I notice my fists are clenched and my pulse is racing. If the context is one in which I think I have been unjustifiably slighted, and thus in which there are grounds for anger, I conclude I am angry. In another context, suddenly noticing the same physiological signs may lead me to conclude that I am sexually excited, or that I am terrified by some mysterious threat. No specific feeling by itself is sufficient to justify the ascription of a particular emotion. Given the right conditions, it is possible that the same feeling could be evidence for some other ascription or could be explained in some other way.

It might be objected that people often feel angry when they have no reason for anger. An emotion wells up inside a person and he or she is overcome. One doesn't judiciously decide whether or not one has been slighted, and if so, whether the slight was justified. Passions are experienced as involuntary. Our experiencing of them contrasts with the theoretical distancing suggested by talk of inference, judgment, and ascription. Even the involuntary rise of anger, however, might contain an inferential component, as Aristotle's analysis would suggest. A judgment that an unjustified slight has occurred may be presupposed by the anger, even though the individual may be unable to formulate such an inference in the cool terms that are appropriate to reflection, and even though he may deny that such an inference is required for his feeling. To the psychoanalyst, a welling up of angry feelings for no ostensible reason requires an explanation, and that explanation is likely to include the postulation of unconscious beliefs and inferences that are ascribed on the basis of the evidence (Collins, 1969).

Emotion words are employed, not as simple descriptions of bodily changes, behavior, or dispositions to behave, but as interpretations and explanations of those phenomena. The

same data in different contexts provide evidence for the attribution of different emotions. Neither internal introspective
evidence nor observation of behavior is sufficient to determine
the appropriate use of an emotion word. Some such evidence is
necessary, but no particular feeling, behavior, or disposition to
behave is sufficient. There would be reason to doubt that a
man loved his wife if there were no evidence at all of this love.
Any particular action or set of actions could, however, under
the right conditions, be evidence for some emotion other than
love. The same behavior or physiological response may, in
different settings, be correctly interpreted as anger, indignation,
exasperation, or annoyance. These interpretations are not
guesses as to the private internal feelings of the person but
attributions of emotion words that are appropriate to the
context.

Sometimes the attribution of an emotion turns primarily
on matters of fact. For instance, I may believe that my
claustrophobic friend's fear of squash courts is unjustified. As
a matter of fact, they pose no real danger for him. In a cool,
reflective period outside, he may also admit that there is no
danger. When he tries to enter a court, however, the fear that
wells up inside him is partly constituted by the belief that the
situation is extremely threatening, a belief that has a practical
influence on his actions though he may doubt it in the daylight.
Once again, an unconscious belief must be ascribed to him in
order to account for his fear. At other times, these judgments
and beliefs are based on assessments of worth rather than on
facts. I may regard my friend's contempt for speculative
philosophy or his pride at having perfectly mastered parallel
parking as unjustified. In these cases, our disagreement is not
over the facts, but over our evaluations of them.

I weigh alternative ascriptions of emotions to myself in
much the same way. Often my interpretation of my own feelings or behavior requires assessments of value or the making
of choices. Were someone to ask whether or not I hope that

the Democrats win the coming election, I would not introspect in order to discover the requisite feeling of hope in my breast. Although I might consider my behavior ("I registered as a Democrat, so I guess I hope that they will win"), I am more likely to consider the merits of the alternative outcomes, assess them, and decide which I prefer. I don't search my feelings. If I wonder how much I trust another person, I don't examine my trust; rather, I assess the available evidence that would bear on his trustworthiness.

Were emotions bodily changes, sensations, or impressions, these inferences and the conceptual constraints that govern the ascription of emotion terms could not be accounted for. A pang is neither reasonable nor unreasonable, but fear and pride may be. If emotion words functioned as simple reports of physiological or psychological events, it would make no sense to say that someone ought to feel ashamed or that another's fear is unjustified. The primary function of language used to attribute emotions to oneself or to another is not to name particular states or to describe phenomena. It is to explain a bit of behavior or a physiological change by setting it within a larger context. Having had my attention called to my accelerated pulse and clenched fists in a context in which I have been insulted, I attribute those phenomena to anger and come to experience my anger.

The relation between an emotion and its object is a conceptual one. As Aristotle said, anger is always directed toward a specific person. Fear is always fear of something. One has pride in a particular state of affairs, and one hopes for an outcome that can be specified. Some emotions that appear to lack objects do in fact have them. Even though there may be objectless anxiety or dread, for instance, such cases are exceptional. The emotion may have an object that is specifiable but indeterminate, such as death or emptiness. Where emotions have objects, the relation between an emotion and its object is a logical one. The rules governing the proper use of emotion

terms set constraints on what kind of object a particular emotion may take. The emotion is identified by reference to its
proper object. Pangs or twitches may be specified without reference to concepts, but the identification of emotions requires
such reference. Unlike sensations, emotions are essentially
directed to objects.

> It is not in general possible to ascribe a piece of behavior or a
> sensation to a particular emotional state without at the same
> time ascribing an object to the emotion. If a man runs past
> me I can say nothing about his emotions unless I know
> whether he is running from A or running towards B; no flut-
> terings of the heart or meltings of the bowels could tell me I
> was in love without telling me with whom. (Kenny, 1963: 60)

I might feel pain, wonder what caused the pain, and consider a
number of hypotheses. Did it result from my having bumped
the desk with my knee this morning, or ought I to attribute it
to a muscle spasm or to arthritis? But I cannot feel love and
cast about in order to determine the object of my love. Unlike
pain, love is not the name of a sensation that can be specified in
the absence of an appropriate object. I may notice flutterings,
consider indigestion and other possible explanations, and settle
on the hypothesis that the flutterings are elicited by the person
of whom I am thinking and conclude that I am in love. But the
attribution of love requires reference to a person and assumes
an explanation of the feeling. I don't immediately perceive it as
love and then search for a cause and an object.

An emotion and its object are conceptually related as a result
of the rules that govern the proper use of emotion terms.
Hume was mistaken in his portrayal of the relation between an
emotion and its object as a causal and contingent one. Causal
hypotheses do, however, play a significant role in my identification of my own emotional states as well as those of others. I
become aware of a vague feeling and search for the best
explanation of that feeling. That explanation may lead me to
attribute an emotion to myself of which I was previously

unaware. I may decide, on the basis of his statements and his behavior, that a person is afraid of the devil and his evil powers. I don't ascribe to that person an objectless fear that I take to be contingently connected with the devil; I ascribe to him fear of the devil. Reference to the devil enters into the description of his emotion, and the emotion and the devil are conceptually related. We can say that the devil is the object of the emotion. My ascription of that emotion to the person, however, is a hypothesis to account for his behavior and his utterances. As a hypothesis, it is contingent and corrigible. He and I may both attribute his accelerated heart rate to his fear of the devil. Our hypothesis is a causal one and may be mistaken. His further hypothesis that the devil's actions caused his fear is surely mistaken and one that I may not accept. But the relation between his fear and the devil is not hypothetical but conceptual.

Spinoza stressed the fact that among the beliefs that are assumed by particular emotions are beliefs about the causes of the emotions themselves.[6] He defines love as "pleasure accompanied by the idea of an external cause" (Spinoza, 1982: 113). In order to experience love of a person, object, or activity, I must feel pleasure and attribute my pleasure to the object of my love. Reference to an object alone is not sufficient to warrant the ascription of an emotion. I cannot identify my anger just by saying that it is directed toward Cleon. In Aristotle's words, some justifying grounds for the anger must be assumed. I must believe that Cleon has insulted me. The identification of a mental state as an emotion requires reference to a proper object of the emotion and to certain beliefs that are presupposed by the emotion. Among those beliefs are typically beliefs about the causes of the state itself. The causal beliefs are hypotheses, but the connection between the emotion and its object is a conceptual one. This distinction will prove to be important for the differentiation of the tasks of description and explanation in the study of religious experience.

A Psychological Critique of the Traditional View

The inadequacy of the view of emotions as impressions or intuitively known inner states has also been demonstrated by recent work in social psychology. Aristotle recognized that emotional states have both physiological and cognitive components. We have seen that people often attribute emotions to themselves or others in the absence of any feeling or any sort of physiological change. Ascriptions of emotion are often made to explain behavior rather than feelings. I may conclude that someone is angry or jealous even in the face of his sincere denial of any feeling of anger or jealousy. People may be unaware of their own emotions. When a person reports a feeling of anger, jealousy, joy, or love, however, he or she is aware of feeling an emotion. Aristotle's analysis shows that these emotional experiences have both a material and a conceptual component, but it says nothing about how these are related.

On the basis of an ingenious set of experiments, the social psychologist Stanley Schachter (1971) has advanced a two-factor theory of emotion, in which he distinguishes between physiological arousal and cognitive appraisal. Schachter began by reconsidering James's claim that emotions are the feelings or perceptions of bodily changes. If emotions were identical with bodily changes, then different emotions would be associated with recognizably different bodily states. Walter Cannon (1927, 1929) cast considerable doubt on James's theory by noting the following points: the total separation of the visceral from the central nervous system does not alter emotional behavior; the same visceral changes occur in very different emotional states and in nonemotional states; the viscera are relatively insensitive structures; visceral changes are too slow to be a source of emotional feeling; and the artificial induction of visceral changes that are typical of strong emotions does not produce the emotions (Schachter, 1971: 1).[7]

Schachter hypothesized that the specific character of emotional states may be determined by cognitive factors. In an earlier study, Marañon (1924) had injected subjects with adrenaline in order to excite the sympathetic nervous system and had discovered that this sympathomimetic arousal was not sufficient to produce emotion. Schachter proposed a two-factor theory in which emotion consists of: (1) a general and diffuse pattern of arousal in the sympathetic nervous system, and (2) a cognitive label, or an explanation by which the subject understands this arousal. The label or cognition would determine whether the arousal was experienced as anger, joy, bliss, or awe. To test his theory, Schachter designed an experiment in which the physiological arousal and the cognitive factors could be independently manipulated.

This theory of the dual determinants of emotional state led Schachter to predict that if a person were to find himself in a state of arousal for which no explanation or appropriate cognition were immediately available, he would feel pressured to understand and to label his feelings. He would require some way to account for what was happening to him. Schachter hypothesized that

> ... he will label his feelings in terms of his knowledge of the immediate situation. Should he at the time be with a beautiful woman he might decide that he was wildly in love or sexually excited. Should he be at a ... party, he might, by comparing himself to others, decide that he was extremely happy and euphoric. Should he be arguing with his wife, he might explode in fury and hatred. ... In any case, it is my basic assumption that emotional states are the function of the interaction of such cognitive factors with a state of physiological arousal. (Schachter, 1971: 3–4)

This line of thought led to the following predictions. First, "given a state of physiological arousal for which a person has no immediate explanation, he will 'label' this state and describe his feelings in terms of the cognitions that are available to him" (Schachter, 1971: 4). The same state of arousal might elicit any one of a number of emotional labels, depending on the cognitive context. Second, given a state of physiological arousal for which an individual has an appropriate explanation, no interpretative need will arise, and he is unlikely to seek labels from the context. Third, given a constant cognitive context, the individual will react emotionally only to the extent that he experiences physiological arousal.

Schachter and Singer (1962) tested each of these predictions by administering disguised injections of adrenaline, informing some subjects about the effects that they would experience, misinforming others, and leaving the remainder ignorant. They then manipulated the cognitive context in each condition by controlling the environment so that the most salient cues suggested a particular emotional state. The aim was to manipulate physiological arousal and the available cognitive labels independently, with the expectation that persons who did not possess a sufficient explanation of what was happening to them would draw on the clues provided in the environment in order to understand their arousal. A confederate of the experimenter, waiting in a room with the subject, acted euphoric and frivolous in some conditions and insulted and angry in others. The result was a striking confirmation of Schachter's hypothesis that emotion is a combination of nonspecific physiological arousal and contextually determined cognitive labels.[8] Subjects who did not expect arousal symptoms tended to experience the emotion portrayed by the confederate. Those who were told the appropriate effects to expect from the injection (heart palpitations, tremors, flushing, etc.) were much less likely to share the confederate's mood. They already had a satisfactory account of what was happening to them. Later experiments have shown that arousal created by drugs, physical exercise, or natural hormonal changes can be labeled anything from euphoria, humor, love, and sexual attraction to hunger, anxiety, conflict, anger, and menstrual distress.

The subjects in the ignorant and misinformed conditions in Schachter's experiment were confronted with arousal symptoms that were unexpected, and they needed to account for those symptoms. They adopted the hypothesis that was suggested by the cues in their immediate environment. Those in the condition in which the confederate appeared to be expressing indignation and anger judged themselves to be angry and attributed their arousal to that anger. Those in the euphoria condition interpreted their arousal symptoms as evidence of euphoria. An identical diffuse arousal of the autonomic nervous system was explained and thus identified differently when the cognitive cues were varied. The subjects searched for plausible causes to which to attribute their anomalous bodily feelings.

The importance of causal attribution and of the subject's adoption of a hypothesis to account for what was happening to him does not conflict with the philosophical point that the relation between an emotion and its object is a noncontingent and grammatical one. The emotion can be identified only by reference to its object and grounds, and this identification is independent of whether or not the object exists outside of the subject's thought and of the validity of the grounds. A person might be afraid of a ghost. His fear and the ghost are conceptually related in that reference to the ghost is necessary in order to identify his fear. This holds even though there are no ghosts and his fear is unfounded.

Someone might object that although the foregoing analysis is appropriate for such relatively simple emotions as anger, fear, and joy, it is inadequate for such complex moods as melancholy, dread, care, and gladness; and that the latter are more significant than the former for understanding religious experience.[9] I suspect it would be impossible to formulate a criterion of simplicity which would capture the suggested distinction. However that may be, these complex moods and affections provide additional support for the proposed analysis. Just as there is no evidence for different states of mind or body that correspond to the several forms of despair detailed by Kierkegaard, it is unlikely that such terms as sorrow or melancholy are names that are employed to report different internal states. Their use for making subtle discriminations derives from the complex and sometimes incompatible interpretations and assessments of one's self, one's fellows, and one's surroundings which constitute these moods. The assessments and interpretations are formative rather than consequent. The suggestion that fear and anger are simple impressions has seemed plausible to many. If they are not simple but assume rather sophisticated conceptual distinctions and judgments, then a similar analysis is surely required for the complex affections with which phenomenologists of religion have chiefly been concerned.

A Classic Conversion Experience

Given the results of Schachter's experiments, it seems quite plausible that at least some religious experiences are due to physiological changes for which the subject adopts a religious explanation. Bodily states that elicit evaluative needs are not limited to arousal of the sort produced by an adrenaline injection. Certain classical meditation states function to decrease heart rate and to dampen rather than arouse autonomic functions. Laboratory-induced sensory deprivation has resulted in subjects' reports that are often quite similar to classical descriptions of mystical experience. Any significant physiological change from equilibrium could have the effects Schachter ascribes to arousal and, if the person were uninformed with regard to the origin of the change, would give rise to the need for a label or explanation.

In his chapter on conversion in *The Varieties of Religious Experience*, James quotes at length from one Stephen Bradley's report of his conversion experience. Bradley had just returned from a revival service in which the preacher had been unusually forceful and in which the sermon was based on a text from Revelation. Bradley had been impressed, but he claimed that his feelings were unmoved.

I will now relate my experience of the power of the Holy Spirit which took place on the same night. Had any person told me previous to this that I could have experienced the power of the Holy Spirit in the manner which I did, I could not have believed it, and should have thought the person deluded that told me so. I went directly home after the meeting, and when I got home I wondered what made me feel so stupid. I retired to rest soon after I got home, and felt indifferent to things of religion until I began to be exercised by the Holy Spirit, which began in about five minutes after, in the following manner:

At first, I began to feel my heart beat very quick all of a sudden, which made me at first think that perhaps something is going to ail me, though I was not alarmed, for I felt no pain. My heart increased in its beating, which soon convinced me that it was the Holy Spirit from the effect it had on me. I began to feel exceedingly happy and humble, and such a sense of unworthiness as I never felt before. . . . My heart seemed as if it would burst, but it did not stop until I felt as if I was unutterably full of the love and grace of God. In the mean time while thus exercised, a thought arose in my mind, what can it mean? And all at once, as if to answer it, my memory became exceedingly clear, and it appeared to me just as if the New Testament was placed open before me, eighth chapter of Romans, and as light as if some candle lighted was held for me to read the 26th and 27th verses of that chapter, and I read these words: "The Spirit helpeth our infirmities with groanings which cannot be uttered." And all the time that my heart was a-beating, it made me groan like a person in distress, which was not very easy to stop, though I was in no pain at all, and my brother being in bed in another room came and opened the door, and asked me if I had got the toothache. I told him no, and that he might get to sleep . . . .

I now feel as if I had discharged my duty by telling the truth, and hope by the blessing of God, it may do some good to all who shall read it. He has fulfilled his promise in sending the Holy Spirit down into our hearts, or mine at least, and I now defy all the Deists and Atheists in the world to shake my faith in Christ. (James, 1902: 190–193)

Bradley's testimony reads like a textbook example designed to illustrate Schachter's theory. He notices his heart rate suddenly increase. He looks to discover the cause of it and, in the context of having just returned from the revival service, attributes it to the Holy Spirit. The palpitations are attributed to an external force, not to pain or an ailment, and thus present no need for alarm. But he must still make some sense of this force. A thought arises in his mind: What can it mean? He sees clearly a passage in Romans that confirms the attribution of his stirrings to the Holy Spirit. Eventually this leads Bradley to "defy all the Deists and Atheists in the world to shake [his] faith in Christ." What began as mysterious palpitations ends with attributional certainty.

Bradley, like so many prospective devotees before and since, could not understand his feelings in naturalistic terms. Religious symbols offered him an explanation that was compatible both with his experience and with his antecedent beliefs. He did not consider explanations involving Krishna, Zeus, or the Qur'an. The content of the scripture and the experience of being moved or physiologically aroused were confidently linked. These are the two components required by Schachter's theory. It seems likely that religious concepts and doctrines often provide labels for experiences of arousal which initially appear to be anomalous. Bradley's testimony is striking in part because of his conscious recognition of the physiological effects and explicit acknowledgment of a search for a hypothesis by which to account for them. More often the interpretation is simultaneous with the recognition of the symptoms, so that the subject reports an immediate perception of the palpitations as the work of the Holy Spirit. In settings in which religious experiences are sought or anticipated, the explanatory scheme is firmly in place prior to the experience. Revivalists understand this, as do gurus and spiritual directors.

The experience of Pentecost among the disciples of Jesus may be amenable to a similar explanation. As Luke describes it, the disciples were gathered together shortly after Jesus' death. The setting was a religious one. Suddenly a sound came from heaven, and the disciples experienced voices speaking through them. Luke reports that "All were amazed and perplexed, saying to one another, 'what does this mean?'" (Acts 2:12–13, RSV). Some observers provided a naturalistic explanation, accusing the disciples of drunkenness. But Peter, noting the early hour, rejects this hypothesis and quotes from the words of the prophet Joel: "And in the last days it shall be, God declares, that I will pour out my spirit upon all flesh, and your sons and your daughters shall prophesy, and your young men shall see visions, and your old men shall dream dreams" (Acts 2:17). This interpretation carries the authority of the Hebrew prophets. It is provided in order to account for an arousing experience that was unsought and unexplained. Peter's interpretation relates the disciples' shared experiences to the tradition of Yahweh's promise and to their conviction of its fulfillment in Jesus, a tradition and a conviction that had recently been threatened by Jesus' death and apparent defeat.

In the case of Stephen Bradley, our information is insufficient to enable us to account for his initial symptoms. Perhaps they were due to the excitement of the revival meeting, though he claims to have been unaffected at the time. In the case of the disciples, it is not surprising that their reunion after the death of their teacher, in the setting of a religious festival, should have been a moving one. In both cases the arousal was interpreted in religious terms and attributed to divine activity, and in both cases that attribution produced conviction and behavioral consequences.

The results of a controversial experiment in the psychology of religion may also be subject to reinterpretation in the light of Schachter's theory. Pahnke (1970) attempted to induce experimentally a form of mystical experience with the aid of psilocybin. In the setting of a Good Friday service, theology students received either psilocybin or a mild control drug, nicotinic acid. The results show that the subjects receiving the hallucinogen labeled their experiences in religious terms to a significantly greater extent than did those who received the placebo; and their reports of their experiences showed a significantly greater coincidence with nine characteristics previously gleaned from the reports of classical mystics. Pahnke's experimental design can be viewed in retrospect as parallel to that of Schachter, but with attention to a different dependent variable. Pahnke sought to maintain a constant cognitive context (the Good Friday service and the use of seminarians for subjects) and manipulated the arousal agent. Clark (1970: 191) calls attention to the fact, omitted in the published accounts, that one of Pahnke's subjects seems to have been immune to the religious effects of the hallucinogen because of a firmly held naturalistic interpretation. This subject was skeptical from the outset, was randomly selected for the experimental condition, and did not report any of the characteristics of religious experience. Although one subject is statistically unimportant, the case does provide some evidence for a Schachterian interpretation. The subject was unwilling or unable to adopt the attributions suggested by the context, and so the effects of the psychedelic drug were not experienced as mystical or religious. Pahnke's conclusion that mystical experience might be caused by some quality of the hallucinogen is then called into question. Perhaps psilocybin functions only as a rather powerful agent of arousal, differing only quantitatively from the arousal produced by the nicotinic acid. The attributional or interpretative component might then be the crucial factor in those experiences that were reported in terms reminiscent of classical mystics.

The history of religion is replete with the religious labeling and explanation of anomalous bodily states and activities. Gershom Scholem (1973: 125–138) has shown that the abnormal physical and mental condition with which the seventeenth-century Jewish mystical messiah Sabbatai Sevi was afflicted is well documented and was widely known before his association with Nathan of Gaza. Nathan provided a religious explanation of Sabbatai's pathology, declaring him to be the messianic figure awaited by those who adhered to the Lurianic school of Kabbalah. This explanation was eagerly accepted by the prophet himself and by hundreds of thousands of followers.[10]

Any bodily changes or feelings may be accounted for in religious terms when the subject's past experience and present context makes such an account plausible and compelling. The common element in religious experience is likely to be found, not in a particular physiological or even mental state, but in the beliefs held by the subject about the causes of that state.

Attribution of Causes

Emotions assume particular concepts and beliefs. They cannot be assimilated to sensations or simple internal events that are independent of thought. Reference to rather complex concepts and beliefs is required in order to specify an emotion. That much was clearly understood by Aristotle, though it was neglected by those working in the empiricist tradition. Spinoza, however, in his theory of the emotions, stressed a further point. Among those beliefs to which reference must be made to identify an emotional state are beliefs about the causes of the state itself. Love is pleasure accompanied by the idea of an external cause. It would make no sense for me to say that I was proud of the table without my assuming some story that establishes an appropriate connection between myself and the table. Perhaps I repaired the table, or my son built it. Were I to acknowledge that my pride was independent of any facts about the table or my relation to it, my emotion would be irrational.

The role of inference and the explanation of one's own physiological and mental states in determining emotions was demonstrated by Schachter's work. Subjects sought explanations for what was happening to them. The hypotheses they adopted to account for their arousal determined the specific emotions they experienced. The accuracy of their causal attributions is irrelevant for the identification of their emotions. If a subject believed that the experimenter's insults caused his symptoms, it was that belief that entered into his experience of anger. Aristotle correctly observed that in order to specify an emotion it is necessary to specify the quality of the feeling, the object of the emotion, and the rational grounds by which the subject justifies the emotion. We can now see that among those grounds are the subject's beliefs about the causes of his state.

An individual's beliefs about the causes of his bodily and mental states enter into the determination of the emotions he will experience. The attribution of causes of one's experience will also prove to be crucial for the identification of an experience as religious. Among the criteria for such an identification is the subject's belief that his experience cannot be accounted for without reference to religious concepts and beliefs. We are constantly monitoring ourselves and searching for the best explanations of our own behavior as well as of what happens to us. A person identifies an experience as religious when he comes to believe that the best explanation of what has happened to him is a religious one.

Schachter's work on emotion is part of a more comprehensive research program in social psychology known as attribution theory.[11] This program is actually a loose coalition of theories concerned with the ways people perceive the causes of their bodily states and behavior. One component in that coalition, known as self-perception theory (Bem, 1972), is an account of the ways people monitor themselves and form self-concepts. It can be seen as an extension of Schachter's demonstration that people interpret diffuse physiological arousal in the light of the context in which they find themselves. Self-perception theory suggests that among the phenomena that require interpretation are actions as well as states of physiological arousal. According to the theory, evaluative and interpretative needs are salient not only in situations of unexplained arousal states but intermittently throughout the course of all human activity. Furthermore, the explanations a person adopts to account for his behavior will also affect his future behavior.

The central propositions of self-perception theory are as follows:

> Individuals come to "know" their own attitudes, emotions, and other internal states partially by inferring them from observations of their own overt behavior and/or the circumstances in which this behavior occurs. Thus, to the extent that internal cues are weak, ambiguous, or uninterpretable, the individual is functionally in the same position as an outside observer, an observer who must necessarily rely upon the same cues to infer the individual's inner states. (Bem, 1972: 2)

This theory has been used to explain results from a series of controversial attitude-change experiments originally designed to test the theory of cognitive dissonance (Brehm and Cohen, 1962; Festinger, 1957). It had been discovered, for example, that people who are paid a small amount to make a statement with which they disagree will later agree more with the statement than will people who were paid a larger amount for the same task (Festinger and Carlsmith, 1959). Bem suggests that this might result from an inference made by the experimental subjects on the basis of observing their own behavior. The inferences might be expressed as follows: (in the low-incentive condition) "I must have believed the statement I made if I was willing to make it for such a small fee"; (in the high-incentive condition) "I must really not have believed the statement if they had to pay me to make it."

Later experiments have provided other significant examples. In one, children were induced to believe that they were moral by seeing themselves resist a forbidden toy. In another, children's intrinsic interest in new art materials was shown to be undermined if external rewards were offered for playing with the materials (Lepper, Greene, and Nisbett, 1973). It seems that if no rewards were given the children believed they painted for fun only, but when prizes were offered they believed they painted mostly for extrinsic reasons. The important consequence was that children who believed themselves to be intrinsically interested continued to play with the art materials on their own when the experiment was over, whereas those who received extrinsic rewards no longer cared about painting when prizes were not forthcoming. Weiner (1972, 1974) has developed an attribution theory of achievement motivation and has provided evidence for the claim that different beliefs about the causes of one's behavior have direct consequences for future behavior.

Bem (1972) reviews many more studies that support self-perception theory. The central claim of the theory is a conclusion we arrived at earlier in our examination of the use of emotion words. People come to understand their own emotions, beliefs, and attitudes by attending to evidence in much the same way that they ascribe these states to others. There is no sharp distinction between first- and third-person ascription of emotions, attitudes, or even beliefs. We make inferences and adopt hypotheses in order to arrive at an understanding of our own attitudes and behavior. Bem says we infer to internal states on the basis of observable behavior "to the extent that internal cues are weak, ambiguous, or uninterpretable." Schachter designed his experimental situation so that the symptoms experienced by his subjects would be ambiguous or uninterpretable in terms of what they were given to believe. Such emotions or attitudes as love, trust, or faith are complex states for which there are no definitive physiological or other internal marks. No internal cues will tell me I am in love in the relatively unambiguous way I come to know my left foot is in pain. We must employ whatever evidence is available to us in order to ascribe emotions, attitudes, and even beliefs to ourselves or others. A four-year-old acquaintance of mine, when asked by someone whether or not she believed in Jesus Christ, reasoned aloud: "My mother is Jewish, and my father is Christian; that makes me half Jewish and half Christian, so I guess that I half believe in Jesus." Such patterns of inference are more widespread than one might imagine. Instances of sudden conversion to or from a religious tradition are few compared to cases in which a person comes to discover, on the basis of his observations of his behavior and spontaneous responses over a period of time, that he has lost his faith, or that the religious beliefs of the tradition in which he was raised are more firmly entrenched in his patterns of thought and action than he realized.

Nichiren Shoshu is one of the fastest growing of Japan's "new religions." It is a Buddhist sect committed to spreading the message that salvation can be attained by faith in the Lotus Sutra, and especially by repeated chanting of the title of that sutra: *nam myoho renge kyo*. A typical meeting of an American Nichiren group consists of about an hour of chanting, a short break for sidewalk evangelism, additional chanting, testimonials, questions and answers about the doctrine and practices of the movement, followed by a strong appeal for commitment from the new prospects.[12] The emphasis on testimonials provides an opportunity for prospects and members of the group to hear their peers interpret their experiences within the supportive context of the meeting. The commitment asked from the prospective members is behavioral; they are to engage in chanting for an extended period. Chanting the *daimoku* (*nam myoho renge kyo*) is the central activity of both public and private worship. It is completely standardized and, for Americans at least, almost totally free of cognitive content. Even for Japanese members the phrase is a title with no propositional meaning ("adoration to the lotus of the wonderful law"). The contents of the sutra remain unknown to most American adherents, and they are not encouraged to study it. The chanting itself is believed to be efficacious. The chanting is directed toward the *gohonzon*, a black box containing a small scroll on which is printed a mandala said to derive from Nichiren. Thus the devotee begins with an attributional *tabula rasa*, fervently chanting meaningless symbols before a "black box." Each service opens with an hour of chanting that appears to arouse the devotees and create a strong sense of participation in a group effort.

Many religious communities urge prospective converts to engage in ritual action or discipline before they acquaint themselves with the supporting doctrine. The regimen might consist of yogic exercises, martial arts, chanting *hare krishna* or *nam myoho renge kyo*, ingesting drugs, embarking on pilgrimages to sacred shrines, or, as in this case, engaging immediately in proselytizing. Each of these activities engages a person. Once involved in action, he is more susceptible to adopting the beliefs of the community in order to justify his actions and explain his feelings. Proselytizing is particularly effective in this respect. Studies have shown that people who voluntarily agree to represent a position with which they differ, and who are given insufficient reward for this behavior, will alter their beliefs in the direction of the position they represented in order to justify their own behavior.

Chanting and proselytizing are strongly commended to the prospective convert with only the most rudimentary justification. "Try it. It will change your life." Curiosity about the belief system is initially discouraged. Emphasis is placed entirely on the claims for the efficacy of the activity. When a colleague and I inquired about the meaning of the chant on a visit to a Nichiren meeting, we were told that this should concern us only after we had experienced the power of the chanting to produce benefits in our lives. This response suggests that the beliefs eventually satisfy adherents because they make sense of an activity to which they have already committed themselves and for which they have as yet insufficient justification. This suggestion is related to Bem's interpretation of the experiments in which subjects engaged in activities with insufficient justification and later attributed increased significance to these activities in order to make sense of their actions.

Once the attribution is made, confirming evidence is much easier to find. At one session we attended, the leader invited a new prospect to chant for just one hundred days and see what would happen. Chanting involves, initially, an hour or more both morning and evening. If the prospective convert decides to try this "experimentally" for one hundred days, the re-arrangement of his life and the persistent chanting, which cannot be justified on any other grounds, present a surd that is quite salient for him. It is likely that before the experimental period has elapsed the potential convert will be attracted by a set of beliefs which give meaning to the apparently meaning-less activity in which he has been engaged and around which he has reordered his life. Schleiermacher (1958: 60) says that spiritual exercises are an expression of piety but play no role in its origin. The causal arrow runs only in one direction. In fact, however, commitment to a regimen of such exercises can lead to the adoption of beliefs that justify that regimen and the resultant feelings. Schleiermacher's refusal to allow that such a state might be genuine piety only confirms what we have already discovered, that his criteria for identifying piety or the religious consciousness include a requirement about the cause of that consciousness.

The testimonials are especially interesting. At one meeting a young man explained that he had recently suffered from test anxiety during a college mathematics exam. He was unable to concentrate, and he perceived himself as failing. Rather than simply giving up or fighting himself to regain control of his attention, he began to chant *nam myoho renge kyo* and "to trust the rhythms of the universe." Suddenly, according to his report, he became calm and the answers came to him as if from outside himself. His report was greeted with enthusiastic applause by his fellow chanters, a reception that undoubtedly encouraged him to make similar interpretations and reports thereafter.

This relatively simple testimony combines the labeling of a state of physiological arousal and the attribution of causality to an external source. Weiner and Sierad (1974) have shown that

characteristic behavior patterns related to achievement motivation can be altered by varying the extent to which subjects
attribute success or failure to factors that are or are not under
their own control. In this case, the arousal, stemming from
test anxiety, is explained as a function of the person's being
"out of harmony with the universe." Chanting is therefore
indicated, and it allows one to give up the struggle and to let
the burden be borne by the cosmic rhythms. The obsessive
focus on the self and the possibility of failure is removed, and
relaxation results. James (1902: 289) regards this ability to
relax and to abandon responsibility as "the fundamental act in
specifically religious, as distinguished from moral practice." He
says that it antedates all theologies and is independent of
beliefs, but we can see that this ability is a consequence of
one's beliefs about the causes of one's behavior. After the fact,
success on the examination is attributed to an outside power.
The willingness to trust may be born out of despair at no other
alternative, but following one success the convert will be more
willing to put his trust in the efficacy of the chant on similar
occasions in the future.

Our "knowledge" of our own attitudes, beliefs, emotions,
and desires is often arrived at by inference from observation of
our own behavior as well as of our bodily states. We constantly
monitor our actions as well as our feelings and make causal
attributions that enter into the determination of our experience and that have direct behavioral consequences. Beliefs
about the causes of one's experience are themselves constitutive of the experience. This is especially true in the case of
religious experience.

Neither the felt quality of an experience nor its intentional
object is sufficient to identify it as religious. Often such an
identification depends on beliefs about the cause of the experience, as we saw in Schleiermacher. This is certainly the case
in theistic traditions. Jonathan Edwards (1959) says that true
religion consists of holy affections and that those affections are

holy that arise from divine operation on the heart. If we confine ourselves to Christianity and look at three descriptions of religious experience which differ greatly but have been influential for the identification of religious experience in modern Protestantism, we shall find that no common sensible quality or intentional object can be discerned, but that the three instances share a claim about the causes of the experiences. Two of the examples are reports of discrete experiences; the third is an attempt to identify the religious moment in experience. The first example is the conversion of Saul of Tarsus, which has served as a model or template for Christians seeking to identify religious experience. The second is John Wesley's Aldersgate experience, and the third, of a very different sort, is Schleiermacher's description of the common element in piety, the feeling of absolute dependence. Paul describes his experience as an experience of Jesus in which he saw a heavenly light and heard Jesus' voice. Wesley's experience, like that of Stephen Bradley, had no such determinate content. It was not an experience of Jesus or of any other intentional object of that sort. He felt "his heart strangely warmed" and had a new sense of assurance and trust. Schleiermacher's description is not of a discrete datable experience at all but of the religious moment in human consciousness.

In his letter to the Galatians, Paul says only that "he who had set me apart before I was born, and had called me through his grace, was pleased to reveal his Son to me, in order that I might preach him among the Gentiles" (Galatians 1:15–16, RSV). Luke records three versions of the experience (Acts 9:1–22; 22:4–16; and 26:9–18). They differ as to whether or not those accompanying Paul saw the heavenly light or heard the voice, but for Paul the experience was both visual and aural.

> Now as he journeyed he approached Damascus, and suddenly
> a light from heaven flashed about him. And he fell to the

> ground and heard a voice saying to him, "Saul, Saul, why do you persecute me?" And he said, "Who are you, Lord?" And he said, "I am Jesus, whom you are persecuting; but rise and enter the city, and you will be told what you are to do." (Acts 9:3–6, RSV)

Paul saw a light, and he perceived it as a "light from heaven." He heard a voice that he identified as the voice of Jesus. He reported to the Galatians that God had revealed his Son to him. He experienced Jesus, or the risen Christ.

Wesley's experience took place in a religious setting during the reading of Luther's preface to Paul's epistle to the Romans. Wesley's report of it in his journal sets the experience within the context of his thoughts and persistent self-examination over a considerable period of time. The actual experience is datable, but it is not a vision or a hearing of voices. Rather, it is a sense that came over him.

> In the evening, I went very unwillingly to a society in Aldersgate Street, where one was reading Luther's Preface to the Epistle to the Romans. About a quarter of nine, while he was describing the change which God works in the heart through faith in Christ, I felt my heart strangely warmed. I felt I did trust in Christ, Christ alone for salvation; and an assurance was given me that he had taken away *my* sins, even *mine*, and saved *me* from the law of sin and death. (Wesley, 1964: 66)

The immediate cognitive context, and his preoccupations, were religious. The occasion was the feeling of his heart strangely warmed, but the experience itself was Wesley's new sense of assurance and trust. It was an experience *of* assurance in a quite different sense from Paul's experience *of* Jesus.

The feeling of absolute dependence is described by Schleiermacher (1963: 16) as "the self-consciousness which accompanies all our activity, and therefore, since that is never zero, accompanies our whole existence, and negates absolute freedom." It is "the consciousness that the whole of our spontaneous activity comes from a source outside of us in just the same sense in which anything towards which we should have a feeling of absolute freedom must have proceeded entirely from ourselves." And that source is what we call "God." This is not a report of an experience, and it is never by itself sufficient to fully determine a conscious experience; rather it is intended to be a description of a moment in all human consciousness.

These descriptions are not strictly comparable. Two are reports of discrete experiences, and one is a characterization of the pervasive sense of finitude in human existence. But they illustrate the futility of searching for some common sensible quality or intentional object for religious experience, even when we confine ourselves to Christian theism. We have a flash of light accompanied by words perceived as having come from the risen Christ, a heart strangely warmed, and a sense of utter dependence. Were one to identify a common component, it would have to be that suggested by Edwards. These experiences are identified as religious because Paul, Wesley, and Schleiermacher each believed his experience to have been caused by God. The experience Schleiermacher describes is in fact the consciousness that all we do and all that impinges upon us is dependent on the divine causality. He says that the religious person perceives every event as a miracle in the sense that he believes everything to be traceable to God as its source. Paul believed that his vision and the words he heard were God's revelation of his Son to him, and Wesley and Bradley perceived the strange sensations in their hearts as the work of the Holy Spirit.

Even those who claim that the common element in religious experience can be described in phenomenological terms that are neutral with respect to the causal explanation of that experience often incorporate causal claims in the identifying descriptions they give of religious experience. We have seen that this is true of Schleiermacher. Looking again at Otto's instructions to his reader, quoted at the beginning of this chapter, we find another instance of the same phenomenon. Otto has formulated the rules for the identification of the numinous moment in experience in such a way as to prevent the "reduction" of religious experience by its being subsumed under any explanatory or interpretative scheme.

> ... for it is not easy to discuss questions of religious psychology with one who can recollect the emotions of his adolescence, the discomforts of indigestion, or, say, social feelings, but cannot recall any intrinsically religious feelings. (Otto, 1958: 8)

The rules have been drawn up so as to preclude any naturalistic explanation of whatever feeling the reader may have attended to in his or her own experience. Such restrictions guarantee ineffability and mystery. If it can be explained, it is not a religious experience. The criterion by which the experience is to be identified precludes certain kinds of explanation. What purports to be a neutral phenomenological description is actually a dogmatic formula designed to evoke or to create a particular sort of experience. By ruling out certain kinds of explanations, the formula guarantees that any experience so identified will not be explicable in naturalistic terms. Thus an explanatory criterion is built into the identifying description, and warnings about reductionism are invoked to protect that criterion. This is sufficient evidence that, despite protests to the contrary, a claim about the cause of the experience is central to Otto's identification of an experience as religious. In this respect Otto is not alone.

IV.
MYSTICISM

Concepts that are offered as descriptions or even as contributions to the theory of religious experience sometimes function in an evocative manner. They serve to establish conditions for the identification of an experience as religious in such a way as to insure that it be of a certain character. Schleiermacher's instructions to the reader for identifying the moment that precedes the differentiation of consciousness, and Otto's incorporation into his instructions for the identification of a religious experience the condition that it not be amenable to naturalistic explanation, both serve to illustrate this phenomenon. Both restrict the conditions under which an experience can be properly identified as religious so as to guarantee that the experience picked out will not be subject to classification under our ordinary descriptive or explanatory categories. The anomalous character of the experience is guaranteed by the rules that govern the employment of the terms by which a religious experience is identified. Language purportedly descriptive and neutral with respect to evaluations or explanations of the experience actually conditions that experience and places constraints on what kinds of explanation are deemed appropriate. In this chapter the formative influence of religious language and the shaping of an experience by the rules that govern its identification will be illustrated by examining two marks that are widely acknowledged to be characteristic of the experiences reported by mystics: ineffability and noetic quality.

The Search for a Mystical Core

Reports of mystical experiences have been of special interest to those studying religious experience and, more recently, to students of comparative religion. These reports seem to point to an experience, or to a family of related experiences, that can be differentiated from the interpretations placed on it in various religious traditions. Though there are differences, it has seemed to many that Hindu, Buddhist, Islamic, Jewish, and Christian mystics testify to a common experience. Many attempts have been made to describe this experience, and to distinguish it from the parochial interpretations associated with the various religious traditions (Otto, 1932; Smart, 1958, 1965; Staal, 1975; Stace, 1960; Underhill, 1911; Zaehner, 1957). There has been debate over how this core experience ought to be described and whether it consists of one or several fundamental types of experience (Smart, 1965; Zaehner, 1957). Some have thought that the ubiquity of the experience in different cultural settings provides support for the claims made by mystics for the revelatory character of their experiences.

In *The Varieties of Religious Experience,* James construes mysticism rather broadly. He says that personal religious experience has its root and center in mystical states of consciousness and that a consideration of these states is a consideration of the general claim that religious experience can yield knowledge. He proposes four marks of a mystical experience, two primary and two secondary (James, 1902: 380–381). The primary marks are its ineffability and a noetic quality. The experience defies verbal expression, and it seems to the mystic to be a state of knowledge or insight, revelation or illumination. These two characteristics taken together, James says, will entitle any state to be called mystical in the sense in which he is using the term. The secondary marks, which are usually found to be characteristic of such states, are transience and passivity.

This characterization is, of course, not unique to James. Classical studies of mysticism, including his, have been broadly phenomenological. Their aim has been to distinguish a single core or several fundamental types from the interpretations placed on the experience by the mystic in the light of his or her attitudes and beliefs. A difficulty arises, however, from the fact that these attitudes and beliefs are typically adopted prior to the experience rather than subsequent to it. The experience is shaped by a complex pattern of concepts, commitments, and expectations which the mystic brings to it. These beliefs and attitudes are formative of, rather than consequent upon, the experience. They define in advance what experiences are possible.

Attempts to differentiate a core from its interpretations may cause the theorist to lose the very experience he is trying to analyze. The terms in which the subject understands what is happening to him are constitutive of the experience; consequently those in different traditions have different experiences. Jewish and Buddhist mystics bring entirely different doctrinal commitments, expectations, and rules for identifying their mental and bodily states to their experiences, and thus *devekuth* and *nirvana* cannot be the same. It might indeed be possible to produce cross-cultural documentation of some common physiological states or mental images in the experiences of mystics. But to focus on these, as some theorists have done, is not to delineate a core but to attend to something other than the experience. A decelerated heart rate may be common to some mystics and to all athletes at the height of training, and it may be a natural endowment of some individuals in contrast to others. Deautomatization (Deikman, 1966) may occur as a consequence of a psychotic break, of finding oneself in a completely unfamiliar and possibly threatening environment, or of preparation through spiritual exercises. But to attend to such phenomena while disregarding the content of the mystic's beliefs and the expectations he or she brings to the experience is to err in one's priorities. What others have dismissed as interpretative overlay may be the distinguishing mark of the experience.

Steven Katz (1978) recognizes that the mystic's experience is conditioned by the complex preexperiential pattern of beliefs, attitudes, and expectations which he brings to it. He illustrates this by contrasting the Jewish mystic's nonabsorptive encounter with God, on the one hand, with the unitive experience of some Christian mystics, on the other, and both of these with the insight into the impermanence of all things which constitutes the state of nirvana for the Buddhist. The fact that Jewish mystics do not experience union with God is best explained by reference to parameters set by the tradition that has formed their beliefs about persons and God and their expectations for such experiences.

> That is to say, the entire life of the Jewish mystic is permeated from childhood up by images, concepts, symbols, ideological values, and ritual behavior which there is no reason to believe he leaves behind in his experience. Rather, these images, beliefs, symbols, and ritual define, *in advance*, what the experience *he wants to have*, and which he then does have, will be like. (Katz, 1978: 33; original emphasis)

In a similar fashion the experience of the Buddhist is shaped by his tradition.

Often, the structuring of an experience according to the particular tradition is done quite explicitly and self-consciously. Most mystical traditions place great emphasis on the importance of a qualified teacher or spiritual adviser for the novice. In Judaism, for instance, autodidacticism is suspect. Guides, gurus, and spiritual advisers in the several traditions do not teach mysticism in general but specific ways to specific goals. Detailed regimens are prescribed to prepare a disciple. Such regimens are employed warily by Buddhist meditators in order to create occasions for the application of Buddhist doctrine and to arrive at discernment (Gimello, 1978).

Those who have tried to distinguish a core experience from the diverse interpretations that can be placed on it would not, of course, deny that these interpretative schemes are pre-experiential. The Kabbalistic doctrines employed by a Jewish mystic to interpret his experience form part of the set he brings to that experience. Some theorists (e.g., Stace, 1960), recognize the presence of such preexperiential patterns and their influence on the experience but still claim that a core can be differentiated from its interpretations. Katz points to what he regards as "a clear causal connection" between the antecedent beliefs and commitments one brings to an experience and the resultant experience. He seems to think he can show causal influence by demonstrating temporal priority. In fact, the connection between the mystic's antecedent beliefs and his experience is not a causal one but a conceptual one. As we shall see, the relevant conceptual connection includes a judgment about causes.

The logic that governs the concepts by which people interpret their experiences in different traditions shapes those experiences. Any attempt to differentiate a core from its interpretations, then, results in the loss of the very experience one is trying to analyze. The interpretations are themselves constitutive of the experiences. Devekuth could not be imagined in isolation from the tradition of beliefs and practices in which it is sought and attained. To isolate some bodily or mental state and refer to it as devekuth apart from any reference to a formative tradition would be to lose the experience. One cannot attain nirvana by accident. This is a logical matter, not just a contingent fact (Smart, 1958: 64). Nirvana is identified by reference to the rules that govern the behavior required to achieve it, and to the doctrines assumed by those rules. The rules that govern the practice and goals of mystics in particular religious traditions condition the experiences that are available to them.

If there is no core experience, and if mystical experiences vary substantively from one tradition to another, what justification is there for continuing to employ the phrase *mystical experience* at all? Katz calls for a pluralistic account of these experiences and a halt to any search for common characteristics. If there is nothing common to the experiences of nirvana and devekuth, and nothing that these share with others that have been classified under the rubric mystical experience, why continue to use the concept? No doubt a history of the phrase *mystical experience* could be written which would parallel Smith's (1964, 1979) research on *religion* with many of the same findings. The concept is very likely an artifact of the past two centuries of European scholarship on the subject.[1] But the results of such a history would be as inconclusive as those of Smith. The fact that the concept is of recent vintage means only that we cannot accurately ascribe it to people in other cultures and other periods. It does not mean that we cannot employ it to refer to a particular pattern of phenomena.

Although the search for an unmediated core that can be distinguished from the interpretations placed upon it may be futile, there do seem to be expressions, experiential reports, and practices that are sufficiently similar across different traditions to warrant use of the term *mysticism* and attention to some common characteristics. One can employ the results of phenomenological analyses without subscribing to the conviction that these represent some fundamental uninterpreted experience. The two primary marks suggested by James are themes that recur regularly in such reports and analyses. Stace (1960: 131–132), for example, gives a central place in his list of common characteristics to ineffability and the related notion of paradoxicality, and to a sense of objectivity or reality. Accordingly, let us focus on the two characteristics of ineffability and noetic quality, considering how each might best be construed.

Ineffability

James regards ineffability as "the handiest of the marks by which I classify a state of mind as mystical."

> The subject of it [a mystical state] immediately says that it defies expression, that no adequate report of its contents can

be given in words. It follows from this that its quality must be directly experienced; it cannot be imparted or transferred to others. In this peculiarity mystical states are more like states of feeling than like states of the intellect. No one can make clear to another who has never had a certain feeling, in what the quality or worth of it consists. (James, 1902: 380)

James treats ineffability as if it were a simple property of the experience, or a phenomenological characteristic that could not be further analyzed. He takes the fact that the experience defies expression to mean that it can be known only by acquaintance and thus is closer to feelings than to states of the intellect.

By contrast, Katz is critical of those mystics or theorists who invoke such pseudoqualities as ineffability, paradoxicality, and a sense of objectivity. He regards the first two as functioning only to inhibit careful analysis and the third as a hopelessly vague concept that has different meanings in different contexts. According to him, the terms *paradox* and *ineffable* are mystifying ploys, serving only to cloak experiences from investigators and to render their comparative study impossible (Katz, 1978: 54). If, however, the characterization of their experience as ineffable or paradoxical is widespread among mystics themselves, as indeed it seems to be, we would do well not to dismiss these concepts too quickly but to attend to the role such character- izations play. I shall argue that ineffability is not a simple unanalyzable characteristic of the experience, as James implies, but that it is an artifact of the peculiar grammatical rules that govern the use of certain terms in particular religious contexts. I shall also argue that terms like *ineffable* and *paradoxical* are not imprecise and vague. On the contrary, they are quite precise. They often serve, however, to constitute an experience rather than to describe, express, or analyze it. They are conditions for the identification of an experience as mystical.

Ineffable is properly a relative term. Nothing can be either effable or ineffable *tout court*. Something is ineffable with respect to a particular language or symbol system, as a sound is ineffable with respect to talk about colors, or the square root of minus one cannot be represented in the system of real numbers (Danto, 1973). But what would it mean to say that something was absolutely ineffable, or ineffable with respect to all linguistic schemes? Paul Henle (1948) has argued that this would be impossible because, as in the example of the sound or the square root of minus one, we would need some way to identify or to represent that which we assert to be ineffable. Furthermore, to take seriously the mystic's claim that his experience is absolutely ineffable would be to credit him with a knowledge of all possible grammatical and symbolic devices. The experience might be ineffable with respect to some, but not to all. Richard Gale (1960) has suggested that to call an experience ineffable is just to ascribe value to the experience; it is an honorific title. Ninian Smart (1958: 69) also regards the term as a sort of intensifier that is expressive rather than descriptive. Danto suggests that absolute ineffability might be understood by reference to the space between language and the world which Wittgenstein attempts to display in the final pages of the *Tractatus*. Stace says only that the ineffability of the mystical experience differs from ordinary kinds of ineffability. But these suggestions are not very helpful.

Since something can be ineffable only with respect to a particular symbol system, the ineffability of an experience must result from its logical or grammatical component. If it is to be an identifying characteristic of mystical experiences that they are ineffable, then the rules that govern the use of the concepts that inform those experiences must be such as to preclude the experience being captured in words. The answer to Henle's query about how an experience could be said to be ineffable with respect to all possible symbolic systems without assuming a knowledge of all such systems is that the experience is constituted, in part, by an implicit rule or operator prescribing that for any symbolic system the experience is ineffable with respect to it. The component of the experience which insures ineffability is a grammatical rule; it is prescriptive rather than descriptive. It is a criterion for the identification of an experience as mystical.

In many religious traditions, grammatical rules embedded in doctrine and ritual preclude the attribution of any name, label, interpretation, or description to a particular experience or religious object. The rules that govern these terms render them systematically anomalous, enabling them to function as placeholders that repel any determinate description or label. A particularly striking example can be found in the opening sentence of the *Tao te Ching*, in which it is said that the *tao* that can be put into words is not the *Tao*. This sentence is not descriptive but prescriptive. It is a rule that governs the use of the term *Tao*. The term then acts as a formal operator, or placeholder, systematically excluding any differentiating description or predicates that might be proposed. The term functions in this way regardless of its meaning or connotations. *Tao* means "path" or "way," but the term *god*, with its connotations of personal agency, serves as a placeholder in the work of Dionysius the Areopagite and the tradition of the *via negativa*. The meaning and connotations of these terms are very important for the traditions out of which they come; they shape the ways people understand themselves and their experience. But the placeholder function is common to these terms, despite the substantial variation in their meanings. The tetragrammaton YHWH, with associated prohibitions against images and the utterance of the holy name, may serve the same function in the context of the early religion of Israel and in later traditions of Jewish mysticism.

Meister Eckhart wrote of the Godhead: "If I have spoken of it, I have not spoken, for it is ineffable" (Clark, 1957: 83). A famous passage in the Upanishads says there is no better description of Brahman than *neti-neti* (not-this, not-this).[2] Nagarjuna says of *śunyātā* (emptiness or voidness) that it is empty even of itself.[3] In each of these cases, the role of place-holder preempts any ordinary connotations a term might have and gives it a special logical function. It serves to maintain, and perhaps even to create, a sense of mystery. The effect is as if Schachter had designed his experiment in such a way as to discredit any possible labels the subjects might employ to explain their arousal, rather than providing labels for them to adopt. All determinate predicates are precluded. Thus the term is prescriptive and evocative rather than descriptive.

Katz recognizes the possibility that such predicates as *ineffable* might function in this way, but he views the consequences for the researcher as entirely adverse and regards this possibility as sufficient evidence to discredit those predicates and to warrant our disregard for them.

> *A fortiori* it would appear that to take the mystic's claim seriously, i.e. that his proposition "x is PI" ["x is paradoxical and ineffable"] is a true description, turns out to have the damaging implication that one cannot make any reasonable or even intelligible claim for any mystical proposition. The proposition "x is PI" has the curious logical result that a serious interpretation of the proposition neither makes the experience x intelligible nor informs us in any way about x, but rather tends to cancel x out of our language—which, of course, is what most mystics claim they want. (Katz, 1978: 56)

He concludes that this is no foundation on which to build an analysis of mysticism. But perhaps it is a beginning. The opening sentence of the *Tao te Ching* does serve to cancel the term *Tao* out of the language, at the very moment of introducing it. It strips it of all possible characterization. The result, however, is quite unlike it would have been had that sentence been omitted entirely. It is not actually dropped from the language; rather it stands there as a placeholder, repelling all attributions. That initial sentence plays a very important role. It formulates the rule by which the term *tao* will be governed in this context.[4]

Some philosophers have argued that to say "God is ineffable" is self-contradictory, because one is simultaneously denying that anything can be predicated of God and predicating something of him, namely, ineffability. We can now see, however, that this is no ordinary predicate. It is an operator designed to achieve the result it is supposed to describe. It is prescriptive and evocative rather than descriptive or analytical. Words are required in order to formulate the rules that guarantee ineffability. The examples cited above should be regarded not as regrettably imprecise descriptions of some state that defies description but rather as precise formulae that rule out in advance the appropriateness or adequacy of any description that might be proposed. William Alston (1956: 319) suggests that those who say that God is ineffable are not actually saying anything about God but expressing their determination not to count as a predicate anything that is said of God. He is correct to note that such a determination is implied by the use of the predicate, but the matter is a logical one rather than a psychological one. The meaning of the term ought to be attributed, not to the determination of individuals, but to the grammatical rules that govern the proper use of *ineffable* in such contexts.

The term *God*, in conjunction with prohibitions against idolatry, may function in monotheistic contexts in a manner similar to that of *Tao*. If it is taken to be a proper name that is used to refer to one being among others, or as a noun that refers to a particular kind of being or an aspect of the cosmos, it no longer serves its function as a placeholder. Placeholders do not represent. Their function is served precisely by the rules that deny them any representational role. Their opacity maintains a sense of ineffability. To the extent that such words are not completely opaque—that *tao* connotes "way" or "path," and that *god* connotes personal agency—they allow determinate attributions, and predicates can be ascribed to the religious object. They then lose some of their anomalous or transcendent status, while gaining plausibility by becoming more fully integrated into the interpretative or theoretical schemes of which they are a part. God becomes an entity in a metaphysical system, and claims about his existence and nature are supported by that system. When the religious object becomes too domesticated in this manner and threatens to lose its anomalous or transcendent status, an Amos, a Luther, or a Kierkegaard arises to proclaim that God's ways are not our ways and that God is "wholly other."

In contexts other than the mystical, the religious object is often designated by terms or phrases that function as place-holders, or as operators that preclude all determinate predicates. Schleiermacher's use of the term *whence* to designate that toward which the feeling of absolute dependence is directed is a case in point. Any determinate specification of the source upon which we are dependent is precluded. Anselm's famous formula *aliquid quo nihil maius cogitari possit* (something than which nothing greater can be conceived) is carefully constructed so that no matter what is conceived, that is not God. Karl Barth's (1960: 73–89) idiosyncratic construal of Anselm's phrase as a proper name is designed in part to expunge from it even the ordinary meanings we associate with the words that constitute the phrase. David Burrell has recently argued that Thomas Aquinas has no doctrine of God and that he refuses to provide one. According to Burrell's reading, *esse* functions as a placeholder, and the ascription to God of such predicates as *simple, good, limitless, unchangeable,* and *one* serve as systematic reminders that nothing can be said of him.

> In fact, all we can do is acknowledge that the statements which purport to describe God truly will fail to do so if the God they would describe is the true one. For the true God cannot be circumscribed by any set of statements. (Burrell, 1979: 68)

Any statement that purports to describe God must necessarily fail. The transcendental predicates and what has been mis-construed as Thomas's doctrine of analogy function to insure that the religious object eludes all concepts and predicates. Burrell argues that Thomas's refusal to permit any description or conception of God was motivated in part by considerations arising from the mystical strain in his spiritual life.[5]

The common feature of each of these examples is the employment of a term or phrase to identify God as a religious object in such a way as systematically to preclude all determinate attributions and thus to guarantee, in advance, ineffability. These terms, and the rules that govern their use, play an active role in establishing the conditions under which one can think of God or identify a moment of one's experience as religious. They direct one's attention to a point that is systematically emptied of all content. Schleiermacher's instructions for the identification of the religious moment in consciousness function in a similar way.

> Your thought can only embrace what is sundered. Wherefore as soon as you have made any given definite activity of your soul an object of communication or of contemplation, you have already begun to separate. It is impossible, therefore, to adduce any definite example, for, as soon as anything is an example, what I wish to indicate is already past. (Schleiermacher, 1958: 41–42)

For the identification of a moment of one's experience, these instructions are analogous to Anselm's formula and Thomas's employment of *esse* and the divine attributes. They guarantee ineffability.

Many of the terms employed in the literature of the history of religions to capture a universal feature of religious experience or practice also appear to function as placeholders. Though purportedly descriptive, they are lifted out of their original contexts and employed in ways that empty them of their original meanings and suggest that they are indefinable. Otto's *numinous* is the most obvious example, but such terms as *mana, tabu, baraka,* and *wakanda,* each of which has been used to designate the essence of religious belief or practice, function in

similar ways.[6] Each has a meaning in the linguistic context
from which it is derived, but each is employed as a technical
term for the characterization of religion in a treatise written in
a modern European language. Each is left untranslated, as an
exotic word that contributes to a sense of mystery. Though
numen fits Otto's purposes, he is not primarily interested in its
meaning within the context of Roman religion. He employs it
as a surd, heightening its mystery by the rules he formulates
for its use. Owing in part to Otto's influence, the words *holy*
and *sacred* have come to function in the same way.

Otto, like Schleiermacher in *On Religion*, is trying to communicate what he takes to be the essence of religion by evoking it in the reader. He assumes it can be known only by
acquaintance. The term *numinous* is not a descriptive one but a
placeholder meant to convey a sense of the mystery that characterizes religious experience. The term is not as much about
religious experience as it is a surrogate for that experience. By
precluding all determinate labels, and thus all demystification,
Otto gives the term a role that resembles that given to *Tao* in
the opening sentence of the *Tao te Ching*. The latter, of course,
in its context of tradition and ritual, has more force than the
former, but both serve as placeholders. Their function is
evocative rather than descriptive.

Such terms as *numinous*, *holy*, and *sacred* are sometimes
employed as if they were descriptive. Reference is made to various manifestations of the sacred, and the term is treated as if
it were a theoretical concept. The resultant "theories" of religion are, like the concept of the numinous, designed to evoke
that which they are supposed to describe or explain. We have
seen, however, that direct acquaintance is neither necessary
nor sufficient for understanding religious experience. Such
experience includes a cognitive component that can be analyzed
and rendered intelligible even in the absence of direct acquaintance with the experience. Fear of reductionism leads some
historians and phenomenologists of religion to believe that the

sense of mystery that characterizes the experience must itself be reproduced in the description of that experience.[7] For that reason, many purportedly theoretical terms employed for the characterization of religion are actually surrogates for religious language. They are intended to evoke rather than to describe or analyze.

Another illustration of the refusal, in advance, to admit the adequacy of any determinate characterization of a religious experience can be found in the only public lecture that Wittgenstein delivered. In a lecture on ethics he tried to elucidate the notion of absolute value by reference to three experiences: wonder at the fact of the world's existence, the sense of being absolutely safe, and the feeling of guilt. None of these experiences, he says, can be represented sensibly in words. The verbal expressions we give of them are strictly nonsense. Moreover, he rejects the suggestion that a correct analysis of religious and ethical concepts could ever enable us to discover what we mean when we say that an experience has absolute value.

> Now when this is urged against me I at once see clearly, as it were in a flash of light, not only that no description that I can think of would do to describe what I mean by absolute value, but that I would reject every significant description that anybody could possibly suggest, *ab initio*, on the ground of its significance. That is to say: I see now that these nonsensical experiences were not nonsensical because I had not yet found the correct expressions, but that their nonsensicality was their very essence. (Wittgenstein, 1965: 11)

The essence of such experiences is constituted by the fact that significant descriptions of them are precluded. The empty placeholder enters into the logic of the experience. Any description with a significant content is, by that very fact, judged to be inadequate. It is a misrepresentation of the experience.

Could a mysterious and ineffable experience be created by manipulating conditions in such a way that a subject would have no determinate label for what was happening to him, or so the object of his attention would be emptied of its ordinary meanings until it served as a placeholder? An experiment could be designed along Schachterian lines which would systematically discredit any label the subject considered. The preparatory regimens and disciplines developed in the various religious traditions for the pursuit, enhancement, and interpretation of mystical experience include manipulations of this sort. Meditation on a mantra, an icon, a doctrine, a name, or a still point, until the object of meditation loses all its ordinary connotations and serves only to empty the mind by excluding all distinctions, is an exercise that is common to many mystical traditions. Typically, the focal object of the meditation is not important in itself but is employed as a tool for excluding all extraneous thought, especially the ordinary inferences we make and explanations we adopt about ourselves and our world. The object of such meditation, whatever it might be, fulfills the function of an empty placeholder. Though its content may be significant for the specific religious tradition in which it is employed, that content is irrelevant for the sense of mystery that James regards as one of the two distinguishing characteristics of the mystical experience.

The description of mystical experiences as paradoxical can be analyzed exactly as we have analyzed the concept of ineffability. Stace (1960: 212) calls paradoxicality one of the universal characteristics of all mysticism. He criticizes both apologists and skeptics who try to explain away the paradox. Stace contends that mystical paradoxes are flat logical contradictions, and the difficulty of finding language adequate to the mystical experience is a logical one rather than a case of the incommunicability of a feeling or sensation. He says that the experience itself is paradoxical.

> The paradox which he [the mystic] has uttered has correctly described his experience. The language is only paradoxical because the experience is paradoxical. Thus the language correctly mirrors the experience. (Stace, 1960: 305)

Stace is correct to see that the matter is a logical one. But his claim to have distinguished a core experience from the interpretations that can be placed on it detracts from his insight into the grammar of the experience. He often claims that the experience is extralogical; he writes that "Laws of logic do not apply to mystical experience" (Stace, 1960: 304). If the experience were extralogical, what would it mean to characterize it as paradoxical? Paradox, like contradiction, is a predicate applied to sentences or propositions. By definition, a paradox entails a logical or grammatical structure. Such a term could properly be applied to the mystic's experience only if that experience were constituted by certain thoughts, beliefs, and attitudes.

Paradox is essential to the mystical experience. Stace's insight is correct, but he reifies the concept of paradox and treats it as a quality inherent in the experience rather than as a feature of the rules governing the identification of an experience as mystical. The subject of the experience perceives ineffability or paradox as a quality of the object of the experience. Peirce (1934: 5.398) observes that the indeterminate character of our thought often leads us to claim that the object of that thought is essentially mysterious. The mystery, however, lies neither in the object nor in some moment of experience which transcends logic and language. James was correct to single out ineffability as a key characteristic of the mystical state, but he was wrong to construe it as a simple property of a feeling or a sensation that could not be put into words. Ineffability is a logical matter. Nagarjuna's tetralemma, the *via negativa*, the speculations of Eckhart or the Kabbalah, or the rules that govern the use of such terms as *Tao, Brahman, śunyātā, esse,* or *God* can all produce and enhance a sense of mystery or ineffability. The terms *ineffability* and *paradox* themselves shape the expectations of seekers. They enter into the criteria by which a person might identify his experience as mystical, and thus they determine the conditions under which a mystical experience can occur. Like the opening line of the *Tao te Ching*, they insure that no experience of which a determinate description can be given will count as a mystical experience. With such a rule in force, ineffability is guaranteed.

Noetic Quality

The second of James's two primary marks of the mystical experience is its noetic quality. The mystic regards his experience as a source of knowledge and insight. James also refers to a "consciousness of illumination" as an essential mark of mystical states. Stace reports that all mystical experiences include a sense of objectivity or reality. Katz judges such characterizations as "a sense of objectivity or reality" to be hopelessly vague. He says that every mystic makes claims to objectivity despite the fact that their views of reality contradict one another, and therefore it is not reasonable to assume that they experience the same reality (Katz, 1978: 50). Once again, Katz thinks such considerations justify and even require that the analyst disregard the mystic's claim. To disregard it, however, is to miss an important component of the experience. The proper question is not whether the "realities" posited by different mystics can be compared; it is whether their experiences can be compared, including the sense of objectivity which is a part of those experiences. Attention ought to be directed to the role the claim of noesis plays in shaping those experiences.

Mystics judge their experiences to be revelatory, productive of insight into the true nature of reality, and not artifacts or projections of their own subjective mental states. This is an important feature of the experience. In most traditions a novice engages in elaborate preparations. Not only is he fully steeped in the attitudes and beliefs of his tradition but he subjects himself to manipulations that he knows will have a considerable effect on his physiological and mental state. For example, he might engage in prolonged fasting, chanting, orison, dancing, sensory deprivation, or various forms of yogic meditation. The seeker is not unaware that these exercises might contribute powerfully to the resultant experience, but it is a *conditio sine qua non* of that experience that he view these manipulations as catalysts, not as sufficient causes. The experience must be perceived by the subject as providing access to some reality beyond himself and his conscious preparations. He must attribute the experience not to the fasting, the exercises, or the chanting alone, but to some power that transcends these natural causes.

The mystic's identification of his experience requires a commitment to a certain kind of explanation or, what comes to the same thing, the exclusion of a particular kind of explanation. He must identify his experience under a certain description, and that description must preclude naturalistic explanation. The assumption that the experience cannot be exhaustively accounted for in naturalistic terms is included in the criteria for identifying an experience as mystical. Not surprisingly, then, it turns out that mystical experiences elude natural explanations.

This explanatory commitment can be illustrated by the logic of the term *miracle*. I could not identify an event as a miracle and then proceed to explain it in naturalistic terms. The question of whether or not a miracle can be explained is not an empirical one. That it cannot be explained follows from the grammar of the concept. Of course, any particular event that has been labeled a miracle might turn out on closer examination to be susceptible of naturalistic explanation, but then it is no longer to be regarded as a miracle. The term does not have a simple descriptive use but is employed to identify events under a certain explanation. A miracle, by definition an exception, presupposes rules according to which such exceptions can be identified. The capacity to identify a miracle requires a distinction between natural and supernatural explanation and a judgment that the former is inadequate to account fully for the latter.

Astor and Bingham may travel together to Lourdes and witness a person's astonishing transformation from crippling disease to radiant health. Astor may experience that transformation as a miracle, while Bingham, equally astonished, views it as an event that is anomalous with respect to the present state of medical knowledge but will doubtless one day be explained. Only Astor has had an experience of a miracle. Their different experiences are constituted, in part, by different beliefs about the explanation of the event. It is their beliefs *about* the explanation which differ because, by hypothesis, neither *has* an explanation. Their different beliefs about the appropriate kind of explanation lead them to identify the event differently. Any event one could imagine, even a deep voice from heaven speaking biblical Hebrew, could only be experienced as a miracle by a person who judged that it eluded and even precluded all naturalistic explanation. It would not be experienced as such by one who viewed it as anomalous with respect to our present knowledge but amenable to explanation in terms of natural causes—as, for instance, we view cancer. This explanatory commitment enters into the identification of a miracle. "Nothing is esteemed a miracle if it ever happen in the common course of nature" (Hume, 1975: 115).

Mystical experience is more complex, but it can be illumined by the logic of miracle. The phrase *mystical experience* can be construed as either (1) a simple description of certain mental and/or physiological states, independent of any judgment about their explanation, or (2) not a simple description but, like *miracle*, a phrase that includes among the rules for its proper application an explanatory commitment—namely, the judgment that whatever physiological or mental states are being identified as mystical could not be accounted for in naturalistic terms.

The literature on mysticism includes examples of both alternatives, but most recent treatments construe the experience as one that can be described without any explanatory commitment. Stace (1960: 29) even adopts at the outset of his study a "Principle of Causal Indifference": If the phenomenological characteristics ascertained from the descriptions given by two mystics exactly resemble one another, then it cannot be said that the experiences are different, or that one is "genuine" and the other is not, merely because they arise from dissimilar conditions. But the analogy with miracle would suggest that a judgment about these conditions is itself a part of the experience. As with Astor and Bingham at Lourdes, a judgment that what has taken place eludes naturalistic explanation is required for the experience to be identified as, and thus to be, a mystical one. To adopt Stace's principle would be to preclude consideration of such a judgment and thus to insure that one would not be studying a mystical experience. That would be like trying to study the perceptions of Astor and Bingham without reference to their judgments about how the event ought properly to be explained.[8]

I have translated James's phenomenological characterization of the mystical experience as having a noetic quality or a sense of objectivity into a description of a judgment made by the person who has the experience. The phrases James employs reify that judgment and suggest an added quality that can be called a sense of reality but cannot be analyzed further. In fact, nothing is added. But the person who undergoes the experience judges it to be revelatory, rather than an artifact of his own subjective states. Compare the following: you are skiing down an icy slope; you are having the experience of skiing down an icy slope; you are dreaming that you are skiing down an icy slope; your brain is being stimulated by a neurosurgeon so as to simulate the experience of skiing down an icy slope. The picture might be the same in each case, but your judgment about the connection of that picture with the rest of your experience differs, and so your experience differs. The difference of felt quality between the several states is accounted for by a difference of judgment.

It might be argued that no judgment about the explanation of the experience is required in order to make it a mystical experience. An interpretation is sufficient. That is to say, it is sufficient for the subject to regard the experience from a perspective other than that of ordinary natural explanation but without rejecting such explanations. He might view the experience in religious terms. This would be one way among others of interpreting his experience. It need not be seen as a judgment about the validity of natural explanations. It need not require an explanatory commitment at all.

This same issue has been raised with regard to the identification of a miracle, and it might be helpful to return briefly to that example. Hume (1975: 115n) defines a miracle as "a transgression of a law of nature by a particular volition of the Deity, or by the interposition of some invisible agent." Attention to the phrase "violation of the laws of nature" has led to much irrelevant speculation about whether the laws of nature are statistical rather than mechanical, thus allowing for occasional anomalies, and about whether an event must be unique and the violation of natural law nonrepeatable in order for it to be described as miraculous (Smart, 1964: 26–56; Swinburne, 1970: 23–32). The distinction between mechanical and statistical laws is beside the point, however. A miracle must be judged anomalous with respect to natural explanations. The statistically deviant molecule or photon does not leave the realm of the natural, and its path is not to be regarded as miraculous. Neither is uniqueness crucial. Eyewitness testimonies to two resurrections from the dead would not lead to the establishment of a new natural law, though they might inspire a more active search for explanations than a single report would warrant. Kant (1960: 81) describes miracles "as events in the world the operating laws of whose causes are, and must remain, absolutely unknown to us." The requirement that they must remain absolutely unknown distinguishes them from the many events for which we as yet have no explanation. Miracles are events that are deemed to elude our ordinary explanatory schemes.

Schleiermacher disagrees. He is among those who have argued that a miracle need not be a violation of or inconsistent with natural laws or explanations. It is enough that an event be interpreted in religious terms, and perhaps that it elicit wonder. The best statement of this position is to be found in his second speech in *On Religion*.

> What is a miracle? What we shall call miracle is everywhere else called sign, indication, Our name, which means a wonder, refers purely to the mental condition of the observer. It is only in so far appropriate that a sign, especially when it is nothing besides, must be fitted to call attention to itself and to the power in it that gives significance. Every finite thing, however, is a sign of the Infinite, and so these various expressions declare the immediate relation of a phenomenon to the Infinite and the Whole. But does that involve that every event should not have quite as immediate a relation to the finite and to nature? Miracle is simply the religious name for event. Every event, even the most natural and usual, becomes a miracle, as soon as the religious view of it can be the dominant. To me all is miracle. In your sense the inexpressible and strange is miracle, in mine it is no miracle. The more religious you are, the more you see miracle everywhere. (Schleiermacher, 1958: 88)

Whereas I have argued that *miracle* is a term that cannot be employed for descriptive purposes alone but is properly used to identify an event under a certain causal explanation, Schleiermacher suggests that it refers to an event under a

certain interpretation, and that it remains neutral with respect
to causal accounts or explanations. Tillich (1951: 130) appears
to agree with Schleiermacher when he describes a miracle as
"an event which is astonishing, unusual, shaking, without con-
tradicting the rational structure of reality." Though it is not
altogether clear what is meant by "the rational structure of
reality," he seems to hold that an event need not elude
naturalistic explanation in order to qualify as a miracle.[9]

Schleiermacher's position makes it impossible to distinguish
the miraculous from the marvellous, or finally, from any other
event. "Miracle is simply the religious name for event. . . . To
me all is miracle." He recognizes and accepts the implications
of his argument when he says that the term "refers purely to
the mental condition of the observer." It is an interpretation
under which the observer views an event, but it entails no
judgment as to the proper explanation of that event. We do
sometimes apply the term *miracle* to childbirth, marvellous feats
of skill, or astonishing and welcome coincidences, where we
would not deny that a sufficient explanation could be given in
naturalistic terms. But these uses of the term are surely
derivative.

A scenario constructed by R. F. Holland (1967) nicely
illustrates the issue. Holland claims that contingencies and
coincidences viewed religiously may be miracles.[10] He imagines
a case in which a distraught mother watches a train come
miraculously to a halt only a few feet from where her child has
been caught on the tracks with his toy car. She regards the
incident as a miracle and continues to do so even after she
learns that the stopping of the train was due to natural causes
entirely unrelated to either the child's plight or her concern. A
sudden stroke caused the engineer to faint, and the brakes
were applied automatically.

The mother's continued identification of the event as a
miracle can be understood in any of three ways. (1) She
believes that the natural explanations are insufficient to account
for exactly why the train stopped where it did rather than a

few feet farther down the track and attributes that apparent
coincidence to divine governance. (2) She employs the term
miracle honorifically to refer to the marvelous coincidence that
saved her son, much as we might say that the halting of the
train was providential. (3) The constellation of emotions of
fear, relief, and gratitude elicited in her by the series of events
is so powerful as to remain even after the implicit belief
in divine action which initially informed the gratitude has
been discarded. In the first instance, she would be invoking
some power beyond the natural to explain the event; in
the second, her use of the term *miracle* would be derivative and
metaphorical; and in the third, her emotion would assume
belief in some supernatural power, though she no longer
consciously defends such a belief. The difference between
these three alternatives has implications for the interpretation
of the explanatory commitment that is assumed by a subject's
identification of his experience as mystical.

Despite his denial that any explanatory commitment is entailed, we saw that Schleiermacher's description of the religious consciousness implicitly ascribes to the subject a belief in
a power that transcends the nexus of natural causes. The
object of the feeling of absolute dependence is a "whence," or
source that is not a part of this world but on which the world
and everything in it depends. All finite existence is grounded in
the infinite, and everything is ultimately to be attributed to the
divine causality (Schleiermacher, 1928: 4.4, 46.2; 1950: 39;
Harvey, 1962). Schleiermacher is a proponent of what James
(1902: 520–523) refers to as universalistic, as opposed to
piecemeal, supernaturalism. The fabric of natural causes is not
rent, but the entire natural order depends on divine causality.
His statement that anything is a miracle as soon as the religious
view of it is dominant can now be seen to include reference to
a causal explanation. The "religious view" is a perception of the
world as absolutely dependent upon a source that is not itself
part of that world. The causal judgment is then disguised by its
inclusion in an allegedly phenomenological description of the

pious consciousness or the feeling of absolute dependence. Both the perception of an event as miraculous and the distinctive moment in the religious consciousness assume this implicit judgment.

The third way of construing the mother's continued identification of the preservation of her son's life as a miracle may be relevant to Schleiermacher's account. He regards the distinctive moment of religious consciousness as a moment that is prior to thought and independent of belief, though we have seen that reference to concepts and to an implicit belief about causes is incorporated into his criteria for specifying the sense of the infinite or the feeling of absolute dependence. Schleiermacher might erroneously regard these feelings and emotions as primitive and independent of speculative thought because he is confusing psychological and logical priority. These emotions are now firmly entrenched in the lives of persons and communities even when explicit assent is no longer given to the beliefs they presuppose. Religious emotions and practices that were shaped in a culture in which belief in divine governance was assumed and supported may be preserved and transmitted even when many would no longer subscribe to those beliefs or to the arguments that once legitimated them. The concepts and beliefs might then appear to derive from the emotions and to give them expression, even though an adequate analysis of the emotions would require reference to the concepts and beliefs. In such a situation, the emotions would be psychologically prior to but logically dependent upon the concepts and beliefs. The relevance of this possibility for the identification and explanation of religious experience will be explored more fully in chapter six.

The subject's identification of his experience as mystical entails the belief that it cannot be exhaustively explained in naturalistic terms, just as the identification of an event as a miracle implies that it is anomalous with respect to the natural order. Two questions immediately arise: (1) What is meant by the phrase "in naturalistic terms"? that is, What boundaries of the natural are presupposed? and (2) What is it in the mystic's experience that is to be explained? that is, What is it that cannot be accounted for in naturalistic terms? The form of the answers to the two questions is the same. In each case the point is a logical one, having to do with the conditions under which an experience might be identified as mystical, and is independent of the content of particular situations.

The term *miracle* implies that any event to which it refers exceeds explanation in terms of natural causes, and this holds irrespective of where the boundaries of the natural are drawn. As Hume saw, a miracle is, by definition, an anomaly. This holds regardless of what nomos it is anomalous with respect to. The concept of miracle is parasitic upon conceptions of the natural order. What people call a miracle may vary according to their familiarity with and explanations of the objects and events in the world around them, but it will always be something they judge to be anomalous with respect to the natural order. If comets and eclipses are judged to be exceptions to that order, they may be perceived as miracles and attributed to divine activity. When it is recognized that their motions can be subsumed under natural laws, they will no longer be considered miraculous. Considered in themselves, events identified as miracles are often trivial. Their significance lies in their anomalous status. Geertz (1973: 101) describes a toadstool in the Javanese village in which he was doing fieldwork which grew larger and more rapidly than the astonished inhabitants of the village thought that toadstools were wont to do. They were anxious and demanded a special explanation. Our expectations and norms for the growth of flora and fauna are probably less restrictive than those of Geertz's villagers, so the precocious fungus would not elicit in us the same reaction. The conditions under which people are astonished depend on their beliefs and expectations about what is normal. If the identification of an experience as mystical entails the judgment that it cannot be exhaustively accounted for in naturalistic terms, this entailment will be invariant across different conceptions of the natural. What is required is that something be judged anomalous with respect to the natural order, regardless of what substantive conception of the natural order is assumed.

Were precognition or extrasensory perception to be reliably established under stringent laboratory conditions, this would not provide evidence for the existence of forces outside the natural realm. It would merely require a revision of our understanding of the forces that exist in nature. Psychologists would be obliged to take account of the new evidence and to modify their theories accordingly, just as physicists took account of electromagnetic phenomena when they were first discovered and revised their conceptions of physical interaction. Such a change would not be a small matter. The integration of the theory of electromagnetic interactions and classical Newtonian physics is not yet complete. But no newly discovered phenomenon could provide evidence for belief in a supernatural order. Nor could a mystical experience, described without reference to its constituent beliefs, be evidence for the inadequacy of naturalistic explanation. If, however, the experience is in part constituted by the belief that natural explanations are insufficient to account for the event, then the identification of the experience as mystical entails, for the one who undergoes it, the inadequacy of such explanations.

If *miracle* is used of events that are deemed to be anomalous with respect to the natural order, what is it in the experience of the mystic that is judged to elude psychological explanation? It must be some physiological or mental state, but exactly what state it is may vary from one context to another. We constantly monitor our own states and behavior, as Stephen Bradley and Schachter's subjects did, making causal attributions and seeking explanations for what happens to us and for what we do. This ascription of causes determines, in part, the emotions we feel. People seek the best explanation for what is happening to them, and the concepts and beliefs employed in that explanation are often drawn from the immediate context.[11]

Preparation for mystical experience within a religious tradition typically includes two components: (1) a disciplined activity designed to produce a change from the physiological and mental equilibrium that constitutes normal consciousness, and (2) intensive study, usually under the tutelage of a guide, guru, or spiritual director, of the doctrines and beliefs of the tradition within which the mystic will interpret and understand what is happening to him. The altered state may be achieved by meditation on a mantra, koan, or icon, by fasting, engaging in yogic exercises, sensory deprivation, or by any of a variety of other means. The actual effect produced may vary from one situation to another. It might include decelerated or accelerated heart rate, a state of quiet pause or one of excitement, visions or the emptiness that results from extended meditation on a sound or a still point. These phenomena may all be functionally equivalent. Any of them might provide the occasion for the mystic's perception of what is happening to him as a breakthrough, an insight, or an experience of a reality that is fuller than that with which he has to do in normal states of consciousness. It is this perception, with its constituent beliefs, and not the specific state that occasions it, which is critical for the mystical experience. While further investigation may reveal some physiological characteristics that are common to the experiences of mystics, those do not enter into the sense of ineffability and the noetic quality that James regards as the distinguishing marks of the experience.

The two secondary marks by which James characterizes the mystical state, transience and passivity, are also related to the noetic quality of the experience. Passivity conveys the sense of being grasped and of being subject to some power beyond oneself. Both passivity and transience reflect the perception that the experience is not under the subject's voluntary control. It cannot be manipulated or guaranteed by the subject's decision or by causes that he might set in motion. He can prepare himself for it, but the experience is finally not subject to his control. The rules for the identification of an experience as mystical include the condition that he judge it to be something other than an artifact of his own thought and actions. Each of the distinguishing characteristics of mystical experiences is best construed, not as a simple unanalyzable quality of the experience, but as a conceptual constraint on what experiences may be identified as mystical. Ineffability and noetic quality, the two marks that James regards as jointly sufficient for the specification of a mystical experience, function to insure that any experience identified as mystical will be anomalous with respect to any determinate description and with respect to any natural explanation. Any experience whose object can be captured in a descriptive phrase or that can be explained in naturalistic terms is, *ipso facto*, not a mystical experience. These criteria are incorporated in the rules that govern the proper use of the phrase *mystical experience*. Far from being more primitive than words, concepts, and beliefs, or transcendent with respect to them, the experience cannot be specified without implicit reference to these criteria. Absolute ineffability can only be guaranteed by a logical placeholder that precludes determinate predication in any symbol system; and anomaly with respect to natural explanations can only be insured by an implicit rule to the effect that if an experience can be explained in such terms, it is not the experience reported by mystics.

Anomaly and Authority

Mystics describe their experiences as anomalous with respect to all symbolic systems and as anomalous with respect to all natural explanations. In our consideration of Peirce's account of the logic of inquiry, we saw that inquiry is elicited by doubt. Doubt arises when we are confronted with some phenomenon or event that is anomalous with respect to our current beliefs. Anomaly gives rise to inquiry, and the aim of inquiry is to fix belief. Schachter discovered that receptivity to and the need for new labels or interpretations occurred under conditions in which subjects were faced with anomalies or surprises. When no appropriate cognition was available, people sought new interpretations to make sense out of what was happening to them and out of their own actions. The role of anomaly and doubt concerning the adequacy of available explanations is crucial for the adoption and discard of religious beliefs.

The anomaly reported by the mystic, or by Astor in describing the miracle he witnessed, is different, however. It is not a provisional anomaly that can be removed by inquiry. The mystic claims that his experience is ineffable, not just with respect to his native tongue or his own capacity to articulate, but with respect to all possible linguistic systems. Astor claims that the event he witnessed is anomalous not only with respect to the present state of medical knowledge but with respect to all natural explanations. Further inquiry might possibly result in an explanation of an alleged mystical experience or of the event at Lourdes. Were that explanation to convince him, however, the mystic would claim either that it was not a genuine mystical experience or that the real experience had not been captured by the explanation. The healing that Astor once took to be a miracle would now be considered a case of mistaken identification.

The anomaly represented by the mystic's claim of absolute ineffability and the anomaly of a miracle are incorporated into the rules for the proper identification of a mystical experience or a miracle. Absolute ineffability can only be guaranteed by an implicit rule to the effect that no symbol system can capture the experience. One cannot identify an event as a miracle and allow that it can be exhaustively explained in natural terms. The identification of an anomaly is determined in part by the conceptual system with which one is operating and by the rules that govern the proper application of concepts like miracle and mystical experience.

Mary Douglas is one of a growing number of social scientists who have turned their attention to the cognitive components of cultural systems. She has been especially interested in the religious significance of cultural anomalies. In an illuminating analysis of the dietary laws of the Deuteronomic code, she demonstrates how each of the forbidden creatures is anomalous with respect to the classificatory structure for animals, birds, and fish which is assumed by that code (Douglas, 1966). She hypothesizes that these creatures were set apart and considered impure because they could not be incorporated adequately in that structure. In the experience of the Lele, an African people, the pangolin, or scaly anteater, is similarly anomalous. It cannot be classified as either an animal or a fish. Here the anomaly is also set apart, but it is worshipped as a sacred object. Douglas suggests that the concern to maintain boundaries and to protect the identity of a nation that had emerged out of a history of exile and conquest caused the Israelites to interpret anything that threatened to dissolve or obscure boundaries as dangerous. The essentially sustaining and peaceful relationships that the Lele enjoyed with their neighbors disposed them to interpret the crossing and eliding of boundaries in a positive fashion, not as a danger but as an unexpected opportunity (Douglas, 1975: 276–318). In both cases the anomalous instance is set apart and treated with respect. The interpretation or labeling of one as taboo and the other as an object of worship is a consequence of the experiences of the respective peoples and their assessments of their situations. The need for new labels and reassessment arises only in the presence of anomaly, however, and of the doubt such cases raise concerning the adequacy of a classificatory and explanatory scheme.

Douglas's work suggests that the sense of the sacred or mysterious is inextricably bound up with the anomalous. A mystery is something that defies classification or explanation. Mystery and awe result when no appropriate label or explanation is available to satisfy inquiry. Schachter manipulated the cognitive context of his experiments so that different labels or interpretations were salient. If the context were arranged so that every candidate for a determinate interpretation was discredited and no labels were available by which to make sense of the experience, the sense of anomaly would be sustained and heightened. The more the need for interpretation is aroused and frustrated, the greater the sense of unease and mystery which is created. As Douglas reports, such situations often lead to respectful behavior and feelings of awe toward the "objects" of these experiences. Whether they are classified as objects of worship or taboo, they are set apart from the world of profane objects and actions.

Both the identification of an anomaly and the attitude that is taken toward it—whether that attitude be worship, avoidance, or a sustained sense of mystery—depend on the conceptual system available to a person for understanding himself and his world. Schachter manipulated labels, and Douglas compared cosmologies in different cultures. Both demonstrated that the sense of anomaly and one's response to it depend on the cognitive context. Otto claims that the experience of the numinous is anomalous with respect to all description and explanation, but we saw that the rules he formulated for the identification of that experience guarantee its anomalous status. The criteria for the identification of an experience as mystical perform a similar function.

In his study of the varieties of religious experience, James turns to mysticism in order to examine the claims of religious persons that they see truth in a special manner (James, 1902: 378). Can the experiences of mystics yield knowledge? We have seen that the subjects of such experiences regard them as having a noetic quality, but can they provide evidence for religious belief? Katz (1978: 22) contends that neither mystical experience nor religious experience more generally described can provide reasons or evidence relevant to the truth or falsity of any religious belief. James is more careful; he recognizes the

need to differentiate between the case of the subject and that
of the observer or analyst. He summarizes his answer in three
parts:

> (1) Mystical states, when well developed, usually are, and
> have the right to be, absolutely authoritative over the
> individuals to whom they come.
> (2) No authority emanates from them which should make
> it a duty for those who stand outside of them to accept their
> revelations uncritically.
> (3) They break down the authority of the non-mystical or
> rationalistic consciousness, based upon the understanding
> and the sense alone. (James, 1902: 422–423)

The experience produces conviction in the subject and is
regarded by him as evidence for his religious beliefs, but it
carries no authority for the observer. At best it may offer a
hypothesis and establish a presumption for those who have
not undergone the experience, but it provides neither reasons
nor evidence to support the claims of mystics.

Mystical states are and have the right to be authoritative for
their subjects. One of these claims is descriptive, the other
normative. The description is accurate, but the claim that the
subjects are justified in regarding their experiences as evidence
for their religious beliefs is not. It is based on an inaccurate
theory about why the experience is authoritative for the subject. James assimilates the experience to that of sensation and
thus regards it as a direct acquaintance that provides evidence
analogous to that of sense perception. For this reason, he says,
the mystic's claims are invulnerable.

> Our own more "rational" beliefs are based on evidence exactly
> similar in nature to that which mystics quote for theirs. Our
> senses, namely, have assured us of certain states of fact; but
> mystical experiences are as direct perceptions of fact for
> those who have them as any sensations ever were for us.
> (James, 1902: 423–424)

These experiences are, he puns, "absolutely sensational in their epistemological quality."

This recognition of the authority of the experience for the subject is important. The experience has a noetic quality. But the explanation that James offers for this authority is based on his erroneous assimilation of the experience to that of sensation and feeling. James makes two errors here. Mystical experience is not a simple feeling that is independent of concepts and beliefs, and sense perception is not authoritative simply by virtue of direct acquaintance with an object.

In accord with his assumption that mystical states are similar to sensations, James attempts to arrange them alongside similar states as one might set the smell of a particular perfume between similar fragrances, or as Hume's missing shade of blue can be placed between two shades that are directly experienced. He treats the sense of profundity allegedly elicited by the sound of the word *Mesopotamia*, the experience of *déjà vu*, alcoholic intoxication, and mystical states as a spectrum. The problem is not that he associates mystical states with lower states of consciousness but that each of these states differs from the others with respect to how it is to be described. The specification of mystical states requires reference to sophisticated concepts and grammatical rules. The ineffability of the mystical experience does not arise from its kinship to sensations but from the logic of the terms by which the subject identifies it as a mystical experience.

The identification of an experience as mystical, as nirvana or devekuth or communion with God, assumes the belief that it is authoritative, revelatory, and that it provides support for the teachings of the tradition within which it is identified and interpreted. Buddhist meditational practices are designed to achieve certain states in order to exemplify Buddhist doctrines (Gimello, 1978). The aim of the meditation is not simply the achievement of the states but the discernment of the truth of Buddhist teachings. The authority of the experience for the subject derives from his identification of the experience under a certain description. That identification assumes the belief that the experience yields knowledge and that it is not an artifact of his preparatory manipulations or subjective states. It follows that the experience will be authoritative for him. But this authority is to be explained not by its similarity to sense perception but by the logic of the description under which he identifies the experience.

Ordinary perceptual experiences also assume beliefs. They presuppose beliefs about the causes of the experiences. One would not identify an experience as a perception in the face of evidence that the appropriate causal relation between the object perceived and the experience itself was lacking.[12] As in the case of mysticism, the identification of a perception assumes certain beliefs about how that experience is to be explained. The experience has no authority for one who does not share those beliefs. The authority of the experience is based not on direct acquaintance but on what is regarded as the best explanation of the experience.

This analysis of the authority of the experience for the subject demonstrates why it carries no obligation for one who has not undergone the experience. It is the subject's identifying description, his belief that the mystical state is one of insight, and his view of the proper explanation of the experience which are constitutive of the experience. The observer must cite the subject's description in order to identify the experience adequately, but he need not endorse that description nor the beliefs it assumes. The experiences of mystics do offer hypotheses, but they do not establish a presumption. They are testimonies not to some direct perception but to the beliefs that enter into the identification of the experience. These issues will occupy us in the following two chapters.

V.
EXPLICATION

The search for a definition that will capture the essence of religious experience is a futile one.[1] As can be seen from attempts to define *religion* or *mysticism*, the meaning of *religious experience* cannot be fixed by appeal to clear and universally shared intuitions. But an explication of the phrase, with the explicit recognition that it is our phrase and that it has a rather parochial location in modern Western culture, might be helpful. What are the criteria by which we discriminate religious experience from moral or aesthetic experience, or from cognate experiences of joy, guilt, or wonder? The meaning of *religious experience* might be elucidated in different ways in different contexts, depending on the inquiry in which one is engaged. Specification of the distinguishing marks of such an experience, or of the conditions under which one would identify an experience as religious, ought to be pragmatic, with attention to the requirements of the inquiry at hand. But we must also formulate common characteristics that conform to, even as they reshape, our intuitions about what is or is not to be called a religious experience. A definition that did not capture those intuitions might be useful as a term of art, but it would not be an explication of our ordinary references to religion and religious experience.

The nineteenth-century interest in specifying the marks of religious experience was aimed at providing a basis for the definition of religion. If the distinctive character of religious experience could be shown, then religious beliefs and practices could be redescribed as expressions of that experience as modified by different languages and cultures. Schleiermacher and Otto were engaged in such a project, and others followed them with attempts to describe the experience of the holy, the sacred, or ultimate value. The aim of distinguishing the religious from other sectors of human experience and thereby precluding reductionist accounts of religion was often shared by those engaged in the descriptive task of comparative religion. A consequence is that efforts to establish a discipline for the comparative study of religion were often conflated with protective strategies that are more properly regarded as theological than descriptive. In our use of the phrase *religious experience*, there is, however, an ambiguity with respect to the conditions under which it is to be applied and the commitments it presupposes. Even James, who differs from the tradition of Schleiermacher and Otto in his opinion that religious experience "probably contains nothing whatever of a psychologically specific nature," preserves the ambiguity.[2] In this chapter we shall consider what is presupposed by the identification of an experience as religious, and in the next we shall turn to the issue of reductionism and the legitimacy of offering explanations of religious experience.

The "Sense" of James's *Varieties*

Like Schleiermacher's *On Religion*, the course of Gifford Lectures that James gave in 1902 and published as *The Varieties of Religious Experience* is a classic and influential study of the subject. Like Schleiermacher, James is convinced that "feeling is the deeper source of religion, and that philosophic and theological formulas are secondary processes, like translations of a text into another tongue" (431). Unlike Schleiermacher, he does not think that religious feeling is psychologically specific. Religious love, for James, is the natural emotion of love directed to a religious object. Religious fear is ordinary fear associated with the notion of divine retribution (27). Schleiermacher claims to have identified a religious moment of consciousness which is never experienced in its pure form but accompanies all other moments and can be described only by a process of abstraction. James, by contrast, is chiefly interested in datable experiences reported in journals and other autobiographical records. He classifies, and tries to understand and assess, events that can be identified as religious experiences. Schleiermacher's work has exerted the greater influence of the two because of the roots of much contemporary theology and the history of religions in nineteenth-century German Protestant thought, but the issues to which James calls attention deserve to be addressed more directly than they have been in the contemporary discussion.

The *Varieties* has been accorded an honored place in the development of the psychology of religion, but its contribution to the philosophy of religion has not been sufficiently appreciated in recent years.[3] The wide selection of reports that James assembled tempts one to regard the volume as an annotated anthology, and the leisurely and anecdotal style sometimes diverts the reader from appreciating the care that has gone into the argument. Even when James is vague, as in his comment that religion is a consciousness of a "More" that is operative in the universe outside the self, he chooses his words carefully and intends them to capture the matter at hand with the appropriate degree of precision. He is an acute observer. We have had occasion to see that accurate observation does not guarantee adequate theory, but James's instinct for the heart of the matter is often correct even when we take issue with the theory he espouses.

Two claims that are central to James's study of religious experience will especially concern us. The first is that religious experience can and ought to be described and assessed without regard to how that experience is to be explained. The second is that religion is a faith-state that is characterized by a noetic quality and is closer to matters of feeling than to the intellect. The proposed restriction on method and the proposed description are in tension with one another. This is due to the fact that an elucidation of what James means by a faith-state or the noetic quality of the experience reveals that certain explanatory commitments are presupposed by the experience. To describe the experience is to cite those claims, and to assess it qua religious experience is to assess those claims.

Unlike Schleiermacher, James does not couple feeling with intuition, nor does he claim any special status for feeling as an exercise of the mind which precedes and informs both knowing and doing. Rather, as we have seen, he regards emotions as perceptions of changes in one's bodily state. But he views religious beliefs as secondary products that would never have emerged had it not been for the prior existence of religious feeling (431). Religious beliefs are overlaid upon a faith-state that is best characterized as affective. It is a state of trust or confidence that forms the ground of religious assurance. When a particular intellectual content is associated with this faith-state, it is invested with conviction and stamped upon belief. James takes this process of association to explain the loyalty of believers to their widely differing creeds (506). In his proposal for a science of religions that would replace theology and the traditional philosophy of religion, James assumes that the comparative, critical, and constructive reflection that would constitute that science presupposes immediate experience as its subject matter (433). The deeper sources of religion lie in feeling and not in the intellect.

James adduces three observations in support of his view that religion is a matter of feeling and not of intellect. The first is the felt quality of the experience. Religious experience seems to the subject to be immediate rather than the result of conscious thought and inference. The second is the authority of the experience. People are not often moved by intellectual arguments about religion. Religious beliefs and doctrines reflect deeper sources in passion and practice. If religious experience cannot provide sufficient authority for those beliefs, intellectual arguments are not likely to satisfy. Third, James contends that a survey of various religious traditions will discover a great variety of concepts and beliefs, but the feelings and the conduct that underlie that intellectual diversity remain constant. Consequently, in order to understand what is distinctive about religious experience and common to the various traditions, one ought to examine feeling and practice rather than beliefs and doctrines. The first two of these observations are familiar. We have seen that the fact that something seems to be immediate does not guarantee that it is independent of concepts and beliefs. We shall return below to the question of the authority of the experience for the subject. But the third claim that James makes is the most interesting. It is a common assumption, informing much recent interest in religious experience and mysticism.[4] Because of its influence, it calls for special scrutiny.

The claim is that a comparison of religious traditions would show religious feeling and practice to be invariant across cultures that display a great diversity of doctrine and belief.

> When we survey the whole field of religion, we find a great variety in the thoughts that have prevailed there; but the feelings on the one hand and the conduct on the other are almost always the same, for Stoic, Christian, and Buddhist saints are practically indistinguishable in their lives. The theories which Religion generates, being thus variable, are secondary; and if you wish to grasp her essence, you must look to the feelings and conduct as being the more constant elements. (504)

James observes that feelings and conduct are the most constant elements of religion; he concludes that they are the most fundamental. The conclusion does not follow from the evidence. But even the estimate James gives of the result of the survey is open to question. The outcome of such a study can easily be an artifact of the manner in which the comparisons are made.

Beliefs, emotions, actions, and practices must each be specified under a certain description. The chief requirement for assessing these phenomena across traditions is that the level of generality by which the beliefs, emotions, and practices are identified be carefully matched. This requirement is often ignored. A feeling or practice may be characterized in very general terms, while beliefs and doctrines are identified by reference to culturally specific concepts. Fear, wonder, hope, a sense of unity, worship, and sacrifice are said to be invariant across different traditions. Stories about Krishna, the eightfold path, the triune God, and Yahweh's election of Israel are tradition specific, whereas the sense of the infinite, the feeling of absolute dependence, and the ineffability and noetic quality of the mystical experience are allegedly universal. Were the comparison to be made between the feeling of devotion to Krishna, the love for Jesus, or the sense of dependence upon Yahweh, and the belief that there is something "More" beyond the visible world, the conviction that naturalistic explanations cannot exhaustively account for experience, or the belief that our present condition is defective and can be rectified only by establishing some kind of relation with ultimate reality, the beliefs would appear to be more universal than the feelings. The result of the comparison depends to a significant degree on the level of generality employed in the description of the feelings, actions, and beliefs. The practice of describing feelings in vague and general terms and beliefs in very specific ones rests on the assumption that feelings and emotions are independent of concepts and beliefs, whereas thoughts are confined to particular linguistic traditions that vary from culture to culture. Once we have seen that emotions also assume certain concepts and thoughts, there is no justification for this asymmetry in the level of generality of the descriptions under which thoughts and feelings are identified. The sense of the infinite or the consciousness of a "More" may appear to be inchoate feelings that have not yet become associated with particular thoughts, but we shall see that such a "sense" is best construed as a very general characterization of a belief.

Suppose we grant to James that the feeling that underlies religion is constant across cultures although the thoughts vary. What is the feeling he takes to be central to religious experience? Rather than being psychologically specific, it is what he calls a faith-state.[5] Faith is a sense, and it is closer to feeling than to intellect. As was the case with Schleiermacher, it is important for James's program to distinguish this sense from thoughts or beliefs. Here also we shall see that this distinction finally will not stand, and that what James refers to as a sense is actually a thought that carries conviction.

The theme of a sense of an unseen reality, or consciousness of a higher power, runs throughout James's characterization of religious experience in the *Varieties*. This sense is first described in the third chapter, after two preliminary chapters on method, and it emerges in the final pages of the book as the sense or consciousness of "More" which James takes to be the essence of religious experience. Chapter three is entitled "The Reality of the Unseen," and James begins it with the statement that the most general characterization of the religious life is as a belief in an unseen order and in the fact that our supreme good lies in adjusting ourselves to that order (53). But such a belief elicits no conviction unless it expresses or is associated with a sense or sentiment of reality.

> It is as if there were in the human consciousness a *sense of reality, a feeling of objective presence, a perception* of what we may call "something there," more deep and more general than any of the special and particular "senses" by which the current psychology supposes existent realities to be originally revealed. (58, original emphasis)

James goes on to speak of an "undifferentiated sense of reality" or "reality-feeling" that is present in nonreligious as well as religious contexts but is necessary for the latter. This feeling

of reality is more like a sensation than an intellectual operation (64). It is as convincing to those who have it as any direct
sensible experience (72). James describes the authority of this
feeling by stressing its similarity to sense experience. In matters of religion and metaphysics, reasons are convincing only
when these inarticulate feelings of reality have been impressed (74).

> We may now lay it down as certain that in the distinctively
> religious sphere of experience, many persons (how many we
> cannot tell) possess the objects of their belief, not in the form
> of mere conceptions which their intellect accepts as true, but
> rather in the form of quasi-sensible realities directly appre-
> hended. As his sense of the real presence of these objects
> fluctuates, so the believer alternates between warmth and
> coldness in his faith. (64)

This sense of the presence of an unseen reality becomes the
thread that runs through the *Varieties*. It is the common
denominator of the experiences that James considers. His ful-
lest description of the religious life is given in a discussion of
saintliness, which he regards as "the collective name for the
ripe fruits of religion in a character" (271). He describes the
"sense of Presence of a higher and friendly power" as the
fundamental feature in the spiritual life, along with a sense of
continuity with this power (273–274). The characterization
appears in the concluding chapter, in which James summarizes
the results of his investigations. The common nucleus to
which all religions bear testimony consists of two parts: a
sense that there is something wrong about us, and a sense that
we are saved by making contact with a higher power of which
we are conscious (507–508). At one end of the spectrum from
the simplest to the most complex which James traces in the
book, is the sense of the presence of an unseen reality, which
appears also in hallucinations and other nonreligious experiences. At the other end is the sense of a wrongness, the
sense of the possibility of salvation, and the consciousness of a
"More."

This theme of a sense or consciousness that is more like a sensation than an intellectual operation runs through James's analysis and surfaces whenever he tries to characterize the common element in religious experience. I have documented it at some length because I want to consider why he uses the term *sense* to describe this moment. What is this sense? When James first introduces the concept of a sense of unseen reality, he offers several examples. The first is that of a friend who reported feeling conscious of a presence in his room one evening after he had gone to bed and again the next night while he was working on some lectures. The friend described both experiences as "intensely more real than any ordinary perception" (60). The second comes from a woman who practiced automatic writing and who had the impression of a presence while she wrote; the impression was impossible to describe but convinced her that her writing was not due to her own subconscious self (62).

What can we learn from these examples? What is the sense of an unseen presence in the room? As James suggests, the experience is familiar enough. In a darkened room, or while attending to something else, I suddenly have the sense that someone is behind me. I feel a presence. In fact, however, this is not a sense or a feeling that is more like a sensation than an intellectual operation; it is a hunch, a thought, an opinion, and it has the epistemic status of a hypothesis. It may not feel like an opinion or hypothesis because of the suddenness and the element of conviction involved. But the sense that there is someone standing behind me is really the thought that someone is there. When I look over my shoulder or turn on the lights, I am engaging in inquiry in order to confirm or disconfirm the hypothesis. Similarly, the woman who has the sense of a presence when she engages in automatic writing is reporting her conviction that the writing does not originate with her but comes from another source. Such experiences have the feel of direct sensations, but they have the epistemic status of hypotheses. They are thoughts, hunches, or guesses. James describes such a moment as a sense or feeling because that captures the felt quality of the experience. It is not reached by conscious inference, and it seems to the subject to carry authority. The observation is well taken, but it ought not to be regarded as evidence that the feeling is a direct sensation in contrast to thought. Nor ought it to be taken as evidence that explanation does not enter into the identification of this sense or feeling. The term *sense* is ambiguous between (1) a phenomenological description, and (2) an identification by reference to the causes of the stimulation of our sensory apparatus. James appeals to the neutrality of (1) while incorporating (2) into the example he gives for identifying such a sense and into his assessment of its authority.

In the previous chapter we saw that James claims that mystical states are, and have the right to be, authoritative for those who have them because they are "as direct perceptions of fact for those who have them as any sensations ever were for us" (423–424). He concludes that the mystic is invulnerable to our criticisms and must be left undisturbed in his faith. For those who have not had the experience, however, the deliverances of mystic states and transmarginal regions of the mind have no such authority. Beliefs cannot be assessed on the basis of their origins.

> To come from thence is no infallible credential. What comes must be sifted and tested, and run the gauntlet of confrontation with experience, just like what comes from the outer world of sense. Its value must be ascertained by empirical methods, so long as we are not mystics ourselves. (426–427)

James's conclusion is marred by an erroneous theory of perception.[6] He is wrong to suggest that the gap is so wide between the first- and third-person cases. Subjects often revise their perceptual judgments. They are not simple givens. Reflection and new evidence may lead me to doubt that I really saw a bear, just as similar considerations may lead an observer to question my claim to have seen it. The fact that a sense of a presence feels like a sensation or perception does not mean that it is incorrigible. A perceptual judgment assumes a claim about the cause of the perception, and that claim is subject to revision. This calls into question a methodological distinction that James makes at the beginning of his inquiry and has important implications for his assessment of the authority of the sense of reality that is an ingredient of the faith-state.

At the outset of his study James draws a distinction that is crucial for his program and that has impressed those who regard him as an exemplary practitioner of the phenomenological method. He distinguishes between existential judgments, which are aimed at establishing the constitution, origin, and history of an object or event, and spiritual judgments, which are attempts to determine its importance, meaning, significance, or value. James views interest in causes and assessment of value as two entirely different orders of inquiry which proceed from diverse intellectual preoccupations (4). Scientific theories as well as religious phenomena derive from natural antecedents, he says, but that fact is of no help in determining their value. He will not confuse the accurate description of an experience, and a consideration of its fruits for life, with an inquiry into the causes of the experience. Those who do confuse the two are guilty of what he calls "medical materialism."

This methodological proposal plays an important role in the *Varieties*. For instance, James entertains a speculative hypothesis to explain conversion experiences as the result of an invasion from subconscious regions of the mind. But the truth or falsity of such a hypothesis is irrelevant, he thinks, to an evaluation of the experience of conversion. Its worth is independent of its origin.

> Our spiritual judgment, I said, our opinion of the significance and value of a human event or condition, must be decided on empirical grounds exclusively. If the *fruits for life* of the state

of conversion are good, we ought to idealize it and venerate it, even though it be a piece of natural psychology; if not, we ought to make short work with it, no matter what super-natural being may have infused it. (237, original emphasis)

When discussing the composite picture of the religious life which he calls saintliness, James first describes the varieties of religious belief and practice and then considers their value. Although the criteria he offers for the assessment of value may be difficult to apply, James is explicit about the fact that he considers such an assessment to be completely independent of any inquiry into the cause or origin of the experience. Attention to the cause of the experience is reductionist, and it misses the significance of the experience qua religious experience for the one who has it.

James regards this empirical approach, with its separation of questions of explanation and evaluation, as essential to his inquiry. He claims to have discovered a distinguished American antecedent in Jonathan Edwards.

In other words, not its origin, but *the way in which it works on the whole*, is Dr. Maudsley's final test of a belief. This is our own empiricist criterion, and this criterion the stoutest insisters on supernatural origin have also been forced to use in the end. . . . In the end it had to come to our empiricist criterion: By their fruits ye shall know them, not by their roots. Jonathan Edwards' *Treatise on Religious Affections* is an elaborate working out of this thesis. The *roots* of a man's virtue are inaccessible to us. No appearances whatever are infallible proofs of grace. Our practice is the only sure evidence, even to ourselves, that we are genuinely Christian. (19–20, original emphasis)

The empiricist criterion, as James understands it, requires that he set aside questions of cause or origin. Why should this be the case? It is by no means obvious that such questions should be excluded from empirical inquiry. Notice that James moves from Maudsley's assertion that a belief must be assessed without reference to its cause to the claim that religious experiences ought to be evaluated in the same way. It is possible that reference to the cause or origin is required for the assessment of some experiences but not for beliefs or for feelings, where the latter are exemplified by pangs and twitches. We shall consider this question in the following section.

In any case, James is wrong to cite the authority of Jonathan Edwards in support of his contention that the origin of religious experience is irrelevant to its assessment. Edwards's *Treatise Concerning Religious Affections* makes exactly the opposite point. The treatise opens with the statement that "true religion, in good part, consists in holy affections" (Edwards, 1959: 95). But what is the criterion for identifying these affections? They are those affections produced by the operation of the Holy Spirit. In the terms of the Lockean psychology that Edwards adopts, genuine religious affections consist in a new sense of the heart, or a new simple idea in the mind. This new sense is analogous to the five ordinary senses, but it cannot be reduced to any of them. Unlike James, Edwards does hold that religious experience is of a psychologically specific nature. The new sense can be directly known only by acquaintance. As the taste of honey differs from all other tastes and cannot be conveyed to someone who has not experienced it, the new sense of the heart differs from all other senses.

Though the new sense can be directly known only by acquaintance, Edwards considers various signs that might be used to discriminate true religious affections from their spurious counterparts. Among the signs that are insufficient for this purpose are emotional intensity, strong bodily effects, obsession with religious doctrine and biblical texts, and the appearance of a loving nature. He then proposes twelve signs that can be considered distinguishing marks of true religious affections. In describing the final sign he states that holy affections can be known only by their fruits. This twelfth sign, and the extended commentary on it, are surely what James had in mind in characterizing Edwards's treatise as he did. Viewed in the light of the full argument, however, a rather different picture emerges.

For Edwards, the chief distinguishing mark of the religious affections is their origin or cause. Holy affections are those that arise from divine influence and operations. This is clearly stated as the first sign:

> Affections that are truly spiritual and gracious, do arise from those influences and operations on the heart, which are *spiritual, supernatural, and divine.* (Edwards, 1959: 197, original emphasis)

Natural affections stem from natural causes, and though Satan is capable of producing counterfeits that imitate genuine religious affections, they lack the supernatural sense that is imparted by the action of the Holy Spirit. God infuses a new principle into the heart of the saint, so that his or her actions spring from a supernatural source.

> The Spirit of God is given to the true saints to dwell in them, as his proper lasting abode; and to influence their hearts, as a principle of new nature or as a divine supernatural spring of life and action. (Edwards, 1959: 200)

The Spirit is united to the faculty of the soul and becomes the source of a new mind.

Each of the signs that Edwards details functions as evidence for the supernatural cause of the religious experience.[7] Because the operation of the Spirit differs in kind from the operation of natural causes, the resultant effects are also qualitatively different from anything in nature. But neither the unique sensible quality, nor the intellectual content, nor the behavioral fruit is itself a criterion of genuine religious affections. These are all cited by Edwards as reliable indicators of the supernatural cause of the affections. James is mistaken in his belief that Edwards is interested only in the fruits and not in the roots of the experience. On the contrary, the fruits are of interest to him chiefly as evidence that warrants the attribution of the experience to a supernatural cause. Far from supporting the contention that inquiry into causes is irrelevant for the description and assessment of religious experience, Edwards's treatise proposes the supernatural origin of the new sense of the heart as the chief criterion for its identification and evaluation.

We have seen that James describes the common core of religious experience as a sense or consciousness of the presence of a reality or power that transcends the self and its ordinary world. This sense or consciousness is said to be more like a sensation than like an intellectual operation. It is formative of, rather than consequent upon, religious belief. But the examples James gives of a sense of reality or consciousness of a presence suggest that intellectual operations are involved, and that what he has called a sense is really a thought or belief. He proposes that questions of origin and questions of evaluation be radically separated in the study of religious experience. But his observation that that experience is characterized by a noetic quality similar to that of sense perception suggests that matters of assessment and explanation cannot be kept as clearly distinct as he would like. To that question we now turn.

Sensible Authority

The analogy James draws between mystical experience and sense perception is weakened by his assumption that perceptual experience is unmediated by concepts and beliefs, but his observation is accurate. The contrast he makes between the authority of the experience for the subject and its authority for an observer is important, and it does parallel the case of ordinary perception. There is a noetic quality to the experience, a sense of authority that distinguishes the attitude of the subject of the experience from that of an observer. An analysis of this characteristic of the experience will demonstrate the impossibility of following James in his proposal to exclude questions about the cause or origin of the experience.

An important distinction that will help to capture the noetic quality or the authority of perceptual experience is that drawn by Chisholm (1957: 43–53) between the epistemic and comparative uses of what he calls "appear words."[8] When I say that the table across the room appears to be round, I am using *appears* to report what I am inclined to believe on the basis of my present sensory experience. I believe that the table is round even though its image on my retina is elliptical. When I say that the tree in the distance appears to be as tall as the one under which I am standing, I am reporting my belief about the actual size of the tree. In both cases I have already made corrections for parallax and distance, and I am stating what appears to me to be the case. Such adjustments have become habitual in my learning to use the relevant words and to report what I see. Now I am making a judgment and a claim. When, however, I report that the table appears elliptical even though I believe it really to be round, or that the stick I have just dropped into the water appears to be bent, I am employing what Chisholm calls the comparative use of *appears*. I am stating that the table looks to me as it would look if it were an ellipse and were viewed under standard conditions, or the stick appears as it would if it were out of the water and bent. I am not making a judgment about the actual characteristics of the table or the stick; I am reporting an image by comparing it with other known images. The epistemic use is a report of what the subject is inclined to believe on the basis of the present experience, and thus it assumes habits of inference and of explanation which are relevant for arriving at beliefs on the basis of this data. The comparative use is a report of how the image appears to the subject, despite what he may believe about the actual state of affairs. The epistemic use assumes a theoretical interest and an inference to the best explanation, whereas the comparative use does not. Ordinary perceptual judgments include an epistemic component. This is what James refers to as the noetic quality of religious experience.[9]

Some philosophers of religion have argued that religious experience and religious faith more generally considered can best be represented as an attitude toward the world which is innocent of theoretical assumptions and, in particular, of any explanatory interests. Following Wittgenstein's discussion of certain examples from Gestalt psychology as illustrations of the phenomenon of "seeing-as," John Hick (1969) characterizes religious faith as "experiencing-as." Wittgenstein (1953: II, xi) considers examples in which the same lines on a page can be perceived in two different and mutually exclusive ways. The figure constructed by Jastrow, for instance, can be seen with equal justification, depending on the context assumed, as either a duck or a rabbit. The observer does not first perceive the figure and then infer that it is a duck or that it is a rabbit. Rather he just sees it as a duck or a rabbit. The perception is immediate.

The religious believer and the atheist, says Hick, both live in the same world, and yet there is a sense in which they live consciously in different worlds. That difference is a result of their experiencing the same phenomena in different ways, and not of their claiming to have discerned new facts or to have some better explanation of the phenomena. Hick claims, for instance, that the Israelite prophets were not engaging in theoretical explanation when they interpreted their history in the light of Yahweh's covenant and his purposes. They just experienced events in that way.

> It is, I think, important to realize that this prophetic inter-
> pretation of Hebrew history was not in the first place
> a philosophy of history, a theoretical pattern imposed retro-
> spectively upon remembered or recorded events. It was
> in the first place the way in which the great prophets actually
> experienced and participated in these events at the time.
> Hosea did not *infer* Yahweh's mercy; second Isaiah did not
> *infer* his universal sovereignty; Jeremiah did not *infer* his holy
> righteousness—rather they were conscious of the Eternal as
> acting towards them, and towards their nation, in his mercy,

in his holy righteousness, in his absolute sovereignty. They
were, in other words, experiencing-as. (Hick, 1969: 32,
original emphasis)

This way of portraying the religious consciousness has two
advantages for Hick, one descriptive and the other apologetic
or protective. Descriptively, it captures the felt immediacy of
that consciousness. The religious person typically does not
regard himself as making inferences or theorizing about explanations when he interprets his experience religiously. The
prophets experienced the events of Israel's history as expressions of Yahweh's purposes. They did not regard themselves
as speculative philosophers of history. Apologetically, the
Gestalt analogy is welcomed by Hick because it suggests that
the religious consciousness can be portrayed as an autonomous
way of perceiving the world. As an attitude that is complete in
itself, it is independent of and cannot conflict with common
sense or the results of scientific inquiry. Some people see the
world in religious terms; others regard it in naturalistic terms.
These are mutually exclusive perspectives, but they can never
come into direct conflict.

Hick's phrase "experiencing-as" is ambiguous with respect to
its epistemic and comparative uses. His employment of the
Gestalt examples suggests that the Hebrew prophets thought
of their interpretation of history as one among a number of
equally legitimate interpretations, much as one can view the
Jastrow drawing as a duck or a rabbit. They were not, he says,
engaged in theoretical explanation. Hosea, Deutero-Isaiah, and
Jeremiah may not have engaged in conscious inference, but
they were convinced that Yahweh was the power to be
reckoned with and that to explain historical events in the light
of his purposes was to explain them accurately. A modern
reader might regard the Hebrew, Babylonian, and Greek views
of nature and history as alternative and equally justified ways
of making sense out of the same events, but the prophets were

convinced that their way of regarding those events was revelatory of the actual nature of the world and its creator.

Gestalt examples ought not to be used to blunt the claim for the authority of the experience that is part of the religious consciousness. When the believer experiences an event as part of God's plan, *experience-as* must be ascribed to him in its epistemic sense. He believes that this event can best be explained by reference to God's plan. In this regard, religious experience is like ordinary perception. When I see something as a table, I am inclined to believe it is a table. My perception includes a judgment about the object.

James understands that the religious consciousness is more than a way of seeing, that it includes a claim about the nature of things.

> What is this but to say that Religion, in her fullest exercise of function, is not a mere illumination of facts already else-where given, not a mere passion, like love, which views things in a rosier light. It is indeed that, as we have seen abundantly. But it is something more, namely, a postulator of new *facts* as well. The world interpreted religiously is not the materialistic world over again, with an altered expression; it must have, over and above the altered expression, a *natural constitution* different at some point from that which a materialistic world would have. It must be such that different events can be expected in it, different conduct must be required. (518, original emphasis)

Religious experience includes a judgment about how things actually are. Stephen Bradley's accelerated heart rate appeared to him to be the result of the operation of the Holy Spirit. His belief that it was to be explained that way was a constitutive part of his experience. Schleiermacher's pious theist experiences every event in the light of the sense of absolute dependence. For him, every event is a miracle. It is to be ascribed to a power on which the entire nexus of natural causes is dependent. Hick does not deny that the prophets believed Yahweh was governing history, but his attempt to capture their faith by the concept of experiencing-as trades on an ambiguity between the epistemic and comparative senses of that phrase in the service of a protective strategy. It obscures the conviction or noetic quality which is an essential part of the experience.

Once we recognize this noetic or epistemic quality in the religious experience, it is not possible to maintain the sharp separation James proposes between inquiry into the cause or origin of an experience and inquiry into its significance or value. When he introduces this distinction, James says that it is drawn in recent books on logic (4). His reference here is probably to Peirce, and to the discussions they had over the years. In his article on the fixation of belief, Peirce argues that beliefs can and ought to be assessed without regard to their origin (CP 5, 358–387). Each of the alternative methods for fixing belief which Peirce rejects involves an appeal to the origin of a belief rather than to the experimental evidence. He is particularly critical of religious traditions on this score. It has often been supposed that if an idea derives from the Bible, from some other appropriate authority, from intuition, or from the natural processes of the mind, it must be true. In opposition to this assumption, Peirce argues that the origin of a hypothesis is altogether irrelevant to the issue of its truth or falsity. A physicist might arrive at a novel hypothesis in a dream, by painstaking calculation, or he might derive it from some mystical interpretation of ancient texts. But the hypothesis must be assessed only according to the results of an experiment designed to test it, without regard for its origin. The justification of a belief and the explanation of how one came to hold it must be kept distinct. The criteria for empirical inquiry are orthogonal to the criteria appropriate for the causal explanation of a belief. The scientist is and should be indifferent to the origin of his hypotheses.

In our discussion of James's distinction between existential and spiritual judgments, we noted that he moved from reference to Maudsley's statement that the final test of a belief is not its origin but the way it works on the whole, to the conclusion that religious experience ought to be assessed in the same manner. Granted Peirce's point that the evaluation of a belief should be independent of its origin, does this apply to religious experience as well? Were religious experience a matter of a simple feeling more akin to a physiological sensation than to an intellectual process, it is possible that it could be evaluated without reference to its origin. A particular shade of blue, the taste of honey, the scent of eucalyptus, or a lowered body temperature or accelerated heart rate can each be described and, for some purposes, assessed without attention to their causes. A high body temperature may be desirable in order to combat a particular virus, and that judgment can be made independently of the means used to achieve that end. A certain shade of blue might be preferred to another. James tries to approach the study of conversion in this manner. After describing conversion as a reorientation of the habitual center of a person's energy, or a restructuring of his field of consciousness, he surveys the evidence and deems it overwhelmingly supportive of the value of conversion for improving the quality of a person's life. A formerly divided self is unified. One whose life was without purpose acquires a focus of excitement and energy which was previously lacking. The analogy is biological. It is as if a particular religious experience functioned to maintain normal body temperature in a context in which the environment was likely to cause it to deviate from normal, or as if a certain set of religious practices operated in such a way as to provide social stability for a community. Religious experiences, as James views them, are for the most part highly adaptive and valuable for human life. But while religious experience can be described and evaluated in this manner for some purposes, such a description and assessment misses what is distinctive about the experience for the one who undergoes it.

If we consider, not a particular shade of blue or a taste of honey, but the perceptual judgment that this sample is blue and this liquid contains honey, then the situation is different. Beliefs can ordinarily be assessed without regard to the origin or cause of the experience that gave rise to those beliefs. But an exception must be made in the case of beliefs that include claims about the cause of an experience. Perceptual beliefs and judgments are of this kind. A perceptual judgment includes an embedded claim about the cause or origin of the perceptual experience. What are the conditions under which we identify an experience as a perception? My having a visual image of a tree, believing that I see a tree, and possessing evidence to justify my belief are not jointly sufficient to constitute a perception of the tree. My belief may be mistaken; perhaps there is no tree there at all. More surprisingly, my having a visual image of a tree, believing that I see the tree, having evidence to justify my belief, and the actual existence of a tree at the point at which I think I see one are not sufficient for the conclusion that I am seeing the tree. Each of these conditions could be fulfilled and yet the circumstances be such that we would not call it a perception.

Consider the following example: I have a visual image of a tree, and on the basis of that image, my beliefs about my visual capacities, my waking state, and other background assumptions, I believe I see a tree thirty yards ahead.[10] It is possible that a tree exactly matching the description of the tree I think I see does stand at that point thirty yards away, thus that my belief is both justified and true, and yet that I have not perceived the tree. Suppose that, unknown to me, halfway between where I stand and the tree is a large mirror. This mirror blocks my vision of the tree but reflects a tree of exactly the same description placed off to the side at such a distance that the reflected image exactly simulates the image I would have received had the mirror not been interposed. I have not actually perceived the tree because the relevant causal conditions have not been fulfilled. The tree has not entered in the requisite way into my coming to believe there is a tree at that spot.

Most important, were the tree that I think I perceive not there, I would have the same experience I now have. Should I come to know the actual conditions that have produced my visual image of the tree and my belief, I would conclude that I had not perceived the tree that I had supposed, but that I did perceive another tree. Reflection on such examples has led to the recent revival of the causal theory of perception.[11]

The authority of the perceptual judgment is dependent on an assumed causal relation. It is the assumption of such a relation which gives the perceptual experience its noetic quality. If James is correct in saying that the noetic quality and the authority of religious experience are analogous to that of sense perception, then a similar assumption about the cause of the experience may be embedded in reports of religious experience. Consider religious conversion. Despite James's characterization of conversion as a shift in the habitual center of a person's mental energy, a subject would not normally label such a shift as a religious conversion if he regarded it as the consequence of his voluntary action. The experience of conversion includes the convert's sense of having been grasped, turned around, or moved by some force beyond his own activity. Stephen Bradley's experience is appropriately included by James in his chapter on conversion. The convert believes his experience has been produced by something outside of him. That belief is itself constitutive of the experience. An assessment of the event as experienced by the subject must therefore include an assessment of the truth or falsity of that belief. It is not sufficient to point out that those who are converted lead more integrated and fruitful lives than they did before the conversion experience.

In chapter one we saw that Schleiermacher's descriptions of the sense of the infinite and of the feeling of absolute dependence include assumptions about the causes of those experiences, even though he denies making any such assumptions. Otto's criteria for identifying an experience of the numinous preclude any experience that can be explained by reference to natural causes alone. Such criteria include an embedded explanatory claim, thus belying his denial of any such interests. In chapter four it was argued that a claim about the causes of a mystical experience is built into the identification of such an experience. James's characterization of the mystical experience as having a noetic quality is meant to apply to the cognitive moment in all religious experience. This evidence suggests that a claim about the cause of the experience may be assumed more generally in reports and theoretical accounts of religious experience. Like the others, James appeals to the authority residing in such an explanatory claim, but he denies that concern with causes or explanations is relevant to the description or assessment of religious experience.

For the subject, the identification of an experience as religious assumes an embedded causal claim; consequently the experience has an epistemic quality, as in the case of sense perception. But what are the conditions under which an observer would identify an experience as religious? Here the cases of sense perception and religious experience diverge in an important way. *To perceive* is what Ryle (1949: 130–135) calls an achievement verb. The criteria for saying that someone has perceived an object include the assumption that the object is really there to be perceived and that he has perceived it. If you claim you see a table, and I think there is no table there to be seen and you are hallucinating, I will not identify your experience as a perception of the table. I will say that you think (wrongly) that you see the table. The identification by an observer of a subject's experience as a perception includes an endorsement by the observer of the subject's perceptual claims. The subject believes the tree or table is there and that he has seen it, and the observer identifies the experience as a perception only if he endorses that belief. If a person erroneously believes he has seen a table, or if he has been to Rouen and is confusing that town with Chartres, we would not claim he has seen the table or the cathedral at Chartres.

One could follow a similar policy with respect to the identification of a religious experience, but the result would be too restrictive. Were we to require the existence of the object or the accuracy of the subject's embedded claim as a criterion for the identification of an experience as religious, then the very existence of religious experiences would depend on the existence of God, Krishna, or other objects people have claimed to experience. Edwards did require that an affection be caused by the operation of the Holy Spirit for it to be identified as a religious affection. By that criterion, the identification of an experience as religious presupposes belief in God and his Spirit. We want to admit, however, that there are religious experiences. Reports of them abound in religious literature. People identify their experiences as religious, though, as we shall see, not often in those terms. But we want to identify certain experiences as religious without committing ourselves to endorsing the claims that are constitutive of those experiences. Perceptual experience and religious experience are similar in that the experience is constituted by certain embedded claims. The subject assumes certain beliefs in identifying his experience as perceptual or religious. But they differ in that the observer's identification of a perceptual experience does, and his identification of a religious experience does not, imply an endorsement of the claims assumed by the subject which constitute the experience.

Religious Experience

We can now return to the question with which we began this chapter: What are the distinguishing marks of religious experience? The aim of the question is not to arrive at a definition that will capture the real essence of religious experience. There is no such essence to capture. Our aim is rather to explicate the concept. What are the tacit rules we employ to determine whether or not something is to be identified as a religious experience? Any characterization depends on the nature of the inquiry and thus must be pragmatic. Edwards was a pastor in the midst of a revival; it was his task to lay down guidelines for deciding which of the surprising occurrences in his congregation were genuine works of the Spirit and which were artifacts of contagious excitement and social pressures. For his purposes, it was appropriate to define genuine religious experience as affections that are produced by a divine operation on the soul. For us, however, that would be unduly restrictive. A social scientist studying various forms of social organization might want to define religion in terms of cult and to specify the distinctive structure and behavior that permit one to identify a cult. Such a definition would be inadequate for religious experience, however, because it does not enable us to understand the experience from the perspective of the subject.

The concept of religious experience is a difficult one to make precise, as much because of the term *experience* as because of anything to do with religion. *Experience* covers a wide variety of phenomena, from ordinary sense experience to dreams, fantasies, and extraordinary states that may be either spontaneously induced or highly contrived. This is not the place to enter into an elaborate analysis of the term. We might agree, however, that anything that is described as an experience must be specified under a description that is given from the subject's point of view. That is, an event may be specified under many different descriptions. It may be specified as an action, which requires reference to the agent's description of the event. For it to be identified as an experience, it must be specified under a description that can be attributed to the person to whom the experience is ascribed. The same event may be described in different ways, as it was experienced by the actor or by different observers. A complex series of events such as a baseball game is experienced differently by each of the players, the manager, and the spectators, and the same can be said for any particular event in the game. To call something an experience requires that it be specified under a description that can be plausibly ascribed to the person to whom we attribute the experience.

I have said that the experience must be identified under a description that can plausibly be ascribed to the subject rather than under a description employed by the subject. There are cases in which we cannot discover what description the subject employed; there are also cases in which the subject cannot articulate his experience but finds that words that come to him upon reflection or are offered by another do capture what he takes to be the experience. In still other cases, we decide that the person has experienced something even in the face of his denials. We have seen that we may have good reason to describe someone as jealous or angry, and even to say that he experienced jealousy or anger, without the requirement that he assent to the description. But the description must be one that can plausibly be ascribed to the subject. That is to say, it must employ only concepts in the subject's repertoire, and any background beliefs or desires presupposed by the attribution of the experience to the subject must be plausibly ascribed to the subject.

Religious experience must be characterized from the perspective of the one who has that experience. It is an experience that the subject apprehends as religious. This is rather close to James's circumscription of the topic of his lectures.

> Religion, therefore, as I now ask you arbitrarily to take it, shall mean for us the feelings, acts, and experiences of individual men in their solitude, so far as they apprehend themselves to stand in relation to whatever they may consider the divine. (31)

We can ignore the restriction to individuals in their solitude, but James identifies religion in terms of the subject's apprehension of his relation to what he considers divine. Both "apprehend" and "consider divine" refer to the subject's descriptions and tacit beliefs.

Even from the subject's perspective, religious content is not enough to identify an experience as religious. The intellectual or imagistic content of an experience does not suffice to identify it as religious. This might do for a historian of ideas or a literary critic who is trying to trace the influence of a particular religious tradition. Buddhist art, Islamic calligraphy, and biblical imagery are all identified by style and subject matter that derive from certain religious traditions and can only be specified by reference to those traditions. But one would not want to characterize religious experience in this way. Were we to do so, visiting Borobodur, listening to Bach, admiring a painting by Piero della Francesca, wishing there were a God, and tracing the history of the concept of nirvana would all be religious experiences. Any of these might be a religious experience, but it is not made such by the fact that the person attends to concepts or images that derive from a religious tradition. The experience must be one that the subject takes to have religious significance or import.

What does it mean to say that an experience has religious import, if this is not to be identified with the subject matter of the experience? This is the noetic quality or authority described above, the basis for the analogy with perception. James's characterization of religion refers to the perspective of the subject and to the subject's judgment about his relation to whatever he considers divine. Religion refers to the feelings, acts, and experiences of persons "so far as they apprehend themselves to stand in relation to whatever they may consider the divine." "Apprehend" includes a judgment about what is real and its relation to the subject. In order to do justice to the authority of the experience, the subject must be convinced that the experience could not be accounted for without reference to religious beliefs. This does not mean only that it could not be described without reference to religious concepts or beliefs. That would be true of Borobodur, of a performance of the Bach B-minor mass, or of an exhibition of Islamic calligraphy. It must also be the case that the experience cannot be explained without such a reference. We saw that the noetic quality of sense perception and of mystical experience assumes a judgment about the proper explanation of that experience. The

subject matter on which attention is focused might not be distinctively religious at all, as in the case of the anomalous toadstool that elicited wonder from Geertz's villagers, but the one
who has the experience must be convinced that it cannot be
exhaustively accounted for without reference to religious
beliefs.

The religious significance of the experience derives from its
noetic quality. The subject apprehends himself and his world in
the light of religious beliefs. The Hebrew prophets regarded
the history of Israel in the light of their covenant with Yahweh.
Buddhist meditation has developed in order to exemplify, and
to enable adepts to apprehend, the truth of Buddhist doctrine.

> In the end, then, the Buddhist world view predominates in
> the Theravāda meditative structure and practice. Whatever
> else it may be or do, Buddhist (Theravāda) meditation is
> viewed as futile unless it brings enlightenment, an illu-
> minative awareness of existence seen through the lens of
> the Four Noble Truths. Whatever use may be made of
> yogic (Jhānic) attainments, they must be subservient to
> this end. Only when the negativity of this world view is
> fully existentialized can the positive apprehension of Nibbāna
> itself be achieved by means of Path realization and fruition
> experiences—experiences not available to mere jhānic adepts.
> (King, 1980: 16)[12]

The intuitions and habitual responses of the adept are redi-
rected in order that he might apprehend his experience in
the light of Buddhist doctrine. Apparently spontaneous experiences, such as that of Stephen Bradley, are also identified by
the subject as religious if they can be accounted for only in
terms of religious beliefs. Schleiermacher and Otto claim the
experiences they describe as religious are independent of religious concepts and doctrine, but we have seen that the criteria
they employ for identifying those experiences assume certain
concepts and beliefs.

A religious experience is an experience that is identified by
its subject as religious, and this identification must be based,

not on the subject matter or content of the experience, but on its noetic quality or its significance for the truth of religious beliefs. But now we must confront a difficulty we have ignored heretofore. Seldom do people actually describe or identify their experiences as religious. In fact, the possibility of doing so is very recent and is restricted for the most part to the modern West. People understand and identify their experiences in terms of the concepts and beliefs available to them. But *religion* is a term that is relatively recent in origin and belongs to the history of Western ideas.[13] Smith (1964) has argued persuasively that this concept was not available to the adherents of most of the traditions we identify as religious. Attempts to translate similar terms from other cultures as "religion" often distort the meaning of those terms. The same is true of our use of *mysticism*. In the previous chapter we spoke of subjects identifying their experiences as mystical. In fact, however, even the possibility of identifying one's experience as mystical is only as recent as the availability of that term. Most individuals whom we might want to call mystics did not identify their experiences as mystical.

In the modern West, at least since the eighteenth century, the concept of religious experience has been available, so people could identify and understand their experiences in this way. James's *Varieties* could only have been written in a culture in which there was some meaning to the concept of religious experience. Although most of James's examples come from Christian cultures, they often diverge from the orthodox tradition, and he views them as exemplifying a kind of experience that has instances in many different traditions. The concept of a religious experience, as distinct from Christian conversion, Buddhist meditation, or Jewish study or prayer, is a recent one. Were we to explicate our concept of religious experience as an experience that the subject identifies as religious, we would be forced to admit that religious experiences have been confined to the modern West. A good case could be made for this conclusion. The criteria that have been proposed by Schleiermacher, Otto, and others for the identification of the religious moment in experience are criteria that have a history and that employ concepts that are recent and culture specific. If only experiences that are apprehended by their subjects in those terms are to be counted as religious experiences, then the phenomenon is a very recent one. If, however, we want to accommodate in our explication of the concept its use to refer to experiences of persons to whom the term *religious* or its counterparts are not available, we must revise our account. The explication, to be useful, ought to capture some of our intuitions about the concept, and one of those is that it should be applicable to experiences outside the modern West.

We might just say that a religious experience is an experience that the subject identifies as Christian, Buddhist, Jewish, Hindu, etc., where the *etcetera* stands for a list of traditions we consider religious. But, of course, these terms also vary in their origins and their availability to members of those traditions. Perhaps most Christians have considered themselves Christians, but the parallel claim cannot be made for Hindus or for followers of Shinto. An experience must be specified under a description that can be ascribed to the subject, and it is the task of the historian of religions to identify the particular concepts and descriptions available to people in particular contexts and to disentangle them from our anachronistic tendency to ascribe our concepts to those people. This is what much of the study of religion is about. Careful textual study of the Pali scriptures, Tibetan commentaries, and Buddhism in East Asia can help us sort out the particular concepts and assumptions that were available to Buddhists at different points in that complex tradition, as well as cases in which scriptural authority and local traditions came into conflict. Much of the same kind of work has been done for Christianity and Judaism.

Often we discover that our anachronistic readings have prevented our understanding the terms in which people identified their experience.

Though this task can never be completed, even when we have sorted out the concepts and assumptions available to people in different traditions for understanding their experience, we must still decide which experiences we will describe as religious. What are our criteria for identifying an experience as religious? We cannot expect this issue to be settled by empirical considerations alone. *Religious* and *religious experience* are our terms; we must examine them and decide how they are going to be used. In this regard, Peter Winch (1958: 15–18) is correct when he says that questions that have been regarded by some social scientists as empirical are in fact conceptual. The dichotomy between conceptual and empirical inquiries which informs Winch's work is a false one, but it is true that no amount of data gathering will, by itself, determine for us what is or is not a religious experience. We must examine our own intuitions about the matter and modify them in the light of investigations into traditions that serve as paradigms of religion (e.g., Buddhism, Judaism, Christianity) and in the light of the goals of our inquiry. We have rejected Edwards's definition because it assumed belief in the existence of God. We have rejected characterizations in terms of subject matter because those were not sufficiently restrictive to accord with our intuitions about what is and is not a religious experience. They did not capture the noetic quality of the experience. We must explicate our use of the concept as best as possible, considering the implications of particular formulations and revising them so that the concept is useful for our purposes. In order that it may be useful, however, it must capture some of our intuitions about the term. Some of these intuitions may be revised, but if the definition strays too far from ordinary usage, though it might be valuable as a term of art, it will not illumine our concept of religious experience.

We have discovered that our concept of religious experience includes a noetic quality or epistemic element, and that that component is best analyzed as an assumed claim about the proper explanation of the experience. We have found this in various guises in Schleiermacher, Otto, and James, and in accounts of mystical experiences. More specifically, we have seen that Otto includes among the criteria for the identification of the religious moment the condition that it cannot be explained exhaustively in natural terms. Schleiermacher describes the experience as one of the utter dependence of oneself and the nexus of natural causes on some other power. James includes in his description of the common element in all religious experience a consciousness of a "More" that is operative in the universe beyond the self and its ordinary world. He thinks it is best understood as a straightforward supernaturalism, though he says this is an overbelief that goes beyond the data. In the discussion of mystical experience, we saw that the noetic quality of the experience seems to derive from an assumption that naturalistic explanations are insufficient. This assumption accords with the way in which the concept of religious experience is ordinarily used. We would think it odd if someone claimed to have had a religious experience and then argued that the experience could be exhaustively explained as the effect of a pill he had ingested. It would be strange for someone to report a religious experience and to subscribe to a psychoanalytic or sociological explanation as providing a complete account of that experience. The words *exhaustive* and *complete* are important here. Mystical regimens and other disciplines for prayer and meditation do prescribe exercises and conditioning that powerfully affect both mind and body, and the meditator is normally aware of such effects. But in the doctrine that governs those practices, and in the beliefs of the adept, those manipulations are viewed as catalysts. They are required for the experience, but they don't constitute a sufficient explanation. If it was thought that an experience could be exhaustively explained by these manipulations, then it could not be apprehended by the subject as religious.[14]

The theories of Schleiermacher, Otto, and James are strongly formed by theism, and the assumption that religious experience cannot be exhaustively accounted for in naturalistic terms is undoubtedly shaped by the same tradition. But the concept of religious experience is ours and is itself a product of the rise of the study of comparative religion in a period during which the appeal to religious experience was a strategy employed by theologians. The echoes of this theistic origin have been preserved in our concept of religious experience, even when those echoes are denied. The concept of natural explanation is itself, of course, parochial. It presumes a somewhat determinate conception of nature as a network of causes, and this can surely not be ascribed to cultures that are far removed from ours either temporally or geographically. How would we judge whether the report of some experience in a tribal society assumes an appeal to some power beyond the natural if there is no conception of the natural in that culture?[15] It would be more reasonable to say that an experience, in order to be identified as religious, ought to be apprehended by the subject as one that can be explained only in terms of the doctrine of his religious tradition. Buddhist meditation states exemplify Buddhist doctrine, though that doctrine may have no place for a distinction between natural explanations and those that appeal to some power beyond the natural. The experience must be apprehended by the subject as fully explicable only in terms of the doctrine of the religious tradition within which the subject stands. Here again, however, we must ask what leads us to identify Buddhism, Hinduism, and Australian totemism as religious traditions, to exclude Marxism, and to have doubts about humanism and some forms of Confucianism.

This is not the place to settle the extension of the term *religion*, and there is no need to settle it once and for all. The meaning of the term will vary depending on the inquiry in

which we are engaged. It is important, however, to recognize
that the concept of religious experience retains echoes of its
origin in a theistic context and of the assumption that a religious experience is one that cannot be completely accounted
for in naturalistic terms. We may want to alter that assumption, but we ought to recognize it. Too often the ambiguity
between a purely descriptive account of religious experience
and the explanatory assumptions embedded in our concept has
been exploited for apologetic purposes. Religious experience
has been described in terms that disclaim any explanatory
interest while the echoes of an embedded explanatory commitment have been drawn upon and appealed to in the name of
combatting reductionism. This attempt to have it both ways
has been rather widespread. We shall see this more clearly in
the following chapter when we examine recent discussions of
the problem of reductionism in the study of religion.

VI.
EXPLANATION

Reductionism has become a derogatory epithet in the history and philosophy of religion. Scholars whose work is in other respects quite diverse have concurred in advocating approaches to the study of religion which are oriented around campaigns against reductionism. These campaigns are often linked to a defense of the autonomy of the study of religion. The distinctive subject matter of that study, it is argued, requires a distinctive method. In particular, religious experience cannot properly be studied by a method that reduces it to a cluster of phenomena that can be explained in historical, psychological, or sociological terms. Although it is difficult to establish exactly what is meant by the term, the label "reductionist" is deemed sufficient to warrant dismissal of any account of religious phenomena.

Questions have been raised about this wholesale rejection of reductive accounts and about the theological motivations that sometimes underlie it, but the issues in the discussion have not been sufficiently clarified.[1] Penner and Yonan (1972), for example, take the problem to be crucial for the study of religion, survey the meaning of *reduction* in empiricist philosophy of science, and deplore the negative connotations that have become attached to the term. But they admit that they have found the issue difficult. They show no appreciation of why the attack on reductionism has such an appeal, and thus they are unable to elucidate the discussion. The warnings against reductionism derive from a genuine insight, but that insight is often misconstrued to serve an apologetic purpose. I shall try to clarify the confusion surrounding the term *reduction* as it is applied to accounts of religious experience and to distinguish between the insight and the misapplications that result in protective strategies. A recent essay in the philosophy of religion devoted to the exposure and critique of reductionism will serve to illustrate those misapplications and strategies.

The Problem

One of the most influential critics of reductionism in the study of religion has been Mircea Eliade. He has argued that the task of the historian of religion is a distinctive one and has contrasted it with what he takes to be the reductionist methods of the social sciences (Eliade, 1969: 1–53). According to Eliade, a historical or sociological approach fails to grasp the meaning of religious phenomena. Like the literary critic interpreting a text, the historian of religion must attempt to understand religious data "on their own plane of reference." He or she should adopt a hermeneutic method. Just as literary works cannot be reduced to their origins, religious phenomena ought not to be reduced to their social, psychological, or historical origins or functions. Eliade (1969: 6) contends that "a religious datum reveals its deeper meaning when it is considered on its plane of reference, and not when it is reduced to one of its secondary aspects or its contexts." He cites Durkheim and Freud as examples of those who have adopted reductionist methods for the study of religion.

Two points are worthy of note: (1) Eliade thinks that what is lost by reductive approaches is the *meaning* of religious phenomena. He praises van der Leeuw for respecting the peculiar intentionality of religious data and thus the irreducibility of religious representations (Eliade, 1969: 35); (2) his examples of reductionist approaches are drawn almost exclusively from history and the social sciences. Theories that purport to account for religious phenomena in terms of their origins or the functions they serve in a particular social context are *ipso facto* reductionist.

Eliade holds further that religious data represent the expression of religious experiences. Religion is "first of all, an experience *sui generis*, incited by man's encounter with the sacred" (Eliade, 1969: 25). In order to understand religious data on their own plane of reference, the scholar must " 'relive' a multitude of existential situations" (Eliade, 1969: 10). Only through such a procedure can the meaning of the data be grasped. To reduce those data to their origins or social functions is to fail to understand them as expressions of religious experience. That understanding can come only from acquaintance. Since Eliade regards religious experience as experience of the sacred, he can summarize his antireductionist position by reference to "the irreducibility of the sacred."[2]

Religious experience is the experience of something. It is intentional in that it cannot be described without reference to a grammatical object. Just as fear is always fear of something, and a perceptual act can only be described by reference to its object, a religious experience must be identified under a certain description, and that description must include a reference to the object of the experience. Eliade employs the term *sacred* to characterize the object of all religious experience. The notorious obscurity of that term need not concern us here, nor need we accept the suggestion that all religious experiences have the same object. The point is that when Eliade refers to the irreducibility of the sacred, he is claiming that it is the intentional object of the religious experience which must not be reduced. To do so is to lose the experience, or to attend to something else altogether.

This point is well taken. If someone is afraid of a bear, his fear cannot be accurately described without mentioning the bear. This remains true regardless of whether or not the bear actually exists outside his mind. He may mistakenly perceive a fallen tree trunk on the trail ahead of him as a bear, but his fear is properly described as fear of a bear. To describe it as fear of a log would be to misidentify his emotion and reduce it to something other than it is. In identifying the experience, emotion, or practice of another, I must restrict myself to concepts and beliefs that have informed his experience. I cannot ascribe to him concepts he would not recognize or beliefs he would not acknowledge.[3] Though historical evidence might turn up to show that Socrates was dying of cancer, no evidence could show that he was afraid of dying of cancer. No such fear could be ascribed to him because he didn't possess the concept of cancer which is presupposed by that emotion.

Consider two examples cited by William James. The first is an experience reported by Stephen Bradley which took place some years before the one considered in chapter three.

> I thought I saw the Saviour, by faith, in human shape, for about one second in the room, with arms extended, appearing to say to me, Come. The next day I rejoiced with trembling; soon after my happiness was so great that I said that I wanted to die; this world had no place in my affections, as I knew of, and every day appeared to me as the Sabbath. I had an ardent desire that all mankind might feel as I did; I wanted to have them all love God supremely. (James, 1902: 189–190)

The second is from Mrs. Jonathan Edwards.

> Part of the night I lay awake, sometimes asleep, and sometimes between sleeping and waking. But all night I continued in a constant, clear, and lively sense of the heavenly sweetness of Christ's excellent love, of his nearness to me, and of my dearness to him. I seemed to myself to perceive a glow of divine love come down from the heart of Christ in heaven into my heart in a constant stream, like a stream or pencil of sweet light. At the same time my heart and soul all flowed out in love to Christ, so that there seemed to be a constant flowing and reflowing of heavenly love, and I appeared to

> myself to float or swim, in these bright, sweet beams, like the
> motes swimming in the beams of the sun, or the streams of
> his light which come in at the window. (James, 1902: 276)

Bradley tells of a vision in human shape, and Edwards reports a lively sense of Christ's love, which seemed to glow like a stream or pencil of light. Each of these experiences can only be properly described by reference to Christ and to Christian beliefs. One might try to separate the description of the core experience from its interpretation and to argue that only the interpretation is specifically Christian. But if the references to the Savior, the Sabbath, and God are eliminated from Bradley's report, we are left with something other than his experience. After deleting references to Christian concepts, we have a vision of a human shape with arms extended saying, "Come." Is this any less informed by Christian beliefs and doctrines than was the original experience? Surely the vision of a person with outstretched arms is not some universal archetype onto which Bradley has added an interpretation in Christian terms.[4] Nor can his experience of comfort and salvation be abstracted from his Christian beliefs. Sarah Edwards's experience is not a vision, but it would be inaccurate to describe it exclusively in general terms and to characterize it only as a lively sense of sweetness, accompanied by the sensation of floating in streams of bright light. Her report cannot be purged of references to Christ and Christian beliefs and still remain an accurate description of the experience.

An emotion, practice, or experience must be described in terms that can plausibly be attributed to the subject on the basis of the available evidence. The subject's self-ascription is normative for describing the experience. This is a kind of first-person privilege that has nothing at all to do with immediate intuitive access to mental states versus mediated inferential reasoning. It is strictly a matter of intentionality. It is like the distinction between the words of a speaker and those of one who reports what he says. The speaker's meaning, and his choice of words to express that meaning, are normative for the reporter. The latter may choose to paraphrase or elaborate, but the words uttered by the speaker are authoritative for determining the message. Where it is the subject's experience which is the object of study, that experience must be identified under a description that can plausibly be attributed to him. In the cases cited above, the subject's own words constitute the description. If, however, an observer or analyst describes the experience of another, he must formulate it in terms that would be familiar to, incorporating beliefs that would be acknowledged by, the subject. If challenged, he must offer reasons in support of his ascription of those concepts and beliefs to the subject. He is not responsible for reasons offered in support of those beliefs.

The explanation the analyst offers of that same experience is another matter altogether. It need not be couched in terms familiar or acceptable to the subject. It must be an explanation of the experience as identified under the subject's description, but the subject's approval of the explanation is not required. Bradley's experience might be explained in terms of the conflicts of early adolescence and that of Sarah Edwards as a consequence of her life with Mr. Edwards. No reference need be made to God or Christ in the construction of these explanations. If the explanation is challenged, the one who proposed it is responsible for providing reasons to support it and for showing how it accounts for the evidence better than any of its rivals does.

Schachter's subjects experienced anger or euphoria. An accurate description of the experience of a subject in the anger condition would require that it be described as anger and that the anger be specified by reference to its object. The subject was angry at the experimenters for subjecting him to insulting questions. The ascription of this anger to the subject assumes he does in fact find the questions insulting and he holds the experimenters responsible for them. He also explains the arousal he feels by reference to the experimenter's insults. Schachter and his colleagues, however, explain the anger in terms of which the subject is ignorant. They explain it in terms of the physiological effects of epinephrine and their manipulation of the cognitive cues in the experimental setting. The subject's explanation of his arousal must be cited in a description of his experience, but it need not figure in the explanation of the experience which Schachter and his colleagues adopt.

In the study of religion considerable confusion has resulted from the failure to distinguish the requisite conditions for the identification of an experience under a certain description from those for explaining the experience. The analyst must cite, but need not endorse, the concepts, beliefs, and judgments that enter into the subject's identification of his experience. He must be prepared to give reasons for his ascription of those beliefs and judgments to the subject, but he need not defend the beliefs and judgments themselves. If he proposes an explanatory hypothesis to account for the experience, he need not restrict himself to the subject's concepts and beliefs, but he must be prepared to give reasons in support of his explanation.

Descriptive and Explanatory Reduction

We are now in a position to distinguish two different kinds of reduction. *Descriptive reduction* is the failure to identify an emotion, practice, or experience under the description by which the subject identifies it. This is indeed unacceptable. To describe an experience in nonreligious terms when the subject himself describes it in religious terms is to misidentify the experience, or to attend to another experience altogether. To describe Bradley's experience as simply a vision of a human shape, and that of Mrs. Edwards as a lively warm sense that seemed to glow like a pencil of light, is to lose the identifying characteristics of those experiences. To describe the experience of a mystic by reference only to alpha waves, altered heart rate, and changes in bodily temperature is to misdescribe it. To characterize the experience of a Hindu mystic in terms drawn from the Christian tradition is to misidentify it. In each of these instances, the subject's identifying experience has been reduced to something other than that experienced by the subject. This might properly be called reductionism. In any case, it precludes an accurate identification of the subject's experience.

Explanatory reduction consists in offering an explanation of an experience in terms that are not those of the subject and that might not meet with his approval. This is perfectly justifiable and is, in fact, normal procedure. The explanandum is set in a new context, whether that be one of covering laws and initial conditions, narrative structure, or some other explanatory model. The terms of the explanation need not be familiar or acceptable to the subject. Historians offer explanations of past events by employing such concepts as socialization, ideology, means of production, and feudal economy. Seldom can these concepts properly be ascribed to the people whose behavior is the object of the historian's study. But that poses no problem. The explanation stands or falls according to how well it can account for all the available evidence.

Failure to distinguish between these two kinds of reduction leads to the claim that any account of religious emotions, practices, or experience must be restricted to the perspective of the subject and must employ only terms, beliefs, and judgments that would meet with his approval. This claim derives its plausibility from examples of descriptive reduction but is then extended to preclude explanatory reduction. When so extended, it becomes a protective strategy. The subject's identifying description becomes normative for purposes of explanation, and inquiry is blocked to insure that the subject's own explanation of his experience is not contested. On this view, to entertain naturalistic explanations of the experiences of Bradley and Edwards is reductionist because these explanations conflict with the convictions of the subjects that their experiences were the result of divine activity in their lives.

Many of the warnings against reductionism in the study of religion conflate descriptive and explanatory reduction. Eliade exhorts the historian of religion to understand religious data on their own plane of reference and contrasts this understanding with the reductive accounts offered by social scientists.[5] Wilfred Cantwell Smith (1976: 152; 1981: 97) contends that a necessary requirement of the validity of any statement about a religion is that it be acknowledged and accepted by adherents of that religious tradition. This is appropriate if addressed to the problem of providing identifying descriptions of experiences in different traditions, but it is inappropriate if extended to include all statements about religion.

For some years Smith has waged a campaign against the use of the term *religion* in the study of what he calls faith and the historical traditions (Smith, 1964, 1979). In criticizing this use of the term, he brings forth abundant evidence to show that it is of rather recent and parochial origin. According to his research, there is no concept in most of the world's cultures and traditions which can accurately be translated by our term *religion*. In other words, there is no evidence to support the ascription of that concept to people outside the modern West. From this evidence Smith concludes that the term ought to be avoided by scholars of the faiths of mankind. Even if the results of his philological researches were granted, however, there would be no more reason to reject *religion* than to reject *culture* and *economy*. The fact that it cannot accurately be ascribed to people in many societies does not require that it be excluded from the accounts we give of those societies. Smith's conclusion follows from his evidence only with the addition of the premise that any account of the religious life, including explanatory accounts, must be couched in terms that are familiar and acceptable to participants in that life. Smith accepts this premise and regards it as a requirement of the comparative study of religion, but we have seen that explanatory accounts are not subject to this restriction.

Protective Strategies

The neglect or refusal to distinguish between descriptive and explanatory reduction constitutes the core of an apologetic strategy. Recognition of the requirement that religious experience and belief must be identified under the description employed by the subject is used to argue that all accounts of religious experience must be acceptable to the subject. This accords with the assumption that in order to understand religious experience one must participate in that experience or reproduce it in oneself.

Smith (1976: 146) explicitly formulates the rule that "no statement about a religion is valid unless it can be acknowledged by that religion's believers." He contends that in order to understand the Qur'an as a religious document, one must approach it in the same spirit as a Muslim would (Smith, 1976: 31). One must read it as if he already believed it to be the word of God. We ought not to study Muslim, Buddhist, or Jewish beliefs and practices but must learn to see the world through Muslim, Buddhist, or Jewish eyes. Understanding requires the scholar to share in the experience or the way of life of a particular tradition and to elicit or reproduce the same in his readers. Eliade describes the task of understanding as a hermeneutic one and exhorts the historian of religion to "relive" the existential situation of those whom he studies.

This requirement gains its appeal from the consideration that a religious experience, belief, or practice must be identified under the description employed by the subject; but it exhibits confusion when it is extended to preclude explanatory hypotheses that differ from those of the subject. In order to understand Astor's experience of a miracle, I must ascribe to him the belief that the event cannot be exhaustively explained in naturalistic terms, but I need not endorse that belief. After accurately citing Astor's description of the event, including his explanation of what he saw, I may go on to propose a competing explanation both of the event and of Astor's perception. To require that any explanation of a religious experience be one that would be endorsed by the subject is to block inquiry into the character of that experience.

A recent work by D. Z. Phillips, entitled *Religion Without Explanation*, provides a clear illustration of the confusion of the concepts of descriptive and explanatory reduction in the service of an apologetic or protective strategy. Phillips argues that any attempt to explain religious experience, belief, or practice is reductive and is for that reason to be rejected. He devotes the first half of his book to a brief survey of what he takes to be reductionist accounts of religion and the second half to an elucidation of religious phenomena which avoids reductionism. Frazer, Tylor, Marett, Freud, Feuerbach, and Durkheim are all labeled conscious reductionists because they attempt to explain religious phenomena in nonreligious terms. Those who assume that religious beliefs and doctrines purport to refer to some object or to describe matters of fact are said to be unconscious reductionists because they construe religious statements as referential rather than expressive. Phillips criticizes both types of reductionists for their failure to accept religious beliefs "at face value." His comments show, however, that he misconstrues both the theories he criticizes and the religious beliefs he is attempting to elucidate. Since the key to his misconstructions lies in a confusion between descriptive and explanatory reduction, they provide a convenient illustration of the importance of this distinction. The confusion can be seen in his criticism of the approaches of Durkheim and Freud and in his misinterpretation of the intentional character of religious experience and belief.

Phillips characterizes Durkheim's theory of religion as follows:

> When one does go below the religious symbol to the reality it represents, one finds it is society itself. Religion is in fact the worship of society. This is an extremely odd claim and it is

not at all easy to understand why anyone should want to make it. (Phillips, 1976: 90)

As an identifying description of primitive worship, this is indeed an odd claim, and it is not one that Durkheim makes. The Australian people of whom he wrote did not identify their practice as the worship of society. The intentional object of their worship or respect was not society but their totemic representations and the animals or vegetables that served as totems for the clans. Given the respect, fear, and authority elicited by these sacred totems, Durkheim set out to offer a hypothesis to explain their force. He argued that the totems were imbued with the power of the social order. The authority of the totems over members of the clans required an explanation in terms of some source or power that could plausibly elicit such fear and respect. The Arunta "worshipped" the totems, but Durkheim hypothesized that the authority of those objects over the clan members was to be explained by reference to the authority of the social order over the individual. One might disagree with Durkheim's hypothesis, but Phillips's dismissal is based on a misunderstanding. He assesses Durkheim's explanatory hypothesis as if it were meant as an identifying description, and he finds it extremely odd. But it was not intended as such a description.

Phillips makes a similar error when he criticizes as reductionist Durkheim's comment that from the fact that a religious experience occurs "it does not follow that the reality which is its foundation conforms objectively to the idea which believers have of it" (Phillips, 1976: 94; Durkheim, 1965: 465). Durkheim is here drawing the required distinction between identification and explanation. The subject's identification of his experience in religious terms makes it a religious experience and is normative for describing that experience. But the subject's explanation may not be the correct one; it may be that the correct explanation requires no reference to religious realities. Astor's perception of what he saw at Lourdes as anomalous with respect to the natural order and consequently demanding a religious explanation constitutes for him a miracle experience, but his perception and its embedded judgment about the proper explanation of the event may be inaccurate.

The same confusion is exhibited in Phillips's remarks on Freud. He correctly notes that a person's beliefs, motives, and emotions must be described in a manner that is intelligible within that person's way of life. A contemporary concept of freedom, or a desire for that freedom, cannot accurately be ascribed to a person in the ancient world. Freud (1950: 27–28) juxtaposes a Maori taboo with an obsessional prohibition experienced by one of his patients. Phillips objects to the comparison between a ritual practice and obsessive behavior.

> Freud does not offer an account of the situations in terms of reasons which have their life within the activities of the tribe. Freud says that it is a waste of time to listen to the reasons of the tribesmen. Notice that he is ruling out their references to the sacred as a possible satisfactory account of their activities. (Phillips, 1976: 61)

Freud does not say that it is a waste of time to listen to the reasons of the tribesmen. That would be uncharacteristic. One of the most important lessons Freud has taught us is to listen carefully to everything, even and especially to what appears to be trivial and unimportant. Close attention is necessary in order to identify accurately the beliefs, intentions, and emotions that are to be ascribed to an individual. But he has also taught us to listen skeptically. One needn't accept the reasons offered by the subject. In the passage to which Phillips alludes, Freud says that we cannot expect the tribesmen to give us the real reason (*die wirkliche Motivierung*) for their prohibitions or the origin of their taboo because psychoanalytic theory would lead us to expect that the real motivation is unconscious (Freud, 1950: 31). The explanation he offers for the practice differs from that of the tribesmen. Whether by choice or by accident, Phillips employs the ambiguous phrase "satisfactory account" in his criticism of Freud for not accepting the Maori reference to the sacred as a satisfactory account of their activities. This phrase is ambiguous with respect to the distinction between description and explanation. If the Maori did make such a reference, it would be necessary to cite that in any adequate description of the Maori practice, but Freud is under no obligation to explain the practice in terms of the sacred.[6]

Phillips construes Freud's theory of religion not as an explanatory hypothesis but as an alternative description of religious emotions and practices. He contends that despite the fact that Freud intended to offer an explanation, he was actually proposing a description of religious emotions and practices which competes with the description employed by the subjects.

> But why can't we say that what we have here is things being looked at from the aspect of the sexual? By looking at things in this way, their aspect changes too. (Phillips, 1976: 69)

Following a suggestion made by Wittgenstein, Phillips claims that Freud's interpretation of emotions and practices in the light of his mythology of the sexual charms people away from the religious alternative but is of no use in elucidating that alternative. But a psychoanalytic explanation is not meant to be an accurate identifying description of a practice from the subject's perspective. Like Durkheim, Freud sought an explanation of the power religious concepts and ritual practices exert over people's lives. Such an explanation must invoke a force or interest that could conceivably have that kind of impact. Sexuality, like the authority of the social order, is a sufficiently powerful force to serve as a plausible explanation, especially in the light of Freud's demonstration of the pervasiveness and strength of libidinal drives.

This misconstruction of Freud's theory of religion as an alternative description of religious phenomena permits Phillips to dismiss it as irrelevant to the study of those phenomena.

Freud did not offer his psychoanalytic account as an accurate representation of the Maori way of viewing the world, nor did Durkheim claim that the Arunta worshipped society. The Maori practices are governed by their concepts, and the Arunta respect and fear totems and totemic spirits. The power of the social order and the pervasive force of the sexual may enter into the explanation of those practices, but not into their identification. One is free to take exception to the theories of religion offered by Durkheim and Freud, but Phillips's dismissal is based on a misrepresentation of their status.

The characterizations of religious belief offered by Phillips are as inadequate as his accounts of the theories of others. The problem arises from his attempt to attribute to believers the neutrality appropriate for the scholar describing religious beliefs. His concern to show that religious beliefs and practices do not presuppose explanatory hypotheses that might conflict with those of science leads him to deny that they entail any assertions at all. They are expressive attitudes and activities. The theories of Durkheim and Freud are explicitly reductionist, but the real problem in the philosophy of religion, according to Phillips, stems from the unconscious reductionists, particularly from those who hold that religious beliefs refer and that they sometimes make claims about the world. He contends that religious language is not referential but expressive. It expresses religious practices and forms of life.

> If we mean by reductionism an attempt to reduce the significance of religious belief to something other than it is, then reductionism consists in the attempt, however sophisticated, to say that religious pictures must refer to some object; that they must describe matters of fact. That is the real reductionism which distorts the character of religious beliefs. (Phillips, 1976: 150)

The meaning of Phillips's title now becomes clear. Not only is any attempt to explain religious phenomena *ipso facto* reductionist but any construal of religious beliefs as themselves assuming explanations is similarly reductive. By precluding explanatory hypotheses about religious phenomena, and by refusing to permit the assessment of religious beliefs as hypotheses, Phillips has adopted an effective apologetic strategy. Conflict between religious beliefs or practices and our theoretical commitments is precluded from the outset.

Like all attempts to block inquiry, this one has its costs. In these terms Phillips cannot accurately account for actual examples of religious belief. For instance, he criticizes E. B. Tylor for attempting to explain beliefs in souls or spirits rather than taking them "at face value." But by taking beliefs at face value Phillips does not seem to mean taking them literally. He says that talk about souls entails neither opinions, hypotheses, theories, nor explanations.

> Talk about the soul is a way of talking about people, a way of talking which, perhaps, is not so familiar as it used to be. What is important to note for our present purposes, however, is that such talk is not based on opinion or on any kind of conjecture about some odd substance inside the body called the soul. Yet, when we listen to Tylor speaking of primitive conceptions of the soul, he speaks of such a substance. He speaks as if the question of whether people have souls is a hypothetical question, an assumption, and in his view one which is empirically false and without foundation. (Phillips, 1976: 39)

Despite his call for beliefs to be elucidated by close attention to details and to their contexts, Phillips does not offer any evidence for his claim. Talk about the soul has probably meant many things in different contexts, and it is highly unlikely that hypotheses about an immaterial substance have not been among those meanings. By taking the belief at face value, Phillips appears to mean construing it in such a way as to preclude its falsity.

Ironically, despite Phillips's contention that religious beliefs are expressive of the attitudes and practices of the religious life and consequently can neither support nor conflict with any theories, his practice suggests that any belief that appears to conflict with our mundane and scientific views requires reinterpretation. Elucidation of religious beliefs is thus dependent on our ordinary and scientific beliefs. Religious beliefs are always to be construed in such a way that they accord with the beliefs we hold to be true. This is clearly a protective strategy. Quine (1960: 59) argues for what he calls "the principle of charity." We ought so to assign meanings to the sentences of an alien language that we ascribe to the speakers of that language beliefs that, in the main, accord with our own. At some point it becomes more plausible to assume we have mistranslated than to ascribe to other speakers beliefs that seem widely off the mark. If our translation leads us to ascribe to the speaker such sentences as "The sunlight is usually brighter at night than in the daytime" or "No one can throw a stone farther than the distance measured by ten paces," then we ought to consider revising the translation to accord with the beliefs that we know to be true and that we ascribe to the speaker. But Phillips is arguing that whenever our understanding of religious doctrines leads to a conflict between those doctrines and what we know or believe to be true about the world, we must reconstrue those doctrines in order to preclude that conflict. This is charity with a vengeance.

In order to give an account of religious belief from the perspective of the believer and to maintain his thesis about religious language, Phillips must elucidate the reality of God or the religious object in a way that requires no reference outside itself and that entails no claim. He tries to do this by exploiting the intentionality of emotion and belief and an ambiguity in our use of the term *real*. The objects of our experiences, emotions, and beliefs are real by the very fact that they inform those states, and therefore the experiences, emotions, and beliefs cannot be identified without mention of those objects. If a person believes in ghosts, those ghosts are real for him.

Insofar as they affect that person's thoughts and actions, they are real *tout court*. A significant part of the world (i.e., that part including the subject's beliefs, experiences, emotions, and actions) cannot be described without reference to those ghosts. In this sense, the ghost of Hamlet's father, Hamlet himself, and unicorns are all real. Brentano, who revived the scholastic doctrine of intentionality and introduced it into the modern discussion, characterized the status of such objects as one of "intentional inexistence" (Brentano, 1874: 115–118). Hamlet is real, though Hamlet does not exist. Phillips ignores this distinction between reality and existence and claims that the reality of an intentional object is the reality a believer ascribes to God.

Phillips introduces an example to make this point. He quotes a comment by Peter Winch on a passage from Simone Weil. Weil said that the longing of a bereaved person for one who has died is not imaginary. The absence of the dead one is very real and is itself a manner of appearing. Winch comments that the dead person is real precisely as the object of the other's longing, since mention of that object is essential for describing the world.

> It is important to what Simone Weil is saying that longing is intentional. I long *for* something or someone. In other words my longing itself, which is undoubtedly something real, cannot be grasped except as a longing for that person. So mention of her is essential to describing the reality of the world as it is for me; she has *not* become something unreal, imaginary, because mention of her is indispensable to describing the world as it is. Her absence is, henceforth, "her way of appearing"; she makes a difference to the world by virtue of her absence.[7]

The deceased is real as an object of the longing of the beloved. Phillips concludes from this that the reality of God and of other objects of religious belief and practice need only be intentional reality and that the question of the existence of such objects outside of those beliefs and practices need never arise. But the reality of God for the theist is not adequately captured by the concept of intentional inexistence, or by the reality of the remembered loved one or Hamlet. The scholar describing the beliefs and practices of another can and must accord intentional reality to the objects of those beliefs and practices, but he must not attribute his indifference with respect to the existence of those objects to the subjects themselves.

I can long for something that does not exist and that is real only as the object of my longing. A person might entertain the concept of God, long nostalgically for the God of his childhood, or wish that there were a Savior to relieve him of his burdens. God and the Savior would be real as objects that must be cited in order to describe accurately his mental states, but they would not be real in the same sense that they were for Bradley and Sarah Edwards. James can be indifferent with respect to the existence and efficacy of the objects of the experiences of those whose reports he has collected, but the subjects of those experiences are not indifferent to their existence. James must cite the Christian belief in God and a Savior to characterize Bradley's experience; he need not endorse it. Phillips erroneously attributes to the subject of an experience or belief an indifference with regard to the existence of the object of that experience or belief which is an appropriate stance for the analyst. If accurate, this move would protect religious beliefs from the results of inquiry, but it does not adequately capture the role of those beliefs in the religious life.

The characterization of reductionism as "an attempt to reduce the significance of religious belief to something other than it is" is crucial to Phillips's apologetic program. It is ambiguous with respect to the distinction between descriptive and explanatory reduction. Phillips characterizes what must be reduced, not as the identifying description of a religious belief, but as the *significance* of that belief. One might identify the experiences of Bradley and Edwards in their own terms and then proceed to offer a natural explanation of those experiences. According to Phillips, such an explanation would reduce the significance of those experiences and would consequently be reductionist. In fact, it would be an example of explanatory but not descriptive reduction. The term *significance* is ambiguous in this context, as is Eliade's use of the term *meaning* for that which is to be preserved. Phillips elicits assent by producing examples of descriptive reduction and then criticizes those who have proposed reductive explanations. This equivocation constitutes his protective strategy.

Force

In order to elucidate an experience, one must identify it under a description that can be ascribed to the subject of that experience. But when the analyst has given an identifying description of the experience, and has cited the relevant concepts and beliefs while withholding his endorsement of those beliefs, has he really captured the force of the experience? Some would argue that he has not, that to describe the experience of Astor, Bradley, or Edwards in such a way as to understand its force, one must have recourse to the kind of acquaintance or participation called for by Schleiermacher and Otto. A commitment by the analyst to a nonreligious explanation is said to preclude appreciation of the authority of the experience for the subject.

In his remarks on Frazer's *The Golden Bough*, Wittgenstein (1979: 1–9) suggests that the story Frazer tells about the King of the Wood at Nemi is impressive in a way that his proposed explanation of the practice of killing the king is not. Wittgenstein concludes that the satisfaction we seek cannot come from any kind of explanation but only from a description that draws connections between our practices and those of the people whom we are trying to understand. The proper identifying description satisfies where the explanation does not. It is implausible to suggest that such gripping practices rest on mistaken perceptions or theories about the world.

> Even the idea of trying to explain the practice—say the killing of the priest-king—seems to me wrong-headed. All that Frazer does is to make this practice plausible to people who think as he does. It is very queer that all these practices are finally presented, so to speak, as stupid actions.
>
> But it never does become plausible that people do all this out of sheer stupidity . . .
>
> I think one reason why the attempt to find an explanation is wrong is that we have only to put together in the right way what we *know*, without adding anything, and the satisfaction we are trying to get from the explanation comes of itself . . .
>
> We can only *describe* and say, human life is like that . . . .
>
> Compared with the impression that what is described here makes on us, the explanation is too uncertain. (Wittgenstein, 1979: 1–3)

The practices themselves are deeper and more gripping than any theories or explanations either we or the practitioners might associate with them.

This is an important point. An explanation must satisfy in that it must account for the force of the experience. It is not necessary for the analyst to share the experience, however, to understand its force. It is the account which must satisfy, and an account can satisfy if it makes clear why the experience has the power it has for the subject. Knowing that my partner takes the log on the trail ahead to be a bear is sufficient for me to understand why it has a dramatic effect on his emotions and behavior. I have elucidated his fear by identifying the object of that fear as he perceives it, and I can see how the fear was occasioned. I can understand his fear without sharing his perception.

The appeal to the force of the experience can be used to serve a protective strategy. Phillips argues that religious beliefs are irreducible in the sense that they cannot be explained in nonreligious terms. The impressive character of any religious belief or practice eludes all attempts at explanation.

> One may be interested in investigating the consequences of various religious beliefs for other social movements and institutions, or the historical development of religious beliefs. Yet, such investigations would not be an investigation into the impressiveness of the beliefs. The impressiveness may be elucidated—we have seen how symbol may be placed alongside symbol—but it cannot be explained. (Phillips, 1976: 151)

Force or impressiveness is not defined independently but is said to be that which is lost whenever an attempt is made to explain religious phenomena. This remark suggests that what is really distinctive about religious phenomena is their resistance to explanation, or their anomalous status with respect to all natural explanations. No attempt to explain them can be permitted without losing their distinctively religious character. The impressiveness of religious phenomena is identified as that which is lost whenever explanations are proposed for those phenomena.

The rejection of any kind of explanation is presented by Phillips as a plea for neutrality with respect to the truth of religious beliefs and a rejection of reductionism of all kinds. In fact, however, it is not a neutral position at all but conceals a substantial commitment. The function of Phillips's remarks is similar to that of Otto's instructions to his readers.[8] If the experience can be explained, it is not religious. Like *numinous* and *miracle*, the *impressiveness* of religious beliefs, as Phillips uses the term, includes in the rules for its proper application the condition that it will be anomalous with respect to any proposed explanation.

The protective strategy Phillips and others adopt is similar in an important respect to the position of Schleiermacher and Otto and serves similar apologetic concerns. Both seek to restrict accounts of religious experience and belief to the perspective of the subject. Schleiermacher holds that piety is a form of immediate self-consciousness which is independent of concepts and beliefs and consequently can only be understood by acquaintance. One must experience it in oneself in order to describe it. Any nonreligious explanation must be ruled out as inadequate to the feeling as the subject experiences it (CF 32.2). Phillips recognizes that religious experience is constituted by concepts and beliefs, and he urges attention to the grammar of those concepts. He argues that the rules of that grammar must govern any account of the experience. If questions are raised about the validity of beliefs assumed by the subject in his identification of the experience, one has imported issues from outside the religious form of life and *ipso facto* shown that one does not understand that life. Both positions assume that religious experience and belief can be understood and assessed only from the inside. Both are then able to say that religious beliefs can never come into conflict with scientific or other nonreligious beliefs. If the possibility of such conflict is entertained, that is evidence that one has not understood the expressive character of religious language. In one case, that language expresses a moment of feeling which is allegedly independent of beliefs and practices; in the other case, it expresses a form of life that is constituted by concepts and practices that can be understood only in terms of the grammatical rules by which they are governed. In both instances, accounts are restricted to those that accord with the perspective of the believer.

When the question of how to account for the force of the experience is not employed in a protective strategy, it is a legitimate one. It is likely that no general account can be given which is adequate to capture the force or impressiveness of different kinds of experience. Let us briefly consider two kinds of experience, ordinary perception and the power of a work of art. Both can be gripping and forceful, though in different ways. The authority of perception consists in what we have called, following James, its noetic quality. In chapter five we saw that this quality is best accounted for by the assumption of a causal connection between the perceptual experience and that which is perceived. I will withdraw my claim to have seen a tree if I learn that my visual image of the tree can be traced to some irrelevant cause and that I would have had the same image even if the tree had not been there. The force of my experience of climbing Mount Rainier, as compared with merely imagining the climb, derives from the judgments I make about the connections between myself, the mountain, and the rest of the world. My judgment about how the image in my mind is caused affects the experience, making it more vivid and gripping than if I believe I am just entertaining the possibility of the climb.

Hume thought that belief in a proposition was to be distinguished from merely entertaining that proposition by the greater vivacity of the impression. He illustrates this by comparing the experiences of one who reads a book believing it to be true and another who takes it to be fiction.

> If one person sits down to read a book as a romance, and another as a true history, they plainly receive the same ideas, and in the same order; nor does the incredulity of the one, and the belief of the other hinder them from putting the very same sense upon their author. His words produce the same ideas in both; tho' his testimony has not the same influence on them. The latter has a more lively conception of the incidents. He enters deeper into the concerns of the persons: represents to himself their actions, and characters, and friendships, and enmities: He even goes so far as to form a notion of their features, and air, and person. While the former, who gives no credit to the testimony of the author, has a more faint and languid conception of all these particulars; and except on account of the style and ingenuity of the composition, can receive little entertainment from it. (Hume, 1965: 97–98)

Hume is wrong on two counts. It is not a matter of common experience that what is taken to be true is more vivid and lively than what is thought to be fiction. Often novels, plays, and films move us more dramatically than do newspapers or history texts. We do experience something we take to be true in a manner that differs from our experience of something we consider fictional, but that difference is not accurately described by reference to the vivacity of the conception. It is a matter of the connections that we believe hold between what we are reading and the world in which we live. If I read in the paper that a portion of the west-side highway has been closed for repairs, I will alter my route when leaving the city. The murder in a mystery novel may be more vividly portrayed than the murder that took place last night on my block and about which I am now reading in the morning paper, but the latter may have a force and effect upon my emotions and behavior which the novel lacks.

The force of the experience is due to judgments and assumptions about the relation of this experience to the rest of my life and to the world in which I live. Those judgments and assumptions are constitutive of the experience. Wittgenstein and Phillips are correct in calling attention to the fact that the force of the experience is a matter of subtle connections between our concepts and the practices that inform our lives, but they are incorrect in claiming that these connections never involve explanations. The difference between my skiing down a slope and my entertaining the possibility of skiing down the slope is not only a matter of logical or conceptual connection. If I take it to be an accurate perception of what is happening to me now because it stands in a certain causal relation to the slope, the snow, and the terrain I am speeding past, the experience will differ considerably from one in which I am entertaining the possibility of that run, either eagerly or with some trepidation, as I ride up the chair lift. The relevant connections are conceptual, but they include conceptions of causes.

Despite Hume's claim to the contrary, novels, paintings, rites, and other works of art move us deeply even when we are aware that they are fictions. Many different theories have been proposed to account for the force of our experience of art, and it is not possible to examine them here. Wollheim (1974:

84–100; 1979) has suggested that the power of a painting, a musical composition, or a ceremony derives from its having been constructed so as to invite the projection and externalization of complex mental states. A work of art succeeds to the extent that it does not foster denial or romanticization but enables a person to experience his or her own inner states with honesty and precision, and so aids in the process of self-discovery. Wolterstorff (1980) has proposed that art is best understood as the creation of possible worlds other than the actual one. Fictional characters are denizens of those worlds, and the power of the work derives from the possibilities presented by those alternatives. In either case, a work of art shows something that is true of ourselves and opens up new possibilities, and it can achieve both functions while we recognize it to be a fiction.

Of the two kinds of force we have considered, the noetic quality of religious experience in theistic traditions is closer to the force of ordinary perception than it is to the power of fiction. To experience God or his providential activity is not, from the subject's point of view, to entertain a possible world in which there is a God and he governs events in the world, nor is it to entertain a concept that permits one to externalize certain hopes and fears by projecting them onto another plane. One might suspect that the proper explanation of religious belief and experience would be found along these lines, but it is not the account that would be given by the believer. The experience has a noetic quality for the subject and is taken to reveal something about the world beyond the individual self. In this way, it is similar to the experience of actually skiing down the slope, as contrasted with that of thinking about skiing down the slope.

Schleiermacher claims to offer an account of piety which is neutral with respect to explanations and beliefs about the world. But causal claims are included in the criteria for identifying either the sense and taste for the infinite or the feeling of absolute dependence. Otto builds an explanatory commitment into his allegedly phenomenological description by his statement that if the experience can be explained in natural terms it is not a numinous experience. Edwards stresses the sensible quality of the new sense of the heart, but that quality and his attention to the fruits of religious affections are significant chiefly as symptoms by which one can discern whether or not the affections have been produced by the Holy Spirit. James writes of a "More" that is operative in the universe outside the self. In each of these instances, despite protests to the contrary, a reference to the causal explanation of the experience is employed to discriminate it from others.

The force of religious experience is best accounted for by the fact that the criteria for identifying an experience as religious include reference to an explanatory claim. The experience is perceived by the subject as eluding explanation solely in terms of his own mental states but as having been produced in such a way that it supports his beliefs about the world, beliefs that are distinctive of the tradition within which it is being characterized as religious. The experience provides support for and confirmation of those beliefs.

Evidence for the hypothesis that the identification of an experience as religious includes an embedded causal claim is of two kinds. First, the descriptions of religious experience which purport to be neutral with regard to beliefs and explanations include disguised explanatory commitments. Second, critics of reductionist approaches claim that the distinctive character of religious experience and belief is lost when the attempt is made to explain them. This shows that what is distinctive about religious belief and practice for these critics is that they are not amenable to nonreligious explanations. These criticisms provide support for the claim that the distinguishing mark of the religious is, after all, a matter of explanation.

Explaining Religious Experience

The term *experience* is ambiguous. When I inquire about what a person has experienced at a certain moment, my question is ambiguous between two meanings: (1) how it seemed to that person at that time; and (2) the best explanation that can be given of the experience. This ambiguity is present in our ordinary talk about perception. I may have been frightened by the bear that I saw up ahead on the trail. My friend points out to me that it is not a bear but a log, and my fear subsides. What did I really see up ahead? By one interpretation of the word *see*, I saw a bear. That is the way I apprehended it, and that apprehension accounts for my fear and behavioral response. By another interpretation, what I really saw was a log, and I took it for a bear. I was wrong about what I experienced, and now that I can explain what happened I can correct my mistake.

This distinction is similar to, but differs from, Chisholm's distinction between the comparative and epistemic uses of "appear" words. It differs because Chisholm suggests that the comparative use, the description of how it appears to the subject, is a report of an immediate experience that is independent of interpretation or other beliefs. No such unmediated experience is possible. The distinction drawn here is between one interpretation, which presupposes a particular explanation of the experience, and another interpretation, also assuming an explanation, which is adopted by another person or by the same person at a later time. The perception of the object ahead as a bear was one explanation, and that was replaced by a better explanation when more information became available. That better explanation led to a reinterpretation of the experience.

It is important to note that both senses of *experience* assume explanations. It is not the case that explanation enters only into the second sense. The first, the description of his or her experience as assumed by the subject at the time of the experience, presupposes an explanation. If the distinguishing mark of the religious is that it is assumed to elude natural explanation, then the labeling of the experience as religious by the subject includes the belief that it cannot be exhaustively explained in naturalistic terms. The attempts of scholars as diverse as Eliade and Phillips to preclude issues of explanation

from entering into accounts of religious experience and belief
are undercut by the recognition that explanatory commitments
are assumed in the identification of an experience as religious.

The distinction we have drawn between descriptive and
explanatory reduction is tailored to meet this ambiguity.
Descriptive reduction is inappropriate because the experience
must be identified under a description that can be ascribed to
the subject at the time of the experience. The experience must
be described with reference to its intentional object. In the
example given above, my fright was the result of noticing a
bear ahead of me. The fact that the analyst must attempt to
formulate a description of the experience which captures the
way it was apprehended by the subject does not mean that no
explanation is incorporated into the subject's description, nor
does it mean that the analyst is not engaged in an inference
toward the best explanation in his attempt to arrive at that
formulation.

The identification of an experience under a description that
can be ascribed to the subject is required before any explanation of the experience can be proposed. Every explanation
assumes a description of that which is to be explained. One
cannot explain phenomena as such but only phenomena under
a description (Danto: 1975: 218–232). An event, action, emotion, or experience can be identified only under a certain
description, and reference must be made to that description in
any explanation that is offered. If the relevant description is
not acknowledged, it will be tacitly assumed. The analyst's
choice of the appropriate description of an experience or action
is not entirely independent of the explanation he goes on to
offer. If a practice is completely baffling to me under a certain
description, and would be recognizable as a practice common to
the culture in which it is ensconced if the description were
altered slightly, then I will be tempted to alter it and to ascribe
the discrepancy to defects in my observation or in the reports
from which I am working. If the evidence for the original

description is compelling, I must accept the anomaly and search further for an explanation; if it is weak, I may adjust the description in the interest of overall plausibility. This is the proper point at which to invoke Quine's principle of charity. I want my total account, with its descriptive and explanatory components, to be the most plausible of the available alternatives. I adjust each until I reach a reflective equilibrium.

The recognition that religious experience is constituted by concepts and beliefs permits an optimism with respect to the descriptive task which would not otherwise be possible. There is no reason, in principle, to despair about the possibility of understanding the experience of persons and communities that are historically and culturally remote from the interpreter. The difficulty is not posed by an unbridgeable gap between an experience that can only be known by acquaintance and the concepts in which that experience is expressed. Because the concepts and beliefs are constitutive of the experience, careful study of the concepts available in a particular culture, the rules that govern them, and the practices that are informed by them will provide access to the variety of experiences available to persons in that culture. Though it may be difficult to reconstruct, the evidence required for understanding the experience is public evidence about linguistic forms and practices. We attempt to formulate a description of the experience from the perspective of the subject, but the evidence is, in principle, accessible to us.

This conception of religious experience also shows that the variety of that experience is much greater and richer than has been suggested by those who claim that a single experience of the numinous or sacred, or a few such types, underlie all the diverse reports in different traditions. Just as the experiences of nirvana and devekuth differ because they are informed by different concepts and beliefs, so the often rather subtle doctrinal differences between religious communities, or subgroups of the same community, will give rise to different experiences.

Kierkegaard was able to distinguish rather precisely several different forms of despair by examining the concepts that enter into those forms. A wide variety of conversion experiences or experiences of religious awe or wonder can be distinguished in the same manner. The catalogue of varieties can never be completed.

If explanation is as central to the study of religious experience as this account suggests, then why has it not been recognized as such? Why is the explanatory component so often disguised or ignored in favor of appeals to a sense or a consciousness that is contrasted with belief? There are two motivations for this procedure: phenomenological accuracy and a protective strategy adopted for apologetic purposes. The first arises from the fact that those who report religious experiences typically take them to be independent of and more fundamental than beliefs or theories. The sense of the infinite or the consciousness of finitude is not apprehended as a theoretical commitment but as an inchoate sense that provides a practical orientation. It seems to the subject to be inaccurate to classify it with inference, inquiry, and hypothesis. Since an understanding of the experience requires that it be identified under a description that accords with that of the subject, it is tempting to assimilate it to the case of sensations, and to assume that sensations are independent of practices and beliefs. For these reasons, phenomenological accuracy appears to some to require that the experience be described so as to make it independent of beliefs.

The appeal to a sense or consciousness that is allegedly innocent of explanatory commitments has an apologetic advantage. If such an appeal could be made, it would be unaffected by any developments in science or other kinds of inquiry. It would, as Schleiermacher said, leave one's physics and psychology unaffected. Religious belief and practice could be seen as derived from this independent experience, and the difficult questions that have been raised for religion by changes in our other beliefs could be circumvented. Rather than seeing the experience as constituted by the beliefs, one could view the beliefs as expressive of the experience. The direction of derivation would be reversed, and that would serve the task of apologetics. If it did not provide a way of justifying religious beliefs and practices, it would at least protect them from the criticism that they conflict with ordinary and scientific beliefs.

As we have seen, the protective strategy used by those who argue that religious experience is independent of concepts and beliefs is parallel to that adopted by those who claim it is permeated by concepts but independent of referential or explanatory commitments. In both cases, accounts of religious experience are restricted to those that would be endorsed by the person having the experience, and consequently the possibility of those accounts conflicting with the claims of the believer is precluded. Whether one describes an allegedly prelinguistic affective experience or confines oneself to elucidating the grammar of a particular religious practice or experience, the result cannot possibly come into conflict with any beliefs or explanations from outside the religious perspective.

A consequence of such strategies is that language that appears to be descriptive may be intended to evoke or reproduce the experience that is purportedly described. Schleiermacher is explicit about his assumption that direct acquaintance is required for understanding the sense of the infinite; thus he sees the need to elicit that sense in his readers. Rhetorical language is carefully constructed, and the speech or essay becomes an edifying discourse, of which Schleiermacher's *On Religion* is a prime example. He regards his evocative language as a catalyst that directs the reader's attention to a sense that is already present but has not been nurtured. In fact, however, the language may be not merely catalytic but constitutive of the experience. If the reader follows Schleiermacher's instruction to attend to the moment before the rise of consciousness and to recognize the unity intuited there, he or she may discover that unity. That discovery ought not, however, to be cited as evidence for the unity of the world or of the infinite. An experience that has been evoked by carefully chosen rhetoric and by assuming a cultural tradition informed by theism cannot be taken as evidence for a unity that is independent of our concepts and beliefs.

Descriptions of doubt, anxiety, or faith in existentialist literature are often employed in a similar way. Kierkegaard displays dazzling literary and analytic skills in the service of edification. His analyses are often designed to elicit experiences and affections in his reader. Just as the spiritual director and the skilled revivalist preacher know how to evoke certain emotions and attitudes, an author can employ rhetorical skills to elicit affections in a reader. That ability presupposes a considerable amount of analysis. Kierkegaard's writings contain very subtle analyses of despair, faith, and doubt. As Aristotle knew, one can often learn more about emotions and attitudes from the orator or poet than from anyone else. Unlike Aristotle's *Rhetoric*, however, Schleiermacher's *On Religion* and most of Kierkegaard's pseudonymous works are written in a rhetorical style intended to elicit that which is being described. Much of the literature in the history and phenomenology of religion can also be viewed in this light. Such terms as *numinous*, *holy*, and *sacred* are presented as descriptive or analytical tools but in conjunction with warnings against reductionism, they function to preclude explanation and evoke a sense of mystery or awe. They are used to persuade the reader that the distinguishing mark of the religious is some quality that eludes description and analysis in nonreligious terms. Otto's use of *numinous* is an example of how one can employ the term to create a sense of mystery and present it as analysis. Such approaches to the study of religion are offered as neutral descriptions, but they assume not only a theory of religion but also religious theory.

We have distinguished the tasks of description and explanation and have argued that explanation is central both to religious experience and to its study. What kind of explanation, then, might we expect to construct for religious experience? An experience or an event can be explained only when it is identified under a description. And we have concluded that the distinguishing mark of religious experience is the subject's belief that the experience can only be accounted for in religious terms. It is this belief, and the subject's identification of his or her experience under a particular description, which makes it religious. If the concepts and beliefs under which the subject identifies his or her experience determine whether or not it is a religious experience, then we need to explain why the subject employs those particular concepts and beliefs. We must explain why the subject was confronted with this particular set of alternative ways of understanding his experience and why he employed the one he did. In general, what we want is a historical or cultural explanation.

This holds both for discrete, datable religious experiences, of the sort on which James concentrates, and for the identification of an underlying and pervasive religious moment in experience. Why did Stephen Bradley identify his accelerated heart rate as the work of the Holy Spirit? What caused Astor to regard what he saw as a miracle whereas Bingham remained skeptical? Why did Schleiermacher apprehend the moment that precedes thought as a sense of the infinite and discern a feeling of absolute dependence which accompanies all consciousness of the polarity of self and world? For Bradley, we would need to know something about Methodist revivalism in early nineteenth-century New England, about the particular meeting he attended earlier in the evening, and about the events in his life up to that moment. To explain Astor's beliefs about what he saw it would be necessary to acquaint oneself with Roman Catholic teachings on miracles, the significance of the shrine at Lourdes, and the details of Astor's background. To explain Schleiermacher's sense of the infinite, his feeling of absolute dependence, and his apprehension of all events as miracles one would need to know more about his early years among the Moravians, his study of Spinoza, and the circle of friends in Berlin for whom he wrote *On Religion*. Each of these instances requires acquaintance with the Christian tradition and with the particular forms of that tradition which shaped the person and his experience.

For experiences sought in highly manipulative settings, as in meditative traditions where the training is carefully prescribed and a person is guided by a spiritual director in the interpretation of the states of mind and body achieved by the regimen, explanations of the sort suggested by Schachter's experiment seem clearly relevant. The novice learns to make attributions that accord with the tradition, and he engages self-consciously in manipulations to attain states that confirm those attributions. For seemingly more spontaneous but still relatively discrete and datable experiences in less contrived settings, one would still look to explain the experience by accounting for why the subject makes these particular attributions. Just as Schachter's experiment sheds light on the experience of emotions in natural settings, attention to the meditative traditions may provide insight into the allegedly natural, spontaneous examples of religious experience. The phenomenologist of religion has often claimed that elaborately contrived ritualistic settings are expressions of the pervasive sense of the sacred or the infinite in human experience, but it seems more likely that the supposedly natural and spontaneous experiences are derived from beliefs and practices in much the same way that an experience is produced in the more disciplined traditions of meditative practice. How did Schleiermacher and others come to think that the sense of the infinite or the sense of finitude was independent of and prior to the beliefs and practices of a culture shaped by theism? His identification of what he takes to be a universal moment in human experience seems clearly to reflect the concept of God as Creator and Governor derived from the Hebrew Bible and the traditions it formed. The consciousness Schleiermacher accurately describes may, upon investigation, turn out to be the product of prior religious beliefs and practices.

Inquiry may demonstrate that some sense or intuition that appears to be independent of beliefs and practices is actually an artifact that developed under particular historical circumstances. Elizabeth Anscombe (1958: 1–19) calls attention to the fact that some of the central concepts of modern moral philosophy, including the distinctively moral uses of *ought* and *right*, have no parallel in Aristotle or in other classical authors. Contemporary moral philosophers debate Hume's claim that one cannot derive ought from is, or Moore's discussion of the naturalistic fallacy, as if they were trying to clarify concepts that are invariant across periods and cultures and that are crucial for moral experience everywhere. Why, then, does that sense of *ought* seem so alien to the moral reasoning we find in Aristotle? Anscombe points out that between Aristotle and Hume our language and practice was shaped by theism, particularly by Christianity. She suggests that the modern concept of moral obligation is not an intuition that is independent of culture and belief, but that it derives from a law conception of ethics, and that that conception assumes belief in a divine lawgiver.

> Naturally it is not possible to have such a conception unless you believe in God as a lawgiver; like Jews, Stoics, and Christians. But if such a conception is dominant for many centuries, and then is given up, it is a natural result that the concepts of "obligation," of being bound or required as by a law, should remain though they had lost their root; and if the word "ought" has become invested in certain contexts with the sense of "obligation," it too will remain to be spoken with special emphasis and a special feeling in these contexts. (Anscombe, 1958: 6)

The concept of ought, and the related sense of obligation, have survived outside of the conceptual framework that produced them and made them intelligible. The moral sentiments Hume describes and maps so well are artifacts that were formed by earlier beliefs and practices.

It seems quite likely that the feeling of absolute dependence and Otto's sense of the numinous are legacies of belief in the God of the Hebrew Bible and Christian tradition and of the practices informed by that belief. These experiences now appear to be autonomous and independent of that belief and that tradition. At a time in which belief in a transcendent Creator and associated metaphysical doctrines have been rejected by many, the habits of interpretation informed by those beliefs remain firmly entrenched in cultural patterns of thought, action, and feeling. Belief in God as Creator once provided the justifying context for these affections and practices. Now the direction of justification is reversed, and attempts are made to defend the beliefs by appeal to the affective experiences and practices. The sense of finitude, the feeling of absolute dependence, the practice of worship, and the grammar that governs the use of the word *God* are appealed to in order to justify the traditional religious statements without which this sense, feeling, practice, and grammar would not be intelligible.

These are only some suggestions of the kind of explanation that might be offered of religious experience. While one might venture a hypothesis to account for Bradley's accelerated heart rate or the recovery that Astor witnessed, that approach will not yield an explanation of their experiences. What must be explained is why they understood what happened to them or what they witnessed in religious terms. This requires a mapping of the concepts and beliefs that were available to them, the commitments they brought to the experience, and the contextual conditions that might have supported their identification of their experiences in religious terms. Interest in

explanations is not an alien element that is illegitimately introduced into the study of religious experience. Those who identify their experiences in religious terms are seeking the best
explanations for what is happening to them. The analyst
should work to understand those explanations and discover
why they are adopted.

CONCLUSION

The program that Schleiermacher inaugurated with his portrayal of religious belief and practice as expressive of an autonomous moment of human experience has been extremely influential for both religious thought and the study of religion during the past two centuries. The felt quality of an experience from the subject's point of view is considered to be the only legitimate account that can be given of that experience, and the result is a protective strategy that serves apologetic purposes. We have seen that the central thesis of Schleiermacher's program cannot be sustained. Religious experience cannot be identified without reference to concepts, beliefs, grammatical rules, and practices. The program requires both that the experience be radically independent of concepts and beliefs and that it be identified under such descriptions as a sense of the infinite or a feeling of absolute dependence. The former is required to show that the experience is original and not an artifact, and the complex descriptions are required in order to show that the object and the authority of the experience are given in the experience and are not dependent on heteronomous ideas or inferences. But these two requirements are incompatible. Schleiermacher's argument that the sense or feeling is independent of culture and that it includes an awareness of reality which is originally given in the experience cannot be maintained.

Most contemporary philosophers of religion would agree that religious experience assumes concepts, grammatical rules, and linguistic practices. Those influenced by Wittgenstein and by recent representatives of the hermeneutic tradition emphasize the impossibility of transcending language in order to discover some aspect of experience which is innocent of conceptual assumptions or grammatical practices. Many of these same thinkers, however, deny that religious experience has anything to do with explanations and with the construction and assessment of hypotheses. Our examination of the conditions under which people ascribe emotions to themselves and others and under which they identify certain moments of experience as religious has shown that these conditions include not only background concepts and rules but also tacit judgments about the causes of their experience. The labels a person adopts in order to understand what is happening to him determine what he experiences.

The word *experience* is ambiguous. It can be used to refer to how something seems or appears to a person, without regard to the accuracy of that seeming or appearing. In the example we have repeatedly considered, the woodsman who momentarily takes the fallen log on the trail to be a bear experiences a bear in this first sense of *experience*. It can also be employed as an achievement word like *see* or *perceive*, where the judgment that someone has perceived something assumes the belief that the object is there to be perceived and has entered into the cause of the perceptual experience in an appropriate way. In this second sense, but not in the first, the statement that Albert had an experience of God assumes that there is a God to be experienced. This second sense includes a judgment on the part of the observer about the accuracy of the subject's understanding of his or her experience. This ambiguity has been exploited for apologetic purposes in the literature on religious experience.

Religious experience, like any experience, must be specified from the subject's point of view. Were we to define religious experience by employing the second sense of the term and including an assumption of the independent existence of the object in the conditions for identifying an experience as religious, we would have to deny that Sarah Edwards had an experience of Jesus or Stephen Bradley had an experience of the Holy Spirit unless we were prepared to accept the theological doctrines those experiences presuppose. But to identify an experience from the subject's point of view is not to exclude issues of explanation. Bradley's belief that what was happening to him was the result of the action of the Holy Spirit in his heart and Mrs. Edwards's belief that it was Jesus Christ whom she encountered are central to and constitutive of their experiences. Their beliefs about the proper kind of explanation to be given of their experiences cannot be separated from the experiences. The experiences have a noetic quality.

Recall Chisholm's distinction between the epistemic and comparative uses of *appears* or *seems*. We sometimes use such words to express judgments about how things actually are, as when we say that the table appears to be round even though the image it makes on the retina is oval. At other times we use these words to describe the image, as when we say the table appears oval even when we know it is round. The noetic quality of religious experience, attested to by such accounts as those of Sarah Edwards and Stephen Bradley, suggests that it is the epistemic sense which accounts for the authority of the religious experience for the subject.

James refers to noetic quality as one of the marks of mystical states of consciousness, where the term *mystical* is extended to capture the "root and center" of all religious experience. These states seem to those who have them to be states of knowledge. The person who identifies his experience as religious does not believe it can be dismissed as an illusion or hallucination. This authoritative component in the experience applies not only to datable events of the sort on which James concentrates but also to the descriptions of religious experience as a moment or aspect of human experience, as in Schleiermacher's portrayal of piety rooted in a sense of finitude or dependence. Schleiermacher might reject the term *noetic* as applied to the sense of the infinite or the feeling of absolute dependence, but he refers in his early work to a unity of intuition and feeling, and he later argues that an accurate description of the experience precludes any attempt to explain it away. The experience is not viewed by the subject as idiosyncratic to him but is taken to be a sense of his dependence on the infinite or on a source that cannot be otherwise specified. Schleiermacher considers the experience to be an awareness of the relation of the individual to the universe, though that awareness is independent of concepts and beliefs and therefore cannot provide knowledge.

This noetic quality, or the sense that the experience is an awareness of something which cannot be explained away as an artifact, is more important for one's identification of his or her experience as religious than is the content or subject matter of the experience. I can call to my mind a picture of the Virgin, but that is not a religious experience. When Alphonse Ratisbonne entered the small church of San Andrea della Fratte and had a vision of the Virgin, it was a religious experience (James, 1902: 223–226). The images may be exactly the same, perhaps modeled after a certain painting with which we are both familiar, but the experiences are vastly different. I believe my image to be the deliverance of imagination and memory, and Ratisbonne took his to be the result of an external intervention that was a sign intended for him. Our judgments about the causes of our respective experiences account for the difference between one of us having a religious experience and the other not. The distinguishing mark of a religious experience is not the subject matter but the kind of explanation the subject believes is appropriate.

This holds not only for dramatic events of the sort Ratisbonne reports but also for the religious moment Schleiermacher claims is present in all experience. I may reflect upon the

Christian doctrine of God and even long for dependence on such a source though I consider my longing to be unfulfilled and belief in God unjustified. My experience is quite different from that of someone who has a sense of his finitude and of his dependence on some source beyond the natural order. The content of the doctrine of God on which we are reflecting may be the same in both cases, and it may engage the affections, but our beliefs about how that "sense" is to be accounted for and assessed will lead to different experiences. The term *religious*, when used to modify *experience*, is not independent of beliefs and explanations but assumes a particular kind of explanation.

This explanatory commitment embedded in the criteria for the identification of an experience as religious may be a legacy of the theistic background shared by Schleiermacher, Otto, James, and other theorists who have contributed to the literature on religious experience. But this does not render that commitment accidental or unimportant. The concept of religion has been shaped by this tradition. It is a product of modern Western, largely Christian, thought of the past three centuries. The concept of religion has developed during a period in which Christianity has been criticized and reinterpreted in the light of modern science, the recognition of the varieties of religious belief and practice in other cultures, and the collapse of the appeal to such traditional authorities as metaphysics, scripture, and ecclesiastical pronouncements.

The concept of religion and the idea of religious experience were both shaped by the conflict between religion and the growth of scientific knowledge. That legacy is implicit in the meanings of the terms as they are employed in the contemporary literature, even though much of that literature is devoted to denying any such legacy. It might be possible to reconstrue *religion* and *religious experience* so as to differentiate them from these issues, but that would be to make of them terms of art, detached from their moorings in the debates of the past three centuries. An explication of these terms as we employ them shows that they are not independent of issues of explanation and beliefs about causes. Proclamations of such independence are themselves attempts to rule out as illegitimate certain kinds of explanation.

Schleiermacher's claim that religious experience is independent of concepts and beliefs functions as a protective strategy. It precludes any conflict between religious belief and the results of scientific inquiry or any other beliefs we might acquire in other connections. He claims that the experience is original, trading on an ambiguity between phenomenological and explanatory senses of *original*. The fact that the experience seems to the subject to be original is taken to exclude other possible explanations. This procedure of invoking a description of the experience from the subject's point of view in order to exclude explanations of the experience from outside the religious perspective is not confined to the tradition deriving from Schleiermacher, nor is it necessarily allied with claims for a prelinguistic experience. Phillips rejects Schleiermacher's thesis that one can identify an experience that is independent of concepts, grammatical rules, and linguistic practices, but he also contrives to exclude explanation as an illegitimate move belonging to another form of life with practices foreign to the religious life. In this way, like Schleiermacher, he excludes all nonreligious explanations of the experience, denies that explanation is at issue, and therefore precludes conflict with the results of science or any other kind of secular inquiry, thus allowing the religious explanation to stand unchallenged. Schleiermacher argues for the autonomy and independence of religious experience, and Phillips argues that religious forms of life and their attendant linguistic practices are autonomous and independent of nonreligious forms and inquiry of all kinds. Each argument is a protective strategy built upon an erroneous separation of the religious life from ordinary belief and inquiry.

Each of these programs results in an artificial block to inquiry which serves an apologetic purpose, but both are grounded in a genuine insight. Religious experience, emotion, action, belief, and practice must each be identified under a description that is available to and can plausibly be ascribed to the subject of that experience, the holder of that belief, or the agent. To identify an experience from a perspective other than that of the subject is to misidentify it. That is the insight. The woodsman in our example experienced a bear even though he and another observer both now know it to have been a log. But neither Schleiermacher nor Phillips acknowledges that in order to identify the experience properly from the subject's point of view it is necessary to ascribe to the woodsman the belief that the cause of that experience was a bear. A judgment about the cause of the experience is implicit in and forms one of the conditions of the experience. The insight that the experience must be identified from the subject's point of view is combined with the erroneous claim that that point of view is innocent of explanatory commitments. It is then employed in the protective strategy built on the claim that the proper description of the experience excludes all explanations of the experience. The explanation employed by the subject remains embedded in the conditions for the identification of the experience, but since its presence is denied, it is not subjected to open criticism and inquiry.

The ambiguities in the use of the terms *immediate, original, interpretation, sense, experience,* and *reduction* all turn on this issue. Each can be read in such a way as to capture the experience from the subject's point of view and remain neutral with regard to the proper explanation of the experience. Or each can be read in such a way as to assume a particular explanation. Schleiermacher takes phenomenological immediacy to be evidence for the assertion that the experience is independent of concepts and beliefs. Representatives of the hermeneutic tradition regard the interpretation of texts, rather than the framing of explanatory hypotheses, as paradigmatic for the interpretation of experience. James thinks that a sense of reality is independent of any judgment or explanation. Those who campaign against reductionism in the study of religion appeal to examples of descriptive reduction to elicit assent, but they are particularly concerned to exclude explanatory reduction from the accounts of religious experience and practice. In each case, the fact that an experience must be specified under a description that can be ascribed to the subject is used to discredit any explanation that might be given of the experience and to say that such explanations are irrelevant to an understanding of the experience as a religious experience. This constitutes the protective strategy.

The fact that the various forms of protective strategy attempt to rule out certain explanations of religious experience provides further evidence for the conclusion that the issue of explanation is central to what the authors of those strategies take to be the distinctively religious. Schleiermacher, Otto, and Phillips all deny that explanation is at issue, and yet they all describe religious experience in such a way as to preclude any natural explanation of that experience. This indirect evidence, in conjunction with our analysis of the noetic quality of the experience, and with the ambiguities in the uses of the key terms mentioned above, is sufficient to demonstrate the importance of the issue of explanation.

Our conclusion that the subject's explanation of his or her experience enters into the conditions required for identifying an experience as religious has important implications for the philosophy of religion and religious thought. One of the major issues addressed by religious thinkers in the West during the past three centuries is that of the conflict between religion and science. Their chief strategy has been to deny that any such conflict exists. Philosophers of religion and theologians have argued that religious experience, belief, and practice have their own integrity and can be understood only from the inside. The object of a religious emotion, belief, or practice is given internally, as is its authority. Any attempt to subject these beliefs or practices to examination from outside the religious perspective is illegitimate. We have seen that Schleiermacher, Otto, James, and Phillips all defend such a position, though on very different philosophical grounds. This strategy has been employed in an even more radical way by Karl Barth, who accuses Schleiermacher and the tradition stemming from him of heteronomy and idolatry because Schleiermacher describes religious experience in terms borrowed from philosophical anthropology rather than in the language of Christian doctrine. But Schleiermacher formulated the rules for identifying religious experience in such a way as to insure its independence of all nonreligious concepts and beliefs. From our perspective, Barth, Schleiermacher, and Phillips employ similar strategies to limit all inquiry and reflection on Christian faith, or religious experience and belief, to internal elucidation and analysis.

We have seen that such limitations are unjustified. The experience to which Schleiermacher appeals assumes certain concepts and beliefs. The authority of religious experience rests upon certain judgments about how that experience is to be explained. The noetic quality cited by James is not given in the experience but assumes a tacit judgment about the kind of explanation appropriate for that experience. The authority of religious doctrine or of the religious form of life cannot be disconnected from other concepts and beliefs. Each of these attempts to restrict philosophical or theological reflection to internal analysis and elucidation fails because the doctrines and experiences to be analyzed assume concepts and beliefs that are not distinctively religious, and because the authority of the doctrine or experience assumes a tacit explanatory commitment.

NOTES

I: EXPRESSION

1. Smith's statement could be disputed by citing Hume's *Natural History of Religion* or any of a number of late seventeenth- and eighteenth-century works. See Manuel (1959). But Schleiermacher was the first to argue for the autonomy of religion and for piety "as a generic something."

2. For a history of the development of the comparative study of religion over the past century, see Sharpe (1975).

3. For recent studies of Kant's argument in *Religion within the Limits of Reason Alone*, see Despland (1973), Michaelson (1979), Wood (1970), and Yovel (1980).

4. Forstman (1977: 65–79) briefly sets *On Religion* in historical context.

5. References to *On Religion* in this section are to Schleiermacher (1958) and are given by page number only.

6. On the difference between the first and later editions of *On Religion*, with special attention to the relation between intellect and feeling, see Brandt (1941: 95–199) and Harvey (1971: 488–512). Quotations in the text have been taken from Oman's translation of the third edition.

7. A mental state is intentional if it can be specified only by reference to an object. For the history of the concept and of different attempts to clarify it, see Aquila (1977), Chisholm (1957, 1967), and Marras (1972).

8. In the first edition the object of religious intuition is the universe, and the concept of God is peripheral.

Anschauen des Universums, ich bitte, befreundet Euch mit deisem Begriff, er is der Angel meiner ganzen Rede, er ist die allgemeinste und hochste Formel der Religion, woraus Ihr jeden

Ort in derselben finden konnt, woraus sich ihr Wesen und ihre Grenzen aufs genaueste bestimmen lassen. (Schleiermacher, 1958: 31)

See Brandt (1941: 95–149) and Harvey (1971: 497–512).

9. References in the text to *The Christian Faith* are given by paragraph and section numbers (e.g., CF 4.4). Quotations are taken from Schleiermacher (1928).

10. Schleiermacher does not deny that speculative theology is possible but only that it can have any bearing on religion or dogmatics (CF 2.1., 4.4).

11. The full title of the work is *The Christian Faith, presented systematically according to the fundamental doctrines of the Evangelical Church.* It was written for the proposed union of the Lutheran and Reformed churches in Prussia.

12. The propositions that comprise the introduction are borrowed from ethics, the philosophy of religion, and apologetics.

By Ethics is here understood that speculative presentation of Reason, in the whole range of its activity, which runs parallel to natural science. By Philosophy of Religion is understood a critical presentation of the existing forms of religious communion, as constituting, when taken collectively, the complete phenomenon of piety in human nature. (CF 2.ps2)

Philosophy of religion is a branch of ethics understood in this sense. Apologetics is a theological discipline that attempts to ascertain the nature of Christianity (CF 2.2, Schleiermacher, 1966: 39).

13. In *On Religion*, Schleiermacher writes:

All is immediately true in religion, for except immediately how could anything arise? But that only is immediate which has not passed through the stage of idea, but has grown up purely in the feeling. (Schleiermacher, 1958: 54)

In *The Christian Faith*, he characterizes the real immediate self-consciousness as one "which is not representation but in the proper sense feeling" (CF 3.2).

14. See Otto (1958) and Wach (1951).

15. For criticisms of Streng's translation and analysis, see Wayman (1969). My point is that there is a discrepancy between the theory of religious language to which Streng appeals and the text he offers as evidence for that theory.

16. References to the *Philosophical Investigations* are to Wittgenstein (1953) and are given by paragraph number in Part I. For discussions of Wittgenstein on avowals, see Aune (1965: 35–57), Hacker (1972: 251–282), and Malcolm (1966: 77–83).

17. Hacker (1972: 277–282) contends, however, that these arguments are independent. It is not clear from the text whether Wittgenstein wants to set forth a noncognitive theory of avowals or is only suggesting this as a possible way of considering the matter.

18. See Alston (1965) and Hacker (1972: 251–282).

19. See note 7 above.

20. Brentano, in Chisholm (1960: 50), refers to the "intentional inexistence" of the object. To speak of intentional objects does not require that one defend a realism with regard to those objects. Intentionality can be characterized in grammatical terms. See Chisholm (1957, 1967).

21. See also Carnap (1935: 26–29).

22. Dogmatic propositions are to be judged according to two criteria: (1) their ecclesiastical value, or adequacy for expressing the emotions of a particular religious community, and (2) their scientific value, which is a function of their clarity and coherence. The best dogmatic propositions are those in which the ecclesiastical and scientific aspects enhance one another (CF 17).

23. For the distinction between descriptive and explanatory reduction, see chapter six.

24. *Erklärung* here appears to mean "explanation." If Schleiermacher intends it to mean elucidation or interpretation, then his appeal to introspective awareness is appropriate. In that case, however, it does not preclude nonreligious explanations of the feeling of absolute dependence.

II: INTERPRETATION

1. See Harman, 1973.

2. In his later notes, Schleiermacher (1959: 163–164) distinguishes between two parts of the psychological interpretation: the technical and the strictly psychological. The former is an understanding of the way the author's language is shaped by his individuality, the latter of the germinal decision (*Keimentschluss*) that underlies this communication. Schleiermacher's fragments have led commentators to reconstruct his theory in different ways (Palmer, 1969: 84–97; Niebuhr, 1964: 77–92; Benson, 1967). Benson's reconstruction is the most thorough, but he distorts by attempting to impose a more rigid order than is justified by the text. He regards the comparative and divinatory procedures as orthogonal to the other distinctions and as prescriptive in contrast to the descriptive status of the grammatical and psychological interpretations. The textual basis that he offers for this reading,

however, does not warrant it. He is overly concerned to impose on the hermeneutic manuscripts a fourfold division that he has extracted from Schleiermacher's philosophical ethics. (See esp. pp. 249–298.)

3. In an influential introduction to his edition of the manuscripts on hermeneutics, Heinz Kimmerle (1959: 9–24) argues that Schleiermacher's focus on the intention of the author emerged only in his later notes and addresses and that this psychologism is not evident in the early notes. Kimmerle, and Gadamer (1975: 162–173) following him, deplore what they take to be the psychologism of the later Schleiermacher and early Dilthey and want to restore the attention to language rather than authorial intent which they find in the early notes.

Kimmerle's interpretation of Schleiermacher's development is not convincing, even on the basis of the textual evidence he cites. For a critical assessment, see Benson (1967: 392–407). Kimmerle's thesis has occasioned much debate, but for our purposes the outcome of this debate is not critical. The emphasis on immediacy and intuition in the hermeneutical tradition is not tied exclusively to Schleiermacher's focus on authorial intent.

4. Berlin (1976). For Dilthey's high estimate of Vico's new science, see Dilthey (1966: 2: 698), cited by Ermath (1978: 376n.).

5. See, for instance, Abel (1948, 1967), Nagel (1953), Wax (1967).

6. One of the best attempts to defend this distinction, with particular attention to an analysis of action, is von Wright (1971). See also Taylor (1971).

7. This was recognized by Hegel (1953: 3–10). See his concept of "reflective history."

8. The contrast between "logical" and "historical" is made by Ricoeur (1976: 90–91). Ermath (1978: 271–290) provides a well-documented account of the development but does not analyze its philosophical implications. Gadamer (1975: 192–194), however, does not think that Dilthey's transition from the psychological approach to the hermeneutic was finally complete. See also Palmer (1969: 98–123).

9. Gadamer's critique of Dilthey's psychologism is a rejection of his individualism, but not of his conception of the aim of knowledge as a kind of participation. Though he shows that the interpreter is ensconced in his own culture and informed by his own questions, Gadamer (1965: 289–290, 369) describes the goal of interpretation as a "fusion of horizons" and a "participation in the communication which the text makes to us." He says that "we know the power of this kind of fusion chiefly from earlier times and their naive attitude to

themselves and origin . . ." (Gadamer, 1965: 289). The dominant metaphors are those of overcoming distance, and the romantic ideal lurks in the background.

10. I owe this example to Arthur Danto.

11. See Ricoeur (1971), Taylor (1979), von Wright (1971).

12. For recent works on historical interpretation and explanation, see Danto (1965) and the articles in Gardiner (1959).

13. References to Peirce will be given by volume and paragraph of the *Collected Papers* edited by Harthshorne, Weiss, and Burks, 1931–1958.

14. The phrase "the myth of the given" is taken from Sellars (1956). This essay is a powerful attack on that myth in all its forms.

15. The failure to distinguish between the logical and psychological sense of *hypothesis* has resulted in considerable confusion in some recent discussions. See, for example, Winch (1970: 88):

The spirit in which oracles are consulted is very unlike that in which a scientist makes experiments. Oracular revelations are not treated as hypotheses and, since their sense derives from the way they are treated in their context, they therefore *are not* hypotheses. They are not a matter of intellectual interest but the main way in which the Azande decide how they should act.

The last sentence in no way rules out the possibility that the logical status of the deliverance of an oracle is that of a hypothesis.

16. See Quine (1981) for his assessment of the contributions of pragmatism to the empiricist tradition.

17. See Abel (1948, 1967), Nagel (1953).

18. See Danto (1970: 121):

Verstehen is understanding how others understand. But, contrary to what critics of it have thought, this does not mean some dubious empathic leap across the barriers of the soul, but rather concerns the manner in which they perceive quite public things. And by and large this comes to the same thing as mastering their language, which conspicuously does not require empathic feats.

III: EMOTION

1. This issue will be examined more fully in chapter five.

2. Davidson (1976) has argued that a cognitive theory of the emotions can be found in Hume. Though Hume identifies pride with a simple impression, Davidson says that he also offers an account of "propositional pride." For a criticism of Davidson's reading, see Baier (1978). See also Ardal (1966).

3. I have altered Rhys Roberts's translation of *phainomenein* from "conspicuous" to "apparent." Fortenbaugh (1975: 12) translates *dia phainomenein oligorian* as "on account of an apparent slight." Freese (Aristotle, 1926: 1378a) renders it "real or apparent" and Kenny (1963: 193) as "what appears to be." Aristotle realized it was the person's thought that he had been slighted that entered into the determination of the anger, regardless of whether or not the slight was intended.

Fortenbaugh also takes *dia* to be causal:

Making use of his own logical tools Aristotle construes the thought of outrage as the efficient cause mentioned in the essential definition. Anger is not a pain which happens to occur together with the thought of such outrage. On the contrary, anger is necessarily caused by the thought of outrage, so that such a thought is mentioned in the essential definition of anger. (Fortenbaugh, 1975: 12)

The thought might, however, be mentioned in the essential definition of anger and be constitutive of the emotion without its being the efficient cause of anger.

4. See Dodds (1964: 28–63).

5. I owe this observation to Arthur Danto.

6. Neu (1977) contains a good exposition of Spinoza on the emotions and a defense of Spinoza's account in contrast to Hume's. Neu argues that Spinoza's theory can illumine the practice of psychoanalytic therapy, in which the patient's thoughts are explored in order to enable him to come to a more adequate understanding of the causes of his mental and bodily states.

7. Mandler (1975: 94–95) points out the fact that Cannon interpreted "bodily changes" exclusively as visceral activity, though James makes no such restriction.

8. For criticism of the Schachter and Singer experiment, see Plutchik and Ax (1967) and comments in Mandler (1975: 92–93). Mandler's book contains an excellent discussion of psychological theories of the emotions and proposes a revised form of Schachter's two-factor theory. Mandler also considers the interaction between arousal and cognitive structures in natural settings. Maslach (1979) is a review of criticisms of Schachter and Singer and a report of attempts to replicate and improve upon the original experiment. Her own use of hypnosis as an arousal agent in order to avoid the introduction of an injection seems highly suspect. Is hypnosis any less artificial than injection? Might it not also alter the subject's normal processes of inference?

Maslach raises some critical questions but does not quarrel with Schachter's basic model.

9. For phenomenological descriptions of such moods, see, for example, Heidegger (1962: 225–311) and Niebuhr (1969).

10. For the definitive account of Sabbatai Sevi and his movement, see Scholem (1973).

For after the beginning of the mass movement in 1666, the believers no longer spoke of an "illness." This term disappears. In their view both phases of the disease were divine dispensations for which they employed theological terms, traditional ones as well as new coinages, corresponding exactly to the modern terms "depression" and "mania." The new vocabulary . . . speaks of periods of "illumination" and of the "hiding of the face" respectively. The anguish of the melancholic sufferings, which all specialists agree are extremely severe though they have no physiological basis, is explained by Nathan in theological terms when in the summer of 1665 he writes about "the severe afflictions, too immense to be conceived, which R. Sabbatai Sevi suffered on behalf of the Jewish nation." (Scholem, 1973: 130)

In speculating about the transformation of Jesus from local exorcist and charismatic wonder-worker to Messiah, Morton Smith writes:

He of course tried to understand himself in terms made available by his own culture, and seems to have thought himself, at first, a prophet, later, the Messiah. He also thought that he had ascended into the heavens, entered the kingdom of God, and was therefore freed from the Mosaic law. (Smith, M., 1973: 140)

11. For a review of attribution theory, see Shaver (1975). For a collection of the major papers contributing to the early development of the theory, see Jones et al. (1972).

12. This description of the American Nichiren Shoshu movement is based on observations made in 1973–1974.

IV: MYSTICISM

1. For a history of the word *mysticism* and its cognates, see Bouyer (1980). Bouyer does not, however, address the question raised here. He is concerned to demonstrate that the roots of Christian mysticism are independent of Neoplatonic and Hellenic influences.

2. *Brhad-aranyaka Upanishad*, II, 3, 6, quoted by Deutsch (1969: 10–11).

3. Richards (1978) argues that the use of the term *śunyatā* (emptiness or voidness) in the Madhiyamika school of Buddhism can be viewed as a form of *via negativa* in its rejection of all positive and

negative possibilities. See also Streng (1967) and the critique by Wayman (1969).

4. In an essay on the logic of mystery in Christology, Katz recognizes what I have called the placeholder function, but again only to dismiss it as mystification. He defines a mystery theologian as one who subscribes to the following formula: "Let θ be any predicate and M any subject; then for any θ, M is no θ" (Katz, 1972: 239). He then claims that such a proposal is senseless, a sign of theological escapism, and that it results only in M dropping out of the language and in consequent obfuscation. But he fails to see the force of such a formula. Only a predicate whose use was governed by rather precise rules could shed its content and thus effectively drop out of the language while remaining very much in it.

5. In an interpretation of Aquinas which has some affinity with that of Burrell, and to which the latter acknowledges his indebtedness, Preller (1967: 156) writes: "In this life 'God' remains a word in *another* language—a word *mentioned but not used in our language*" (original emphasis).

In an earlier work, Burrell (1973) argues that Plato and Aristotle also employ terms that elude and transcend all our ordinary concepts and categories. He regards them as having anticipated in that respect Thomas's use of analogy and perfection terms.

6. For this use of *mana, tabu,* and *wakanda,* see Marett (1914). For accounts of this tradition, see Evans-Pritchard (1965) and Sharpe (1975). For a similar use of *baraka,* see Geertz (1968).

7. The issue of reductionism, and its relation to both description and explanation, will be discussed in chapter six.

8. It might be argued that Stace's principle mandates causal indifference on the part of the analyst but not on the part of the subject. Perhaps a judgment about the proper explanation of the event is included in the phenomenological characteristics that are supposed to resemble one another, and it is the analyst's explanation which is irrelevant for the identification of a "genuine" mystical experience. The phrase "phenomenological characteristics," however, is meant to capture the felt quality of the experience from the subject's point of view when all questions of theory and explanation have been bracketed. It seems clear that Stace means for the principle of causal indifference to apply to the subject as well. Although it is true that the analyst's judgment about the cause of the experience is irrelevant to an identification of the experience as mystical, Stace's reference to

a "genuine" mystical experience is ambiguous at this point. The relation between the subject's and the analyst's criteria for the identification of an experience will be examined in chapters five and six.

9. Kant, Schleiermacher, and Tillich were not chiefly engaged in an analysis of the concept of miracle but in reinterpreting it. Each had set out his own conception of religion and Christianity, and each then proceeded to suggest how such traditional concepts as that of miracle could be understood within the new framework. Both Schleiermacher and Tillich, as theologians, were motivated in part by an apologetic concern to offer a construction of the traditional doctrine of miracles which would be compatible with modern science.

10. Holland (1967: 167) confuses the issue by defining miracle as "something the occurrence of which can be categorized at one and the same time as empirically certain and conceptually impossible." For the sake of this definition, he is willing to reject the principle *ab esse ad posse valet consequentia*. It is difficult to see why he regards the former as more plausible than the latter.

11. For an interesting examination by social psychologists of various strategies of inference employed in everyday reasoning, including reasoning about one's own bodily states and behavior, and the most common kinds of errors, see Nisbett and Ross (1980).

12. The assumptions about the causal explanation of a mental state which are entailed in identifying it as a perception, and the implications for the analysis of religious experience, will be considered in the following chapter.

V: EXPLICATION

1. For a discussion of the distinction between real and nominal definitions, and a defense of the appropriateness of nominal definitions for the study of religion, see Spiro (1966).

2. James (1902: 27). All parenthetical references in this chapter not otherwise identified are to this work.

3. This was not always the case. For recent exceptions, see Wild (1969) and Levinson (1978, 1981).

4. Even Smart (1965), who is critical of most descriptions of a common mystical experience, retains the notion of a core and differentiates it from various levels of interpretation. Otto (1958) describes the experience of the numinous as an experience common to all religious traditions. See also Wach (1951).

5. The concept of a faith-state is taken from Leuba (1896, quoted by James, 1902: 247). James describes it as an "affective experience which, to avoid ambiguity, should, I think, be called the state of assurance rather than the faith state" (247). Its characteristics are (1) a sense of harmony and acquiescence, (2) a sense of perceiving truths not known before, and (3) a sense of the world having undergone an objective change. Despite James's comment, he continues to refer to it as the faith-state.

6. James offers much richer theories of sense perception in *The Principles of Psychology* (1890) and in *Pragmatism* (1907).

Most books start with sensations, as the simplest mental facts, and proceed synthetically, constructing each higher stage from those below it. But this is abandoning the empirical method of investigation. No one ever had a simple sensation by itself. Consciousness, from our natal day, is of a teeming multiplicity of objects and relations, and what we call simple sensations are results of discriminative attention, pushed often to a very high degree. (1890: I, 224)

Only in the *Varieties* does he draw this distinction between a sense that is analogous to sense perception, and overbeliefs that are built on it.

7. The signs Edwards takes to be sufficient for the identification of genuine religious affections differ importantly from those he sees as insufficient. The insufficient signs are marks that could be assessed by anyone and for which reliable public measures could be found: intensity of emotion, great bodily effects, constant talk of Scripture and religious matters, the appearance of a loving nature, and a certain order to the affections. But each of the positive signs incorporates a judgment as to whether or not the affections are produced by the Holy Spirit or grounded in the nature of divine things. If present, they are certain signs of genuine religious affections, but they do not yield criteria that can be applied with certainty. No evidence can enable a person to judge conclusively whether or not a person is saved. Examples of the positive signs are that the affections arise from spiritual and supernatural influences; that they are grounded in the moral excellency of divine things; that they arise from the mind's being enlightened; that they are attended with a change of nature and an evangelical humiliation; and that they naturally beget a spirit of love of the sort that appeared in Christ.

8. By employing Chisholm's distinction at this point, I do not mean to endorse his foundationalist epistemology.

9. James refers to the noetic quality in mystical experience, but he regards mysticism as the name for the special manner in which reli-

gious persons have professed to see truth (378). It is not restricted to a narrow view of mystical experience.

10. This example is derived from those given by Gettier (1963), Grice (1961), and Harman (1973).

11. For the causal theory of perception, see Grice (1961) and Strawson (1974). On proposals for a causal theory of knowledge, see Pappas and Swain (1978) and Shope (1983).

12. See also Gimello (1978).

13. *Experience* is also a recent term. For a brief history of the concept of *Erlebnis*, see Gadamer (1975: 56–66).

14. Wainwright (1981: 54–137) argues that neither the description of an experience as mystical nor the cognitive validity of such an experience is precluded by the fact that the experience can be fully explained in natural terms. To make that argument, he denies that a causal connection with the object is assumed in ordinary sense perception. He considers an example much like the case of seeing the tree and appeals to the reader to agree with his judgment that no causal connection is necessary (Wainwright, 1981: 70). But his example is evidence for the contrary conclusion.

15. Evans-Pritchard (1956) attributes to Nuer religion a dualism that corresponds to a distinction between natural and supernatural, but his categories appear to be imported from his own Catholicism.

VI: EXPLANATION

1. See Fenton (1970) and Penner and Yonan (1972).

2. "To try to grasp the essence of such a phenomenon by means of physiology, sociology, economics, linguistics, art, or any other study is false; it misses the unique and irreducible element in it—the element of the sacred" (Eliade, 1966: xiii).

3. The ascription of unconscious beliefs or desires presents special problems. For a good discussion, see Collins (1969). Even in these cases, the beliefs and desires must be described in terms that the subject would understand and that could plausibly be attributed to him or her.

4. Eliade assumes the existence of archetypal patterns that are given different interpretations in different cultures. See Eliade (1966). The identification of such patterns is highly arbitrary, however, and encourages the scholar to ignore the contextual details of religious experience.

5. Explanatory reduction is permissible, but descriptive reduction is not. Eliade, however, decries explanatory reduction, while his practice

of treating symbols and rites as universal archetypes abstracted from their social cultural contexts, amounts to descriptive reduction. This is precisely the wrong combination.

6. It is unlikely that the Maori employed the concept of the sacred. Freud quotes from Frazer (1911: 136). Frazer drew his information from Taylor (1870), which I have not been able to find. I suspect that *sacred* is a term added by Taylor or Frazer.

7. Peter Winch, "Knowledge and Practice," an unpublished essay on Simone Weil; quoted by Phillips (1976: 125–126).

8. See chapter three.

REFERENCES

Abel, Theodore (1948). "The operation called 'Verstehen.'" *American Journal of Sociology* 54: 211–218.

Abel, Theodore (1967). "A reply to Professor Wax." *Sociology and Social Research* 51: 334–336.

Alston, William P. (1956). "Ineffability." *The Philosophical Review* 65: 506–522.

Alston, William P. (1965). "Expressing." In M. Black, ed., *Philosophy in America*. Ithaca, New York: Cornell University Press.

Anscombe, Gertrude Elizabeth Margaret (1958). "Modern moral philosophy." *Philosophy* 33: 1–19.

Aquila, Richard E. (1977). *Intentionality*. University Park, Pennsylvania: Pennsylvania State University Press.

Árdal, Páll S. (1966). *Passion and Value in Hume's Treatise*. Edinburgh: Edinburgh University Press.

Aristotle (1924). *Rhetorica*. Trans. W. Rhys Roberts. In *Works of Aristotle Translated into English*, vol. 11. Oxford: Clarendon Press.

Aristotle (1926). *The 'Art' of Rhetoric*. Trans. J. H. Freese. Loeb Classical Library, vol. 22. Cambridge, Mass.: Harvard University Press.

Aristotle (1931). *De anima*. Trans. J. A. Smith. In *Works of Aristotle Translated into English*, vol. 11. Oxford: Clarendon Press.

Aune, Bruce (1965). "The complexity of avowals." In M. Black, ed., *Philosophy in America*. Ithaca, New York: Cornell University Press.

Ayer, Alfred Jules (1970). *Language, Truth and Logic*. 2d ed. New York: Dover.

Baier, Annette (1978). "Hume's analysis of pride." *Journal of Philosophy* 7: 27–40.

Barth, Karl (1960). *Anselm: Fides Quaerens Intellectum*. Trans. I. W. Robertson. Richmond, Virginia: John Knox Press.

Bedford, Errol (1957). "Emotions." *Proceedings of the Aristotelian Society*, n.s. 57: 281–304.

Bem, Daryl J. (1972). "Self-perception theory." In L. Berkowitz, ed., *Advances in Experimental and Social Psychology*, 6: 1–62. New York: Academic Press.

Benson, John Edward (1967). "Schleiermacher's Hermeneutics." Ph.D. dissertation, Columbia University.

Berlin, Isaiah (1976). *Vico and Herder: Two Studies in the History of Ideas.* New York: Viking.

Bouyer, Louis (1980). "Mysticism: an essay on the history of the word." In R. Woods, ed., *Understanding Mysticism.* Garden City, New York: Doubleday.

Brandt, Richard B. (1941). *The Philosophy of Schleiermacher.* New York: Harper.

Brehm, J., and Cohen, A. (1962). *Explorations in Cognitive Dissonance.* New York: Wiley.

Brentano, Franz C. (1874). *Psychologie vom empirischen Standpunkte*, vol. 1. Leipzig: Duncker and Humblot.

Burrell, David (1973). *Analogy and Philosophical Language.* New Haven: Yale University Press.

Cannon, Walter B. (1927). "The James-Lange theory of emotions: a critical examination and an alternative theory." *American Journal of Psychology* 39: 106–124.

Cannon, Walter B. (1929). *Bodily Changes in Pain, Hunger, Fear, and Rage.* 2d ed. New York: Appleton.

Carnap, Rudolf (1935). *Philosophy and Logical Syntax.* London: Kegan Paul, Trench, Trubner.

Cassirer, Ernst (1946). *Language and Myth.* Trans. S. K. Langer. New York: Dover.

Cassirer, Ernst (1953–1957). *The Philosophy of Symbolic Forms.* 3 vols. Trans. R. Manheim. New Haven: Yale University Press.

Chisholm, Roderick M. (1957). *Perceiving: A Philosophical Study.* Ithaca, New York: Cornell University Press.

Chisholm, Roderick M. (1967). "Intentionality." In P. Edwards, ed., *The Encyclopedia of Philosophy* 4: 201–204. New York: Macmillan and Free Press.

Chisholm, Roderick M., ed. (1960). *Realism and the Background of Phenomenology.* Glencoe, Illinois: The Free Press.

Clark, James M., ed. (1957). *Meister Eckhart: An Introduction to the Study of His Works with an Anthology of His Sermons.* New York: Thomas Nelson.

Clark, Walter Houston (1970). "The psychedelics and religion." In B. Aaronson and H. Osmond, ed., *Psychedelics: The Uses and Implications of Hallucinogenic Drugs*, pp. 182–195. New York: Doubleday.

Collins, Arthur W. (1969). "Unconscious belief." *Journal of Philosophy* 66: 667–680.

Danto, Arthur C. (1965). *Analytical Philosophy of History*. Cambridge: Cambridge University Press.

Danto, Arthur C. (1970). "Causation and basic actions: a reply en passant to Professor Margolis." *Inquiry* 13: 108–125.

Danto, Arthur C. (1973). "Language and the Tao: some reflections." *Journal of Chinese Philosophy* 1: 45–55.

Davidson, Donald (1976). "Hume's cognitive theory of pride." *Journal of Philosophy* 73: 744–757.

Deikman, Arthur J. (1966). "Deautomatization and the mystic experience." *Psychiatry* 29: 324–338.

Despland, Michel (1973). *Kant on History and Religion*. Montreal: McGill-Queen's University Press.

Deutsch, Eliot (1969). *Advaita Vedanta: A Philosophical Reconstruction*. Honolulu: East-West Center Press.

Dilthey, Wilhelm (1927). *Der Aufbau der geschichtlichen Welt in den Geisteswissenschaften*. Gesammelte Schriften, vol. 7. Leipzig: Teubner.

Dilthey, Wilhelm (1966). *Leben Schleiermachers, Zweiter Band*. Ed. M. Redeker. Gesammelte Schriften, vol. 14/2. Gottingen, Vandenhoeck and Ruprecht.

Dilthey, Wilhelm (1976). *Wilhelm Dilthey: Selected Writings*. Trans. H. Rickman. Cambridge: Cambridge University Press.

Dodds, Eric R. (1964). *The Greeks and the Irrational*. Berkeley and Los Angeles: University of California Press.

Douglas, Mary (1966). *Purity and Danger*. London: Routledge and Kegan Paul.

Douglas, Mary (1975). "Self-evidence." In *Implicit Meanings*, pp. 276–318. London: Routledge and Kegan Paul.

Durkheim, Emile (1965). *The Elementary Forms of the Religious Life*. Trans. J. W. Swain. New York: The Free Press.

Edwards, Jonathan (1959). *Religious Affections*. Ed. J. E. Smith. New Haven: Yale University Press.

Eliade, Mircea (1966). *Patterns in Comparative Religion*. Trans. R. Sheed. New York: Meridian.

Eliade, Mircea (1969). *The Quest*. Chicago: The University of Chicago Press.

Ermath, Michael (1978). *Wilhelm Dilthey: The Critique of Historical Reason*. Chicago: The University of Chicago Press.

Evans-Pritchard, Edward E. (1956). *Nuer Religion*. Oxford: Oxford University Press.

Evans-Pritchard, Edward E. (1965). *Theories of Primitive Religion*. Oxford: Oxford University Press.

Fenton, John Y. (1970). "Reductionism in the study of religion." *Soundings* 53: 61–76.

Festinger, Leon (1957). *A Theory of Cognitive Dissonance*. Stanford: Stanford University Press.

Festinger, Leon, and Carlsmith, J. M. (1959). "Cognitive consequences of forced compliance." *Journal of Abnormal and Social Psychology* 58: 203–210.

Foot, Philippa (1978). *Virtues and Vices and Other Essays in Moral Philosophy*. Berkeley, Los Angeles, London: University of California Press.

Forstman, H. Jackson (1977). *A Romantic Triangle: Schleiermacher and Early German Romanticism*. Missoula, Montana: Scholars Press.

Fortenbaugh, W. W. (1975). *Aristotle on Emotion*. New York: Barnes and Noble.

Frazer, James (1911). *The Golden Bough*. 3d ed. Pt. II, *Taboo and the Perils of the Soul*. London: Macmillan.

Frei, Hans, W. (1974). *The Eclipse of Biblical Narrative*. New Haven: Yale University Press.

Freud, Sigmund (1950). *Totem and Taboo*. Trans. J. Strachey. New York: Norton.

Gadamer, Hans-Georg (1965). *Wahrheit und Methode*. 2d ed. Tubingen: J. C. B. Mohr.

Gadamer, Hans-Georg (1975). *Truth and Method*. Trans. G. Barden and J. Cumming. New York: Seabury.

Gadamer, Hans-Georg (1976). *Philosophical Hermeneutics*. Trans. D. Linge. Berkeley, Los Angeles, London: University of California Press.

Gale, Richard M. (1960). "Mysticism and philosophy." *Journal of Philosophy* 57: 471–481.

Gardiner, Patrick, ed. (1959). *Theories of History*. Glencoe, Illinois: The Free Press.

Geertz, Clifford (1968). *Islam Observed*. New Haven: Yale University Press.

Geertz, Clifford (1973). *The Interpretation of Cultures*. New York: Basic Books.

Gettier, Edmund L. (1963). "Is justified true belief knowledge?" *Analysis* 23: 121–123.

Gimello, Robert (1978). "Mysticism and meditation." In S. Katz, ed., *Mysticism and Philosophical Analysis*, pp. 170–190. New York: Oxford University Press.

Greenlee, Douglas A. (1973). *Peirce's Concept of Sign*. The Hague: Mouton.

Grice, H. Paul (1961). "The causal theory of perception." *Proceedings of the Aristotelian Society*, Supp. 35: 121–168.

Hacker, P. M. S. (1972). *Insight and Illusion*. Oxford: Oxford University Press.

Harman, Gilbert (1973). *Thought*. Princeton: Princeton University Press.

Harvey, Van A. (1962). "A word in defense of Schleiermacher's theological method." *Journal of Religion* 42: 151–170.

Harvey, Van A. (1971). "On the new edition of Schleiermacher's *Addresses on Religion*." *Journal of the American Academy of Religion* 39: 488–512.

Hegel, Georg Wilhelm Friedrich (1953). *Reason in History*. Trans. R. S. Hartman. Indianapolis: Bobbs-Merrill.

Heidegger, Martin (1962). *Being and Time*. Trans. J. Macquarrie and E. Robinson. New York: Harper and Row.

Henle, Paul (1948). "Mysticism and semantics." *Philosophy and Phenomenological Research* 9: 416–422.

Hick, John (1969). "Religious faith as experiencing-as." In G. N. A. Vesey, ed., *Talk of God*. London: Macmillan.

Holland, Roy F. (1967). "The miraculous." In D. Z. Phillips, ed., *Religion and Understanding*, pp. 155–170. New York: Macmillan.

Hume, David (1965). *A Treatise of Human Nature*. Ed. L. A. Selby-Bigge. Rev. P. H. Nidditch. Oxford: Oxford University Press.

Hume, David (1975). *Enquiries Concerning Human Understanding and Concerning the Principles of Morals*. Ed. L. A. Selby-Bigge. Rev. P. H. Nidditch. Oxford: Oxford University Press.

James, William (1890). *The Principles of Psychology*. 2 vols. New York: Henry Holt.

James, William (1902). *The Varieties of Religious Experience*. New York: Longmans, Green.

Jones, E. E.; Kanouse, D. E.; Kelley, H. H.; Nisbett, R. E.; Valins, S.; and Weiner, B. (1972). *Attribution: Perceiving the Causes of Behavior*. Morristown, New Jersey: General Learning Press.

Kant, Immanuel (1956). *Critique of Practical Reason*. Trans. L. W. Beck. Indianapolis: Bobbs-Merrill.

Kant, Immanuel (1960). *Religion Within the Limits of Reason Alone*. Trans. T. M. Greene and H. H. Hudson. New York: Harper and Row.

Katz, Steven T. (1972). "The language and logic of mystery." In S. W. Sykes and J. P. Clayton, ed., *Christ, Faith, and History*. Cambridge: Cambridge University Press.

Katz, Steven T., ed. (1978). *Mysticism and Philosophical Analysis*. New York: Oxford University Press.

Kenny, Anthony John Patrick (1963). *Action, Emotion, and Will*. London: Routledge and Kegan Paul.

Kierkegaard, Søren (1954). *Fear and Trembling and the Sickness Unto Death*. Trans. W. Lowrie. Princeton: Princeton University Press.

Kimmerle, Heinz (1959). "Einleitung." In Schleiermacher (1959), pp. 9–24.

King, Winston L. (1980). *Theravāda Meditation*. University Park, Pennsylvania: Pennsylvania State University Press.

Lepper, M. R.; Green, D.; and Nisbett, R. E. (1973). "Undermining children's intrinsic interest with extrinsic reward: a test of the 'overjustification' hypothesis." *Journal of Personality and Social Psychology* 28: 129–137.

Levinson, Henry S. (1978). *Science, Metaphysics, and the Chance of Salvation: An Interpretation of the Thought of William James*. Missoula, Montana: Scholars Press.

Levinson, Henry S. (1981). *The Religious Investigations of William James*. Chapel Hill, North Carolina: University of North Carolina Press.

Makkreel, Rudolf A. (1975). *Dilthey: Philosopher of the Human Studies*. Princeton: Princeton University Press.

Malcolm, Norman (1966). "Wittgenstein's Philosophical Investigations." In G. Pitcher, ed., *Wittgenstein: The Philosophical Investigations*, pp. 65–103. Garden City, New York: Doubleday.

Mandler, George (1975). *Mind and Emotion*. New York: Wiley.

Manuel, Frank E. (1959). *The Eighteenth Century Confronts the Gods*. Cambridge, Mass.: Harvard University Press.

Marañon, G. (1924). "Contributions a l'étude de l'action émotive de l'adrenaline." *Revue Francaise d'Endocrinologie* 2: 301–325.

Marett, Robert Ranulph (1914). *The Threshold of Religion*. London: Methuen.

Marras, Ausonio, ed. (1972). *Intentionality, Mind, and Language*. Urbana: University of Illinois Press.

Maslach, Christina (1979). "The emotional consequences of arousal without reason." In C. E. Izard, ed., *Emotions in Personality and Psychopathology*, pp. 565–590. New York: Plenum.

Michaelson, Gordon E., Jr. (1979). *The Historical Dimensions of a Rational Faith: The Role of History in Kant's Religious Thought*. Washington, D.C.: University Press of America.

Nagel, Ernest (1953). "On the method of *Verstehen* as the sole method of philosophy." *Journal of Philosophy* 50: 154–157.

Neu, Jerome E. (1977). *Emotion, Thought, and Therapy*. Berkeley, Los Angeles, London: University of California Press.

Niebuhr, Richard R. (1964). *Schleiermacher on Christ and Religion*. New York: Scribner's.

Niebuhr, Richard R. (1969). "The widened heart." *Harvard Theological Review* 62: 127–154.

Nisbett, Richard, and Ross, Lee (1980). *Human Inference: Strategies and Shortcomings of Social Judgment*. Englewood Cliffs, New Jersey: Prentice-Hall.

Otto, Rudolf (1932). *Mysticism East and West: A Comparative Analysis of the Nature of Mysticism*. Trans. B. L. Bracey and R. C. Payne. New York: Macmillan.

Otto, Rudolf (1958). *The Idea of the Holy*. Trans. J. W. Harvey. New York: Oxford University Press.

Pahnke, Walter N. (1970). "Drugs and mysticism." In B. Aaronson and H. Osmond, eds., *Psychedelics: The Uses and Implications of Hallucinogenic Drugs*, pp. 145–165. New York: Doubleday.

Palmer, Richard E. (1969). *Hermeneutics*. Evanston, Illinois: Northwestern University Press.

Pappas, George S., and Swain, Marshall, eds. (1978). *Essays on Knowledge and Justification*. Ithaca, New York: Cornell University Press.

Peirce, Charles Sanders (1931–1958). *The Collected Papers of Charles Sanders Peirce*. Ed. C. Hartshorne, P. Weiss, and A. Burks. Cambridge, Mass.: Harvard University Press.

Penner, Hans H., and Yonan, Edward (1972). "Is a science of religion possible?" *Journal of Religion* 52: 107–133.

Phillips, Dewi Zephaniah (1976). *Religion Without Explanation*. Oxford: Basil Blackwell.

Plutchik, R., and Ax, A. F. (1967). "A critique of 'determinants of emotional state' by Schachter and Singer, 1962." *Psychophysiology* 4: 79–82.

Preller, Victor (1967). *Divine Science and the Science of God*. Princeton: Princeton University Press.

Quine, Willard van Orman (1960). *Word and Object*. Cambridge, Mass.: MIT Press.

Quine, Willard van Orman (1981). "The Pragmatists' Place in Empiricism." In R. Mulvaney and P. Zeltner, eds., *Pragmatism: Its Sources and Prospects*, pp. 21–39. Columbia: University of South Carolina Press.

Richards, Glyn (1978). "*Śūnyatā*: objective referent or *via negativa*?" *Religious Studies* 14: 251–260.

Ricoeur, Paul (1970). *Freud and Philosophy: An Essay on Interpretation*. Trans. D. Savage. New Haven: Yale University Press.

Ricoeur, Paul (1971). "The model of the text: meaningful action considered as a text." *Social Research* 38: 529–562.

Ricoeur, Paul (1976). *Interpretation Theory*. San Antonio, Texas: Trinity University Press.

Rorty, Richard (1980). *Philosophy and the Mirror of Nature*. Princeton: Princeton University Press.

Rorty, Richard (1982). *Consequences of Pragmatism*. Minneapolis: University of Minnesota Press.

Royce, Josiah (1913). *The Problem of Christianity*. 2 vols. New York: Macmillan.

Ryle, Gilbert (1949). *The Concept of Mind*. London: Hutchinson.

Schachter, Stanley (1971). *Emotion, Obesity and Crime*. New York: Academic Press.

Schachter, Stanley, and Singer, Jerome E. (1962). "Cognitive, social and physiological determinants of emotional state." *Psychological Review* 69: 379–399.

Schleiermacher, Friedrich Daniel Ernst (1928). *The Christian Faith*. 2d ed. Trans. H. R. Mackintosh and J. S. Stewart. Edinburgh: T. & T. Clark.

Schleiermacher, Friedrich Daniel Ernst (1958). *On Religion: Speeches to its Cultured Despisers*. Trans. J. Oman. New York: Harper and Row.

Schleiermacher, Friedrich Daniel Ernst (1958). *Über die Religion: Reden an die Gebildeten unter ihren Verachtern*. Hamburg: Felix Meiner.

Schleiermacher, Friedrich Daniel Ernst (1959). *Hermeneutik: nach den Handschriften*. Ed. H. Kimmerle. Heidelberg: Carl Winter-Universitatsverlag.

Schleiermacher, Friedrich Daniel Ernst (1966). *Brief Outline for the Study of Theology*. Trans. T. N. Tice. Richmond, Virginia: John Knox Press.

Schleiermacher, Friedrich Daniel Ernst (1977). *Hermeneutics: The Handwritten Manuscripts*. Trans. J. Duke and J. Forstman. Missoula, Montana: Scholars Press.

Scholem, Gershom (1973). *Sabbatai Sevi: The Mystical Messiah*. Trans. R. J. Z. Werblowsky. Princeton: Princeton University Press.

Sellars, Wilfrid (1956). "The myth of the given: three lectures on empiricism and the philosophy of mind." In H. Feigl and M. Scriven, eds., *The Foundations of Science and the Concepts of Psychology and Psychoanalysis*. Minneapolis: University of Minnesota Press.

Sharpe, Eric (1975). *Comparative Religion: A History*. London: Duckworth.

Shaver, Kelly G. (1975). *An Introduction to Attribution Theory*. Cambridge, Mass.: Winthrop.

Shope, Robert K. (1983). *Analysis of Knowing: A Decade of Research.* Princeton: Princeton University Press.

Smart, Ninian (1958). *Reasons and Faiths.* London: Routledge and Kegan Paul.

Smart, Ninian (1964). *Philosophers and Religious Truth.* London: S. C. M. Press.

Smart, Ninian (1965). "Interpretation and mystical experience." *Religious Studies* 1: 75–87.

Smith, Morton (1973). *The Secret Gospel.* New York: Harper and Row.

Smith, Wilfred Cantwell (1964). *The Meaning and End of Religion.* New York: Mentor.

Smith, Wilfred Cantwell (1976). *Religious Diversity.* Ed. W. G. Oxtoby. New York: Harper and Row.

Smith, Wilfred Cantwell (1979). *Faith and Belief.* Princeton: Princeton University Press.

Spinoza, Benedict (1951). "Theological-Political Treatise." In *The Chief Works of Spinoza,* tr. R. H. M. Elwes. New York: Dover.

Spinoza, Baruch (1982). *The Ethics and Selected Letters.* Trans. S. Shirley. Indianapolis and Cambridge: Hackett.

Spiro, Melford E. (1966). "Religion, problems of definition and explanation." In M. Banton, ed., *Anthropological Approaches to the Study of Religion.* London: Tavistock.

Staal, Frits (1975). *Exploring Mysticism.* Berkeley, Los Angeles, London: University of California Press.

Stace, Walter T. (1960). *Mysticism and Philosophy.* Philadelphia: Lippincott.

Strawson, Peter F. (1974). "Causation in perception." In *Freedom and Resentment.* London: Methuen.

Streng, Frederick J. (1967). *Emptiness: A Study in Religious Meaning.* Nashville: Abingdon.

Swinburne, Richard (1970). *The Concept of Miracle.* New York: St. Martin's.

Taylor, Charles (1971). "Interpretation and the sciences of man." *Review of Metaphysics* 25: 3–51.

Taylor, Charles (1979). "Action as expression." In C. Diamond and J. Teichman, eds., *Intention and Intentionality: Essays in Honour of G. E. M. Anscombe,* pp. 73–89. Ithaca, New York: Cornell University Press.

Taylor, R. (1870). *Te Ika a Maui.* London. Cited by Frazer (1911).

Tillich, Paul J. (1951). *Systematic Theology.* Vol. 1. Chicago: University of Chicago Press.

Tormey, Alan (1971). *The Concept of Expression.* Princeton: Princeton University Press.

Underhill, Evelyn (1911). *Mysticism: A Study in the Nature and Development of Man's Spiritual Consciousness.* London: Methuen.

Wach, Joachim (1951). *Types of Religious Experience: Christian and Non-christian.* Chicago: University of Chicago Press.

Wainwright, William J. (1981). *Mysticism: A Study of its Nature, Cognitive Value, and Moral Implications.* Madison: University of Wisconsin Press.

Wax, Murray L. (1967). "On misunderstanding *Verstehen*: a reply to Abel." *Sociology and Social Research* 51: 323–333.

Wayman, Alex (1969). "Contributions to the Madhyamika school of Buddhism." *Journal of the American Oriental Society* 89: 141–152.

Weber, Max (1968). *Economy and Society: An Outline of Interpretive Sociology.* Ed. G. Roth and C. Wittich. 2 vols. New York: Bedminster Press.

Weiner, Bernard (1972). *Theories of Motivation: From Mechanism to Cognition.* Chicago: Markham.

Weiner, Bernard, and Sierad, J. (1974). "Misattribution for failure and the enhancement of achievement strivings." In B. Weiner, ed., *Achievement Motivation and Attribution Theory.* Morristown, New Jersey: General Learning Press.

Wesley, John (1964). *John Wesley.* Ed. A. C. Outler. New York: Oxford University Press.

Wild, John (1969). *The Radical Empiricism of William James.* Garden City, New York: Doubleday.

Williams, Robert R. (1978). *Schleiermacher the Theologian.* Philadelphia: Fortress Press.

Winch, Peter (1958). *The Idea of a Social Science.* London: Routledge and Kegan Paul.

Winch, Peter (1970). "Understanding a primitive society." In B. Wilson, ed., *Rationality*, pp. 78–111. Oxford: Basil Blackwell.

Winch, Peter (unpublished). "Knowledge and practice." Paper on Simone Weil. Cited by Phillips (1976).

Wittgenstein, Ludwig (1953). *Philosophical Investigations.* Trans. G. E. M. Anscombe. New York: Macmillan.

Wittgenstein, Ludwig (1958). *The Blue and Brown Books.* Ed. R. Rhees. Oxford: Basil Blackwell.

Wittgenstein, Ludwig (1965). "A lecture on ethics." *Philosophical Review* 74: 3–12.

Wittgenstein, Ludwig (1979). *Remarks on Frazer's* The Golden Bough. Ed. R. Rhees. Trans. A. C. Miles and R. Rhees. Retford, England: Brynmill.

Wollheim, Richard (1974). *On Art and the Mind.* Cambridge, Mass.: Harvard University Press.

Wollheim, Richard (1979). *The Sheep and the Ceremony.* Cambridge: Cambridge University Press.

Wolterstorff, Nicholas (1980). *Works and Worlds of Art.* Oxford: Clarendon Press.

Wood, Allen W. (1970). *Kant's Moral Religion.* Ithaca, New York: Cornell University Press.

von Wright, Georg Henrik (1971). *Explanation and Understanding.* Ithaca, New York: Cornell University Press.

Yovel, Yirmiahu (1980). *Kant and the Philosophy of History.* Princeton: Princeton University Press.

Zaehner, R. C. (1957). *Mysticism: Sacred and Profane.* Oxford: Clarendon Press.

INDEX

Designer: U.C. Press Staff
Compositor: Eisenbrauns
Printer: McNaughton & Gunn, Inc.
Binder: John H. Dekker & Sons
Text: 10/13 Palatino
Display: Palatino